LIBERAL BOLSHEVISM

*America Did Not Defeat Communism,
She Adopted It*

ALEXANDER G. MARKOVSKY

Copyright © 2016 by ALEXANDER G. MARKOVSKY

LIBERAL BOLSHEVISM
America Did Not Defeat Communism, She Adopted It
by ALEXANDER G. MARKOVSKY

Printed in the United States of America.

ISBN: 978-1-4575-4852-9

All rights reserved solely by the author. The author guarantees all contents are original and do not infringe upon the legal rights of any other person or work. No part of this book may be reproduced in any form without the permission of the author. The views expressed in this book are not necessarily those of the publisher.

Published by Dog Ear Publishing
4011 Vincennes Rd.
Indianapolis, IN 46268
www.dogearpublishing.net

To my father, who helped me to see the world through the veil of communist propaganda

And to my wonderful daughter, Rebecca

About the Author:

Alexander G. Markovsky is a Russian émigré. He holds degrees in economics and political science from the University of Marxism-Leninism and an MS in structural engineering from Moscow University. He resides in Houston, Texas, with his wife and daughter, where he owns a consulting company specializing in the management of large international projects.

Mr. Markovsky is the author of *Anatomy of a Bolshevik*, published in 2012, and a contributor to FamilySecurityMatters.org. His essays have appeared on RedState.com, WorldNetDaily, Israpundit, Ruthfullyyours, and other websites.

**In 2008 we hoped for the future;
in 2016 we hope for the past**

CONTENTS

Introduction: xi

Chapter 1:
You Have to Know My Past to Understand Your Future 1
    The Way It Was
    The Philosophy of Your Enemies

Chapter 2: Back to the Future 9
    The Future Arrived and It Was Not What We Expected
    The President of the United States!

Chapter 3: Concealed Identity 15
    Who Are You, Mr. President?
    Are You a Socialist?
    Are You a Moderate Republican?
    Are You a Marxist?

Chapter 4: American Liberal Bolshevik 32
    Historical Inevitability
    Philosophy of Poverty
    Fear and Hope
    Effluence and Affluence
    More Power to the Poor

Chapter 5: Building Socialism 58
    Socialism and the Socialists
    Marxism by Any Other Name
    "The Voting Herd"
    The Moral Decay
    Dreams and Reality

Chapter 6: The Three Planks of Liberal Bolshevism 91
    The Liberal Bolshevik's Strategy
    Plank I. Destruction of Wealth

Plank II. Replacement of American Self-reliance with Government Dependence
Plank III. Replacement of a Capitalist Market Economy with a Government-controlled Political Economy
Conclusion

Chapter 7: Capitalism: The Known Ideal 113
Preview
Did Karl Marx Have It Right?
The Centuries of Emancipation
The Spiral of Evolution
Agony of Impotence
Let Capitalism Work
  1. Privatize Government Assets
  2. Regain Energy Independence
  3. Redefine Free Trade
  4. What Is to Be Done

Chapter 8: The President's Socialist Economic Policy—Theater of the Absurd 147
The Biggest Economic Recovery Plan in History or the Biggest Economic Fraud in History
The Church of Global Warming
The Immense Power of Oil

Chapter 9: The Politics of Immorality 176
The New World
What Is "Social Justice," Anyway?
"You Didn't Build That"
Obama's Fairness Doctrine
Inequality: Locomotive of Progress
The Forgotten Seventeenth Amendment

Chapter 10: The Politics of Delusion 204
The Necessary War
World War III
Anatomy of the War

    Standing with Islam
    Romance with Terrorism
    They Want to Die

Chapter 11: The Power of Demagoguery and Lies, or How the Democrats Win 226
    Two Monoliths and a Scam
    Devotion of Black Americans
    The Jewish Question
    "It Is Not Important Who Votes…"
    They Are Ignorant. But They Vote.
    Representation without Taxation

Chapter 12: "Forward" with Socialism 248
    The Second Coming of Barack Obama
    Irreconcilable Ideological Demarcation
    Impending Catastrophe and How to Avoid It
    Strategy for 2016
    The Republican's Road to Calvary

Chapter 13: ¡No Pasaran! 273
    Bolsheviks Are at the Gates

ACKNOWLEDGMENTS 279
BIBLIOGRAPHY 281
Appendix I: "Talk with Bolshevist Head" 287
Appendix II: Sampling of Reports from the 1970s 293
    Warning of Global Cooling

INTRODUCTION

Why should you listen to me?

President Reagan said, *"How do you tell a communist? Well, it's someone who reads Marx and Lenin. And how do you tell an anti-Communist? It's someone who understands Marx and Lenin."* I have been where you are going. I have learned from those who wanted to destroy you. I have been inside this monster and I know him well.

In December 1991, the world watched in amazement and trepidation as the communist empire spectacularly collapsed. Its demise was hailed by the United States as a victory for freedom, a triumph of democracy over totalitarianism. The jubilation proved to be premature, however. The ideas of Marx and Lenin did not die, and the demise of socialism was not irrevocable. Like a deadly bacterium that mutates to become resistant to antibiotics, Marxism adapted to a new reality and, in one of the most dramatic reversals of history, comfortably relocated to the United States, where it acquired a new life and malignancy within the Democratic Party. In 2008 this revolutionary ferment culminated in the election of Barack Obama, the architect of a new, benevolent form of Marxism founded on dependence, hereinafter called Liberal Bolshevism.

Liberal Bolshevism has become the hallmark of the Democratic Party, the manifestation of an epochal shift to an ideology that signifies the total inversion of American historical traditions and values. Nobody has played such a decisive role in shaping the party's ideology as Barack Obama. His principle achievement is that after he is gone, the realities of Obama's "Hope and Change" will continue to emasculate existing institutions—marriage, religion, the free-market economy, the judicial system, and the reliance on individual liberty—as outmoded, unfair, and discriminatory.

As to affirm the Party ideological vitality, the contenders for Obama's legacy Bernie Sanders and Hillary Clinton are charting Obama's ideological vistas masked as Democratic socialism and progressivism. Though, a commonality of the ideological vocabulary of the Democratic Party contenders with Marxism, promising miraculous fulfilment of egalitarian dreams, leaves little doubt about the Party becoming the source and spirit of Marxist awakening.

Most contemporaries, unfortunately, do not see the challenges to the established moral order in an ideological light and believe that this shift is the inexorable product of changing times. Another view holds that it is a conspiracy by unidentified groups of Marxists/Communists/Socialists/Anarchists and the so-called special interests aimed at repudiating the moral status quo. Both assessments are being ground down in the stark realities of Liberal Bolshevism.

As we examine in the course of this book, the Democratic Party has been undergoing an ideological conversion, the impetus of which is traceable to Woodrow Wilson and FDR, veering slowly from liberalism into socialism over several generations, making it difficult for the average citizen to recognize its cumulative effect and comprehend its broader consequences. The waning of moral vigilance has empowered the Democratic Party to accelerate the conversion and bring the country into conformity with a new dispensation. With the chief components of a "fundamental transformation" firmly in place, the Party is on a mission to take the nation in a direction decidedly not in keeping with the course charted by the Founding Fathers. Therefore, it is of paramount importance to recognize the Democratic Party for what it really is, and what Obama's Marxism-sanctioned "fundamental transformation" means for posterity.

Regretfully, the Republican presidential rivals have fixated on pursuing competing aspirations and have not shown any sustained interest thus far in understanding the ideological nature of the proposed transformation, nor the imperative to confront it. They promise to abandon Obamacare, proceed with tax and immigration reforms, improve the economy, etc., thereby emphasizing effect over cause, symptoms over disease. The soaring Republican rhetoric about taking the country back, presumably from the Democrats, is a misdirected and divisive impulse of prevailing during a period of one of the most severe polarizations in the nation's history, when the need for political unity and restoration of faith in American institutions is so great. Should the necessity for such unity be recognized, it cannot be achieved by proclamation of intent, as often happens in politics, but by forging a consensus of national purpose. That itself requires addressing two problems, one chronic and the other short-term. The chronic problem is a failure to recognize that the Democratic Party has not been offering a different philosophy for achieving the same objectives, but for years has had a different philosophy and different objectives entirely. The short-term problem is whether an anti-Marxist, anti-socialist platform can be distilled from the divergent politics of the aspirants for high office.

The Republican strategy, or lack of it, is a classic case of what Henry Kissinger described as "purpose outrunning knowledge." Contrary to the conservative consensus, the country needs NOT to be taken back from the Democrats or undefined "special interests"; the country needs to be taken back—along WITH responsible Democrats—from the jaws of Marxism.

Since my formative years I have had what I call "antagonistic contradictions" with Marxism, which I ascribe to the experience of having grown up in the Soviet Union. For this reason, I find unendurable the thought of this country falling into socialism. Taking the matter grievously to heart, I do not share the President's dream of changing America; on the contrary, I do not want this place of unlimited possibilities to become a place of limited opportunities. My dream is to preserve this "sweet land of liberty" for my children and grandchildren. It is to fulfill this dream that I wrote *Liberal Bolshevism.*

This book is not the biography of an immigrant, although my background is included because I find the President's political views paralleling those with which I grew up. Nor is it an exercise in social philosophy, although clashing social and philosophical theories that eroded the established concept of ethical values have been challenged. Rather, this book is a political exposé of President Obama and the Democratic Party aimed at the hidden nature of Liberal Bolshevism that has eluded the experts and public at large. It is intended to be thought-provoking and insightful.

Hence, not everyone will like this book. It will make some of you uncomfortable. For many it may be an eye opener, to others a source of apoplexy and some may think the author is delusional because nothing of what he envisions could be happening to smart people like us. Yet before the "smart" people get too confident, it is instructive to consider that there have been a few times in history when we have known the smart people to be wrong. Very wrong.

> *The main thesis of this book is to demonstrate how the core philosophy of Marx and Lenin are relevant to understanding Barack Obama's thinking and the Democratic Party's objectives and strategy. It confirms practically what many Americans have long suspected intellectually.*

Liberal Bolshevism is a body of knowledge for conservatives essential to prevent an impending catastrophe and an arresting call to all sincere Democrats and well-intentioned liberals and social-justice supporters to pause, listen, and learn that the road they pave with good intentions is leading all of us to hell. Indeed, through the prism of Marxism, the book sheds new light on the economic stimulus, Obamacare, the war on oil, alternative energies, and economic inequality. Herein, the reader will find a reassessment of accepted postulates exposing socialist ideology and the deeply rooted racism and anti-Semitism of the Democratic Party. The book also challenges vested views of socialism and capitalism. Overall, the work is intended as a dissident course of economics and political education.

In the past years a voluminous body of literature has been published to document President Obama's destructive policies. The authors have enumerated chilling details of his relentless assault on constitutional principles, the free-market economy, and individual freedom. Former members of the administration described the Pres-

Introduction

ident in their memoirs as inept, indecisive, politically oriented, and unfit to govern. But this book goes beyond the obvious to answer the most troubling question: WHY?

Why are the President and the Democratic Party pursuing policies that many Americans see as contrary to American interests and the guiding principles of American idealism? Why is the government running an unsustainable deficit and printing money with no end in sight, leading the country to an economic disaster? Why is the economy not recovering? Why is the President resolute in pursuing alternative energies? Why is the administration waging war on oil? Why is the Democratic Party imposing on Americans universal health care, Dodd-Frank, Cap and Trade, and mountains of new federal regulations? Why are the President and the current candidates for the Democratic nomination spending so much time talking about fairness and inequality? Finally, how does the above fit into Obama's and the Democratic Party's overall strategy to implement the transformation, and what is the legacy the President wants to leave behind?

My unique background and experience give me a special sense of obligation to deliver the message to America that it has been wrong all along about Obama's WHY.

CHAPTER 1

You Have to Know My Past to Understand Your Future

"We are apt to shut our eyes against a painful truth, and listen to the song of that siren till she transforms us into beasts... For my part, whatever anguish of spirit it may cost, I am willing to know the whole truth, to know the worst, and to provide for it."
—Patrick Henry

The Way It Was

Since we are all the products of our environment, whether we wish to be or not, it may be noteworthy to the reader, to understand the environment that shaped my views, values, and convictions. So before we get to politics, I am dedicating this chapter to personal experiences that have led me to present the facts, opinions, and conclusions expressed herein. This is my story.

The country I was born in no longer exists. Sometimes it is hard to comprehend that such a huge empire, one that extended over eleven time zones, from the Bering Strait on the border with Alaska to the city of Kaliningrad in the center of Europe, from the permafrost of Siberia to the warm beaches of Crimea, and with a dozen or so satellite countries, could cease to exist. Once perceived as an economic and military powerhouse threatening to submerge the world, the Soviet Union collapsed within three days like a house of cards. The epitome of Marx's dream and Lenin's artifact of great social experiment in equality and fairness had disappeared into the black hole of history. The world was stunned. The "inevitable worldwide victory" of communism was postponed in perpetuity.

This dramatic event reminds us that empires take centuries to build, decades to decay internally, and only relative moments to topple. Regardless of ideological persuasion, those who seek social experiments to make a better world need to learn this lesson.

The Soviet Union was built on utopian Marxist ideology, and when the ideology was pulled out from under the monolith, there was nothing to hold it together. My father, who had an enormous influence in shaping my views and character, predicted the collapse long before it took place. Unfortunately, he did not live to see the Soviets' demise; he passed away just a few years short of this historic event. Like millions of Russian citizens, my father dedicated his life to building socialism. He defended his country during the Second World War. He rose through professional and Party ranks to become the director of a large construction company as well as a high-ranking member of the Communist Party. Party membership was a way of life for him, the way to support his family and to survive in a highly ideological and often dangerous environment.

All Soviet-era managers had to be members of the Communist Party. My father joked that a rabbi in a synagogue must be a member of the Party because such a position of authority would never be held by a non-Party individual. His civilian post and his position in the Communist Party provided a host of privileges, such as a higher salary, a better apartment, a company car, and access to special stores where high-ranking members could obtain goods unavailable to the general population and at a fraction of the official price. Being a high-ranking member of the Party ensured a relatively good life and a secure future for his children—to the extent that anything or anybody could be secure in the Soviet Union, given the persistent fear of denunciation to the KGB and the possibility of being taken at a moment's notice to the KGB's torture chambers and executed or exiled to the archipelago of prisons and labor camps scattered throughout the country.

I grew up knowing that my father hated the bastards who ran the Soviet state, the Communist Party, and his life. My father never felt free, and he was not free. He, like the rest of us, was the property of the state. The Party told him where to work, how much to be paid, what apartment he could have, what doctor to see, and how to educate his children. He never believed in their "working people's paradise," and he always treated the arrangement as a marriage of convenience. Living with a corrupt system has been the subject of many popular American books and movies, but for many, like my father, it was a real-life dilemma. By day my father and his like-minded comrades enthusiastically supported every Party initiative, be it a five-year plan or condemnation of a new Solzhenitsyn book that none of them had ever read. They were united in their quest to defeat world imperialism and Chinese revisionism, and to "plant the red flag over the planet." At night, they shared anecdotes about Khrushchev's stupidity, Brezhnev's illiteracy, and the futility of communist orthodoxy.

Things changed somewhat after the death of Joseph Stalin and my father enjoyed the period of political thawing that took place afterwards. He appreciated this new, although restricted, freedom to demonstrate his superior rationality supplemented by the sarcastic nature of Jewish humor. I recall an incident that occurred one weekend when he took me to visit a construction site located across the street from KGB headquarters. As we were leaving the site, a KGB general was coming out of the building, his perfectly tailored uniform with golden epaulettes radiating spring sunshine, red stripes on blue pants, and polished shoes all looking ostentatiously and decidedly out of place in the predominantly colorless surroundings.

"Privet [hello], Comrade Markovsky. How are you doing?" the general called to my father. Before my father could answer, the general complained, referring to the new building under construction, "You are blocking our sunlight."

"That is only fair," my father replied. "You people have been blocking me from seeing the sunlight all my life!" They both laughed.

"You know, Gregory, you are very lucky. During the Stalin era, a remark like that, even under the best of circumstances, would get you sent to Siberia."

"I know," my father said. "Back then I would have tried to keep my mouth shut."

I guess my father was torn between prudence and vanity. He always managed to project the image of a courageous and uncompromising communist, but at the same time he was wise to avoid taking an unnecessary risk. My dad had so skillfully navigated between Soviet ideology and his own reality that it would have been impossible to notice the constant inordinate fear he had lived with all his life and comprehend the depth of duplicity and antagonism he carried over the years.

As his son, I grew up watching him don his communist persona to begin his workday, only to shed it at night when surrounded by his family and friends. One day his philosophical dilemma manifested itself in a most unexpected way.

The Philosophy of Your Enemies

I remember vividly that twilight evening at the end of the hot summer of 1964. My father returned home after a late meeting at Communist Party headquarters and asked me to accompany him to his office.

"We need to talk," he said in his commanding tone, which bordered at times on condescension. "I have arranged for you to go to the University of Marxism-Leninism to study political science." "To go *where*???" I whispered, due to lack of air in my lungs. "Are you out of your mind, Dad?" I shouted in anguish. "Why would you want me to waste my precious youth on that communist crap?"

"The Führer," what my father called the chairman of the City Branch of the Communist Party, "has approved your candidacy. It is arranged."

I was shocked to discover that he was completely serious about this. He continued talking, trying to convince me that this was a big deal for a Jewish boy, since the University accepted only "Aryan master race candidates," meaning applicants with a stellar proletarian background, and that "no Jew shall apply." I was incredulous.

"Then by all means I shall be proud," I said, thick with sarcasm, "to study decadent theories and a planned socialist economy, which

I have difficulty understanding due to the complete lack of logic, and I shall appreciate the honor of graduating with a degree in the Art of Demagoguery and Lies."

My father did not smile at my mockery, although I'd heard him utter similar disdain with his friends. He himself repetitively referred to the present day as the dark ages of "Demagoguery and Lies." Then, he added, "There is no contradiction between the accurate assessment of realities and pursuing politically beneficial arrangements." Wow!!! Like a lecture to an untutored student. Then, as if that was not enough, his next words came at me with the force of the Bolsheviks' hammer and sickle. This radical truth became the guiding principle of my life:

> *"Son, that's what the communist ideology is all about. If you want to survive, you have to understand the philosophy of your enemies."* His blue eyes were ice cold and as he continued talking his voice became stronger, *"One should never underestimate the boundless power of demagoguery and lies. It moves nations."*

His voice trembled for a moment and then it was over. He turned around and walked out of the room. This explicit message coming from the mouth of a high-ranking communist who had survived the cataclysms of Bolshevism—the terror, economic destruction, famine, and unlimited power of the state—could not be brushed aside.

Getting a little bit ahead, years later my father demonstrated how well he knew his enemies and how masterfully he could maneuver himself out of an extremely difficult situation. The day of reckoning arrived in November 1975, when my father had to sign a consent form to allow me, his son, to emigrate to Israel. There seemed to be no way out of it and no acceptable solution to the impasse. If he signed the papers, he would be viewed as a coward allowing his son to betray the motherland. As a result, he would lose his Party membership, his job, and the respect and prestige he enjoyed among his colleagues. He would also be denounced by his comrades and become *persona non grata*. He would lose everything he had worked for all his life, including his sizable pension. On the other hand, if he did not sign the papers he was still considered the father of a traitor. The result would be the same; there was no way around it. Or was there? My father requested a meeting with the Party's City Committee. What took place was conveyed to me by a member of the committee, a family friend who witnessed the spectacle "with great trepidation" and, in his own words, "grasped it in its totality."

"Comrades," my father began, "I am suffering a personal tragedy, but the issue I am facing is a lot greater than me. It touches all of us and raises serious questions about the communist future of our country. My son has been seduced by imperialist propaganda and has decided to leave his motherland and emigrate to Israel." He paused and wiped his eyes with a handkerchief. "How did WE miss that? I take complete responsibility for what has happened. I am his father and the blame is mine alone. I thought I did all the right things. My son went to a Soviet school. He was a member of Komsomol [the Communist Party youth organization]. He graduated from a Soviet university, and I even sent him to study Marxism at the University of Marxism-Leninism. Where did WE go wrong with the way we are preparing a new generation to take over the wheel of our beloved socialist country?"

Although my father never mentioned it, the committee was frighteningly aware that the "Führer" had personally approved my candidacy to the university. There was no better way to make the members of the committee suffer wanton humiliation and powerlessness, which my father cunningly exploited.

Cleverly and shrewdly, he demonstrated the highest art of the communists' demagoguery and turned it against them. What was the outcome? Nothing happened, nothing at all. I was allowed to leave the country and my father kept his job and his Communist Party post for a few more years until his retirement. Seeing his skillful maneuver, however, I understood how he had survived and used his knowledge to master the game.

Getting back to my story about having to go to the University of Marxism-Leninism. Needless to say, I was free to do what I was told. To my surprise, I liked it despite the fact that the University was designed to cultivate new citizens—"Homo Sovieticus," as they were called in the West—fanatically committed to communism, religiously wedded to the Communist Party, and prepared to carry out its directives to the letter. At the outset I figured out one very important rule: students must demonstrate religious obedience; no one, under any circumstances, could express any doubts or disagreements with the teachings of Marx and Lenin—this would be a deadly sin. However, "trustworthy" students would get greater access to classified materials. I studied political science and economics. For someone like me, with a capacity to evaluate data and process information analytically, the university was an oasis in the information desert of the country of triumphant socialism. Unexpectedly, I was offered access to publications restricted to a very narrow circle of readers. I gained an understanding of American democracy, economy, and politics, while my studies endowed me with a deep understanding of Marxism-Leninism as a political philosophy, its methods of achieving political objectives, its political economy, and, above all, the Marxist's thinking. The most important element of this knowledge was the realization that Marxists are dogmatic and follow the predictable pattern outlined in the teaching of their gods; as a result, one who understands Marxism-Leninism and the ways those dogmatic philistines think gains a tremendous advantage in foreseeing the outcome of issues.

Equipped with this knowledge, I successfully managed my emigration ordeal, my own fight for survival, through eight years of rejection, including numerous KGB interrogations and arrests. The ordeal took an enormous emotional, psychological, and physical toll on my parents, but in December of 1975, I finally got out of the "big zone," which was what Soviet political prisoners called the Soviet Union (they referred to the labor camps as a "small zones"). Unlike many of my friends, I was never hurt, prosecuted, or incarcerated throughout that period. Contrary to the treatment of other *refuzniks* (a Russian word for those who dared to apply for emigration and were turned down by the authorities), I was not publicly denounced and was even allowed to complete my education, graduating as a civil-structural engineer following my studies at the University of Marxism-Leninism, where I received degrees in economics and political science. Given the political climate in the USSR, the accomplishment was beyond extraordinary.

I am absolutely certain that without the knowledge acquired at the University, I would not be here with you. I would have been dead a long time ago, starved in one of the Soviet concentration camps or disappeared into one of the country's psychiatric clinics. I am sure my father is looking down at me from the heavens and smiling, yet I do not believe he realized at the time just how valuable and far-reaching his decision would be.

With the awareness and experience gained during my life in the Soviet Union, I observe the political landscape through red communist glasses and see the brutal reality that most Americans cannot see and the looming future Americans do not want to see. So, my fellow Americans, relish the experience, put the red-colored glasses on, and see what I see: I have seen this future, and it does not work.

CHAPTER 2

Back to the Future

"The future, according to some scientists, will be exactly like the past, only far more expensive."
—John Sladek

The Future Arrived and It Was Not What We Expected

Very often, contemporaries miss the turning points of history. The depth and historical importance of events are not always fully understood in their time. The election of a black American president was certainly a watershed moment in history. The obvious was acknowledged and widely celebrated; the important had been missed. History was not made by the color of the President's skin; it was made by the color of his ideas. In the euphoria of celebration, the ideology of this new president had not been recognized.

To say that the President of the United States of America is ideologically a Bolshevik, a follower of the socialist theories of Karl Marx and Vladimir Lenin, may sound inconceivable; but to a scholar of Marxism-Leninism, a former Soviet citizen with the ability to see the world through red communist lenses, the American political landscape reveals a frightening reality. The reality is that in 2008, the United States elected a radical socialist government committed to the transformation of the American free-enterprise system into an egalitarian[1] society with a state-controlled political economy[2].

---

[1] *Egalitarian (from the French égal, meaning "equal") society—socialism, communism, or nowadays, in a politically correct universe, referred to as social justice—is based on egalitarianism, a philosophy of economic equality.*

[2] *Political economy (contemporary meaning) is an economy centered on ideology and directed by government planners to address political and social objectives. This kind of economy is based on moral principles and not driven by market forces.*

The tragic irony is that unlike the Russian people, who understood the perils of socialism and fought the Bolsheviks in a bloody three-year civil war that by some estimates took fifteen million lives, freedom-loving Americans, through a lethal combination of ignorance, naiveté, and kindness, voted themselves into socialism, fulfilling Gus Hall's[3] prophetic statement made in 1996: "Socialism in America will come through the ballot box."

Indeed, Communist leaders from Lenin to Brezhnev are sardonically grinning from hell and watching in disbelief as what was impossible for the Soviet Union to accomplish with all its military might and nuclear arsenal is being achieved by a duly elected American president with the support of American voters.

The outcome of the elections confirmed one of Winston Churchill's famous dictums: "No one pretends that democracy is perfect or all-wise." The American people have the constitutional right to be wrong, and they certainly exercised that right on November 4, 2008, and reconfirmed it on November 6, 2012. I keep asking myself: Are we living through a period of historic upheaval, or are current events so preposterous, so improbable, that they simply cannot be? Or has isolation from the world's turmoils that America has enjoyed over the past 250 years inhibited our capacity to understand the vulnerabilities of our republic and the fragility of constitutional restraints? Has it, perhaps, corroded our values and impaired our ability to recognize the danger before us? Have we lost what Alexander Solzhenitsyn called "the measure of freedom"?

Although the present is never a carbon copy of the past, it does provide useful parallels. In the preface to his brilliant book *The American Revolution*, Gordon Wood writes: "Unlike the French Revolution, which had been caused by actual tyranny, the American Revolution was seen as a peculiarly intellectual and conservative affair, as something brought about not by actual oppression but by the anticipation of oppression, by reasoning and devotion to principle...." The key here is "anticipation of oppression," because our country today is filled with such anticipation.

---

[3] *Gus Hall, leader of the Communist Party USA and its four-time presidential candidate.*

The Founding Fathers understood that a government, by its very nature, is an institution of tyranny, and they designed our Constitution to protect citizens from governmental oppression. They even took great pains to protect the republic from the citizens' ignorance. It took many years for a large group of highly educated and dedicated people to amend the Constitution and convince the electorate that American idealism and our social and economic policies required dramatic revisions. They persuaded a significant sector of the population that free individuals cannot govern themselves effectively and that government must play a greater role in order to control the economy and engineer "social justice." This agenda brought with it subsequent changes to the moral principles that guided this country since its inception. The major challenge facing the American people today is to understand the threat to our republic from socialist radicals who refuse to accept the fact that the ills of society cannot be fixed by the government and cannot be cured by legislative action or executive order. If we do not accept this fundamental, our republic may not live much longer. The current socialist administration has enacted a series of laws whose cumulative effect, unless repealed, will change this country forever.

Although the congressional elections of 2010 and 2014 offered some hope that some Americans do get it, the challenges of taking our country back from the political elite remain enormous. The people of California, New York, and other socialist-bloc states heavily dependent on government subsidies, elected the same people who bankrupted their states and thus ensured a continued culture of entitlements. In states where the so-called liberal politicians were voted out of office, they were defeated by only slight margins. The left has amassed enormous power with a constituency that possesses organizational skills and substantial financial strength. The president's re-election in 2012 further dramatized the conversion to a new political reality, serving as recognition that America is facing a crucial moment in history and that hosts of serious and unprecedented challenges lie ahead.

Should the challenges exceed the level of our endurance and the conversion to a new reality is allowed to materialize, America's future will look like the Soviet past and we will become the unfortunate generation, dying bankrupt and telling our children and grandchildren, "Work hard and pay, pay, pay forever for our utopian dream." Or will Americans use "reasoning and devotion to principle" and in "anticipation of oppression" find the moral strength to resist the power of demagoguery and lies, detect the threat and thwart it, and continue on what Alexander Hamilton described as the path to "greater perfection and happiness than mankind has yet seen"?

The President of the United States!

It was November 5, 2008, the day after the presidential election. I walked into the sales office of a luxury high-rise condominium in Houston, Texas, where I had a contract to buy a condo. "The Bolsheviks have taken the White House," I told the sales manager. "The country is toast. I'm bailing out of my contract."

It was depressing and ironic that the bloody Bolshevik revolution in Russia took place on November 7, 1917, and now, ninety-one years later almost to the day, we were facing a bloodless revolution in the United States. All things being relative, I guess the world has changed for the better. A day before, I watched on television as millions of people in Chicago, New York, Los Angeles, all over the USA and the world, cheered the victory of a president who promised to "fundamentally transform America." ABC, CBS, NBC, and other media outlets were elated; their saccharine comments recited the empty rhetoric of Obama's campaign. "People understood his vision of a fairer and more just America and embraced it!" crowed a reporter. A "woman in the street" amplified the sentiment, expressing confidence that Obama would pay off her credit card debt. One of the interviewers, reflecting the prevailing mood, said that she was "looking forward to a new change for a new beginning in our country." "New change." "New beginning." "A fairer and more just America."

It was a crowd comprising uninformed and misinformed people looking at themselves as unfortunate, underpaid, underappreciated victims of capitalism and overwhelmed with jealousy that there are people who are everything they are not. The theatrics were frighteningly familiar. The atmosphere of collective psychosis, which according to *Webster's* dictionary means "fundamental derangement of the mind characterized by defective or lost contact with reality especially as evidenced by delusions," was in full display.

My apprehension about these events emanated from both historical precedent and political prudence. It was apparent that cognitive memories have escaped some people and history lessons have never been learned by others.

It all seemed as if the recurring nightmare I'd had during my first year in New York was coming true. In that dream, the Bolsheviks had taken over the United States and the New York City Communist Party branch had set up its headquarters in the Empire State Building. A huge red flag was planted on top of the building. Roaring cheers and screams of joy swept through 34th Street as people celebrated capitalism's demise. I felt as if I had received an admission ticket to my own nightmare. The excitement should not have been surprising; from ancient times, the most tragic events of history have been made by people who, despite the obvious, failed to forecast the future. Events of the utmost significance, even utterly obvious, are often ignored because they conflict with the prevailing wisdom and the preconception that since we are not stupid, it cannot happen to us, to our people, to our country. But people in this country who had firsthand experience with Salvador Allende in Chile, Hugo Chavez in Venezuela, Fidel Castro in Cuba, and communist regimes in the Soviet Union and China were able to decipher the genuine meaning of the events and saw no cause for celebration. A good friend of mine, Edvig Gershengoren, a Russian émigré who never removed his eyes from the perils of Communism, reflecting on the dominant mood among immigrants from the Communist world, wrote in his blog, "For half of my life I lived in fear, during the other half I have enjoyed freedom and security; now I am afraid again."

Suffice it to say, the scene brought back ugly memories of my own past. Having been raised in the Soviet Union, I had seen this three-part movie before—*Euphoria, Apprehension, and Despair*—and could not be persuaded by popular slogans and empty promises. American values were undergoing a conversion that could result in wholesale constitutional and social changes. The country was facing ambiguous choices and uncertain outcomes. What was certain was that we were entering a period of political upheaval and a protracted economic downturn. As the measures culminating in revolutionary changes to society and the economy were implemented, the effect would be detrimental. Socialists would move to redistribute the wealth, offering more benefits to the masses, providing something for nothing. From ancient Greece to modern Western Europe, the masses have always loved that idea, and the measures have proven to be politically popular. Private investment would dry up—capitalists do not invest in uncertainty, and certainly not in a political economy—thereby causing protracted economic stagnation. Should President Obama be reelected to a second term, erosion in economic performance would most certainly transition into sustained economic paralysis. [*I wrote the preceding in my book* Anatomy of a Bolshevik*, published in September 2012, and every word of this warning was providently and swiftly proven true.*] The administration calls it the New Normal. Yes, indeed, it is the New Socialist Normal.

It was inconceivable and utterly demoralizing that the greatest civilization, the greatest economic and military power on Earth, was going to self-destruct. You may recall the answer that Benjamin Franklin gave at Independence Hall in Philadelphia after the Constitutional Convention of 1787, when Mrs. Powel asked, "Well, Doctor, what we have got, a republic or a monarchy?" Franklin responded, "A republic, if you can keep it." The 2008 presidential election raised a reasonable doubt that America will be able to preserve its unique form of democracy and survive the massive assault on its institutions. For someone who had escaped the Soviet Union thirty-three years earlier and was gazing at the future with bright aspirations, it felt as a farewell to illusions.

CHAPTER 3

Concealed Identity

"Obama is a moderate Republican." Bill Maher
"Obama is a socialist." Sarah Palin
"Obama is a liberal." John Kerry
"Obama is a big-government guy." Bill O'Reilly
"Obama is a Marxist." Glenn Beck
Obama is…

Who Are You, Mr. President?

We can hear the voices. "Who cares about Barack Obama? He will be gone soon." Obama arguably is the most consequential Democratic president of the last century and is an embodiment of the Democratic Party's Marxist ideology. The major consequence of his presidency is that he has launched the country on a course that, if not altered by subsequent administrations, may well culminate in autocratic government and the abolition of civil liberties.

Incredibly, after two terms in office, Obama remains to the American people what Winston Churchill famously described Russia as, "a riddle wrapped in a mystery inside an enigma."[4] Thus we have to unlock the mystery and talk about Obama. But we will not talk about his sealed employment, medical, and academic records; his dubious associations with notorious racist, anti-Semite, and America hater Jeremiah Alvesta Wright Jr.; or unrepentant terrorists

---
[4] The Gathering Storm, *The Second World War, Vol. I, p. 403.*

Bill Ayers and Bernardine Dohrn; or devoted Marxist and member of the American Communist Party Frank Marshall Davis; or former director of the official Palestinian press agency FAFA in Beirut, Rashid Khalidi, and many others.

We will not even talk about Obama's physical birthplace. We will talk about the birthplace of his ideas.

The media imposed their version of a "don't ask, don't tell" policy on Obama. They do not ask; when some people do ask, the media invoke racism—the left's first line of defense when they cannot defend the merits of their position. What seeped through the informational embargo is that Obama attended Columbia and Harvard universities and earned a law degree. But he would not tell us what subjects he studied, what he wrote about, how he managed to get accepted into those prestigious universities, and how he paid for his education. We do know, from his own words, that he studied Marxism:

> *I chose my friends carefully. The more politically active black students. The foreign students. The Chicanos. The Marxist professors and structural feminists and punk-rock performance poets.*

Barack Obama wrote that in his autobiography, *Dreams from My Father*. Why would he choose Marxist professors to be his friends unless he had something in common to discuss?

The stoutest supporter of the President, Harvard historian James T. Kloppenberg, wrote in his glorifying-Obama book, *Reading Obama*: "One of his closest friends from Occidental College [he wouldn't tell us his name] allowed me to read a set of long, remarkable letters that Obama wrote during his senior year at Columbia. Those letters reveal an already mature, penetrating mind and reflect a serious engagement with difficult philosophical ideas." We can only surmise what philosophical ideas were on the future president's penetrating mind; Mr. Kloppenberg would not share them with the American people.

However, judging from the amalgam of Obama's agenda, his stated objectives, and the volubility of the language of Marxism he so skillfully employs, we can interpolate with a reasonable degree of certainty that he studied and wrote about the transformation of capitalism into socialism. Over the process of learning the ABCs of Marxism and interaction with his Marxist professors he grew gradually convinced [he had to] that the general theories of Marx, Engels, and Lenin outlined in *Das Kapital, The Critique of the Gotha Program, What Is to Be Done*, and other communist publications could not be directly applied to the contemporary United States of America. In addition, the Bolsheviks found themselves hideously unprepared to face the formidable task of overcoming capitalism. They had to try method after method until they thought they could find one that served their purpose. Obama wanted to be prepared for what might come later.

The acquisition of this knowledge predisposed Obama to the development of his own ideological doctrine for the fundamental transformation of America. I call this doctrine Liberal Bolshevism or, as a scholar of Marxism and friend of mine called it, Pink Bolshevism. "It is not white, but it is not red either," as he characterized it. I will proceed to describe this distinctive Marxism-Leninism in later chapters. Unquestionably, Obama adopted Marxism as a young man and never wavered in his ideological commitment. Hence, Obama's writings would offer a glance at the evolution of the President's philosophical concepts; regretfully, this intellectual treasure may be lost to future generations.

In *Dreams from My Father*, Obama implies that he dreams of implementing the dreams of his father. Yet the picture he paints of his father, Barack Obama Sr., depicts a man that few would care to emulate. In his personal life, his father was a polygamist and an inveterate alcoholic who in 1982, drunk once more, drove into a tree and killed himself. Was he dreaming of having a harem, or was his dream to be reincarnated as a dolphin swimming in a sea of martinis?

Philosophically, Obama Sr. was a militant socialist and anti-neocolonialist. In July 1965 he published in the *East Africa Journal* the article "Problems Facing our Socialism," where he laid out his Marxist convictions: expropriation of property owned by the rich, resulting in communal ownership of land. He actively supported the so-called African National Liberation Movement of the 1970s. After African countries achieved their independence from the Europeans in the mid-1960s, colonialism as we know it was a thing of the past. But those who fought colonialism were not about to put down their AK-47s and become productive citizens with jobs that paid only a few dollars a day. Hence, a new form of struggle for "independence" emerged: anti-neocolonialism. Anti-neocolonialism was a Marxist movement inspired and supported by the Soviet Union. The objective of the movement was the establishment of Marxist governments in Africa.

The political philosophy behind the African National Liberation Movement was that the former colonial powers were enriched through their savage exploitation of the colonies and, later, by the development and sale of the former colonies' natural resources. Therefore, they should redeem forgiveness from former colonies by paying them back for the stolen goods.

The movement had nothing to do with liberty and everything to do with power and other people's wealth. It was no coincidence that this movement was supported by massive military deliveries from the Soviet Union and the intervention of Cuban combat forces equipped and trained by the Soviets. The Soviet Union used the movement to establish a strategic platform for ideological and military expansion into Africa. In Angola, the Soviets concentrated 300 tanks and 60 helicopter gunships, supported by 15,000 Cuban troops, in preparation for a massive invasion of neighboring countries. The situation began to accelerate to the point of potential disaster for moderate African states.

Kenya's legendary president, Jomo Kenyatta, himself a leader of the anti-colonial movement in Kenya who wrested Kenyan independence from the British Empire and who had enormous influence in Africa, opposed Soviet intervention and requested help from the United States, whose geopolitical interests in containing the proliferation of communism coincided with the preservation of an independent Africa. The United States initiated covert operations to provide military assistance to African regimes. Although American assistance was on and off and, as usual, often a victim of partisan bickering in Congress, it did halt Cuban expansion in Africa. The war went on for fifteen more years, until Ronald Reagan decisively kicked the Cubans and their Russian masters completely out of Africa.

In this context we can get a clearer picture of Obama Sr.'s actual dreams: Capitalism is a tool of exploitation! The future is with socialism! America was preventing the spread of communism in Africa; therefore, America is evil! I leave it to you, the reader, to complete my deductive approach and decide for yourself which of his father's dreams the American president dreams of implementing. That would also explain why Barack Obama joined Jeremiah Wright's church and listened to Wright's disgraceful displays of anti-Americanism and hatred of white people for twenty years. *Jeremiah Wright was singing the song of Obama's father.*

It has been said that a son will have traits similar to his father upon reaching adulthood. Like father, like son. This begs the question: What about Obama's dreams from his mother? She had a much greater influence on her son than did his faraway father. Barack Obama referred to his mother as *"the dominant figure in my formative years.... The values she taught me continue to be my touchstone when it comes to how I go about the world of politics."*

What values did Obama's mother teach her son? Obama's parents were ideological twins. They became acquainted while attending a Russian language class. That fact really caught my attention. Why were those two learning Russian in the 1960s? My Eastern European suspicion tells me that they were planning to enter the University of Patrice Lumumba in Moscow. This so-called People's Friendship University was an educational and research center founded in 1960. Its stated objective at the time was to help nations of the Third World, mainly in Asia, Africa, and South America, by providing higher education and professional training. In reality, the university was preparing leaders of the National Liberation movement. The students were indoctrinated in Marxism-Leninism. Tuition and room and board were paid for. But that is just conjecture.

There is good reason to believe that Obama's mother would continue to instill the ideology of his father in her son long after they divorced. This assertion is evidenced by the fact that when her son's convictions were challenged by his Indonesian stepfather, Lolo Soetoro, she sent him from Indonesia back to Hawaii to live with his grandparents. She was definitely concerned about preserving the seeds of Marxism she had so successfully planted in her son's brain. We must accept it as inevitable that having been raised by Marxists and educated by Marxist professors, Obama embraced Marxism as the "touchstone" to "the world of politics."

Are You a Socialist?

Bill O'Reilly says that Obama is not a socialist because he does not advocate expropriation of private property. Mr. O'Reilly describes Obama as an ideologue and a big-government guy. So do a lot of well-respected and highly educated people who, however, have not been exposed to and are not well acquainted with socialist economics, and only vaguely familiar with the practice of socialism. So, if Mr. Obama is an ideologue, as Mr. O'Reilly believes he is, then to what ideology does he adhere?

Since there is no one universal model of socialism, whether or not a person is a socialist cannot be determined by the single criterion of expropriation of private property. As a political philosophy, socialism offers a surprisingly diverse assortment of entrees for a variety of political tastes. It includes, but is not limited to, state socialism, democratic socialism, social democratic socialism, Christian democratic socialism, National Socialism, Soviet-style revolutionary socialism, and even one with a "human face" (Gorbachev's version). The variants between these political flavors differ by the type of social ownership they advocate, the degree to which they rely on markets versus planning, management of economic enterprises, and the extent of government involvement in ownership and regulation of enterprises. Against this backdrop the most dominant nowadays is democratic socialism, which is a kind of socialist Trojan horse, masked as an alternative to Marxism. Traveling along the egalitarian highway charted by Karl Marx at a slow pace it emulates the strategy developed by the Russian Marxists Julius Martov and Pavel Axelrod (no relation to David Axelrod, Obama's campaign manager, has been established) expecting to make socialism more palatable by installing the Hugo Chavezes of this world through the democratic process (as I shall describe in the following chapters). Theoretically, the differences are superficial. Practically, regardless of how the socialists come to power, they all have one thing in common: control of the economy or, at a minimum, control of the most vital economic activities—energy, finance, and health care—to ensure "fair and equitable" distribution of wealth within society. In his book *To the Rural Poor* Lenin wrote:

> *We want to achieve a new and better order of society: in this new and better society there must be neither rich nor poor; all will have to work. Not a handful of rich people, but all the working people must enjoy the fruits of their common labor. Machines and other improvements must serve to ease the work of all and not to enable a few to grow rich at the expense of millions and tens of millions of people. This new and better society is called socialist society. The teachings about this society are called socialism.*

And Barack Obama said:

> *This is the moment when we must build on the wealth that open markets have created, and share its benefits more equitably.*[5]

Although this priceless gem of Obama's socialist wisdom may sound somewhat different from Lenin's, philosophically they are identical. Both quotes mean taking as much money as possible from productive citizens to share with non-productive or less-productive citizens. Obama shares Lenin's dream of dividing the economic pizza made by others into more equitable pieces, so they can feed everybody. It is worth emphasizing that the President clearly is not talking about creating wealth, which would be capitalism, but rather distributing other people's wealth, which by

---

[5] *July 24, 2008 Speech in Berlin, Germany.*

Lenin's definition is socialism. The overriding impetus of socialism is economic equality.

In order to implement the egalitarian dream, socialist society does not necessarily require government ownership of the means of production. As I pointed out, there are different versions of socialism and most of them offer egalitarianism without the extreme measure of expropriation of private property. Governments have a variety of means to enforce the distribution of wealth accumulated by private enterprises. Among the most powerful tools are taxation and regulation. Private enterprises can simply be regulated and taxed into equality or out of ownership altogether. Therefore, those who necessarily associate socialism with the central planning and expropriation of private property put undue emphasis on the process instead of the outcome.

> *As long as government controls the economy, it is able to replace the free-market capitalist economy with political economy, and being in a position to control profits, the objectives of socialism can be achieved.*

The Soviet version of socialism, revolutionary socialism, was centered on the expropriation of private property by the state as well as the complete abolition of private enterprise by force. However, Lenin urged against immediate expropriation of the means of production and abolition of private property. He wanted to make sure the government took control over the economy first. In his April Theses, published in April 1917, in the penumbra of the October revolution, Lenin wrote:

> *It is not our immediate task to "introduce" socialism, but only to bring social production and the distribution of products at once under the control of the Soviets of Workers' Deputies.*

The fact that Obama and the socialists are not calling for the expropriation of private property does not mean that contemporary socialists are opposed to it ideologically. Perhaps they are following Lenin's directive and wants *"to bring social production and the distribution of products at once under the control of the Soviets of Workers' Deputies"*—in this case the government bureaucrats. In any event, the expropriation of private property cannot be accomplished through the democratic process; it requires a monopoly on the means of coercion and violence—dictatorship. In this view,

> *Obama and the Democratic Party are acting pragmatically on the outer edge of the possible trying to accomplish the achievable while the desirable is still out of reach.*

It has been known that even hardcore committed socialists will sacrifice ideology and tolerate private enterprise if it benefits the state. The Russian Bolsheviks are a case in point. In order to restore the economy after the three-year civil war following the Russian revolution, the Bolsheviks enacted the NEP (New Economic Policy), introduced in the 1920s to extricate Russia from its economic depression. In a rare moment of honesty, Lenin himself acknowledged that NEP was in fact a partial return to capitalism. This new policy lifted restrictions on private property and allowed private enterprises into the economy. It also offered lucrative concessions to the "exploiters of working people"—foreign capitalists. As soon as the country started to recover, the Bolsheviks imposed heavy taxation on private enterprises and drove them out of business.

North Korea is another illustrative example. I am sure that most of the readers think of North Korea as a communist state that forbids ownership of private property and outlaws the free market. You may be surprised to know that approximately 75 percent of North Koreans are independent contractors. After a famine in the mid-1990s, when a million people died, the government decided to lease the means of production to private entrepreneurs. Officially, everything belongs to the government, but in actuality private businesses run the nation's industry and pay bribes to government officials.

Obama's background and affiliations leave no doubts about this president's political pedigree. Since his early years Barack Obama has sought out and maintained relationships with radicals, communists, socialists, and anti-capitalist groups that shared his views.

In 1996, Obama received the endorsement of the Chicago branch of the Democratic Socialists of America (DSA) for an Illinois State Senate seat. Given his agenda, which included universal health care, the huge proliferation of the welfare state, the cap-and-trade bill, and scores of additional regulations and heavy taxation, supplemented by attacks on the private enterprise system, the President would fit in comfortably in a socialist country such as France.

In January 2012 *Forbes* magazine published an article by Paul Roderick Gregory, "Is President Obama Truly a Socialist?" The article incorporates the Declaration of Principles of the Party of European Socialists (PES) issued in November 2011, which summarizes the European socialist agenda that includes the following:

- *A welfare state and state-provided universal access to education and health care will be imposed.*
- *A society must ensure that the wealth generated by all is shared fairly, as determined by the state.*
- *Collective responsibility makes society stronger: people work together and all people are enabled to live a dignified life free of poverty and protected from social risks in life.*
- *The state must insure that economic growth is environmentally "sustainable."*
- *If unfettered by government control, market forces, driven by greed, shift power to the privileged few, deepen economic, geographic, and social inequalities, and create economic crises.*
- *Ensuring long-lasting prosperity, stability—and above all, peace—requires effective coordination in the international realm based on democracy, mutual respect, and human rights.*
- *A strong government must preserve the public good, guarantee the common interest, promote justice and solidarity, and allow people to lead lives rich beyond material wealth, so that each individual's fulfillment is also part of a collective endeavor.*

But does all this amount to qualifications to be a socialist? I do not know about Bill O'Reilly, but there should be no doubt that if the Party of European Socialists were to rate Obama, he would get a perfect score. Should we ask the Europeans about President Obama, they would point out the undeniable fact that he is definitely another "democratic socialist." By contrast, if you are willing, once again, to look at the President through Marxist red lenses you will see that his ideology has a lot more in common with Karl Marx and Vladimir Lenin than with Pierre-Joseph Proudhon[6] or Francois Hollande[7].

Are You a Moderate Republican?

We can conclude with a high degree of certainty that there is no danger that Obama will join the Republican Party in this lifetime.

Are You a Marxist?

A Russian proverb says that one word of truth shall outweigh the whole world. Not surprisingly, President Obama denies he is a Marxist, as in his assertion that *"Contrary to the claims of some of my critics and some of the editorial pages, I am an ardent believer in the free market."* Given the President's socialist policies and pattern of behavior, it sounds as credible as Karl Marx stating, *"If anything is certain, it is that I myself am not a Marxist."* The President exhibits a moral and behavioral pattern that most Americans literally do not understand. For the political pundits who evaluate the President's actions from the standpoint of conventional politics, they look so bizarre that they mystify both his critics and supporters alike.

For eight years the President has been traveling around the country and telling cheering crowds of supporters, with a straight face, that he is committed to bring the deficit down and balance the budget while he has been running the deficit to unsustainable levels. He

---

[6] *Pierre-Joseph Proudhon, a contemporary of Karl Marx, was a French politician, philosopher, and socialist.*

[7] *Francois Hollande is a socialist and the president of France.*

talks about American economic competitiveness as he wastes billions of dollars on green energy that costs consumers and businesses substantially more than conventional sources, making American products and services less competitive. He talks about energy independence, but blocks drilling for oil and building the Keystone pipeline, which would bring cheap Canadian oil to Texas refineries. He says he wants to reduce unemployment, but he has tried to prevent Boeing from opening a new non-union facility in South Carolina. He says he supports Israel, but he wants her to live within her 1967 borders. He says Iran should not obtain a nuclear weapon, but he preserves Iran production capabilities and promises not to use military force against Iran.

It becomes all the more inexplicable since he created the Simpson-Bowles "Deficit Reduction Commission" and then refused to endorse its deficit-reducing proposals. The list of inconsistencies is many miles long and it is not the author's intent to list them all. Republicans criticize the President for unrestrained spending, a staggered economy, and a disastrous foreign policy, depicting him as being in way over his head as he tries ineffectively to stabilize the economy and maintain American prestige in the world. They label the President's policies a colossal failure. Although the President's record makes him vulnerable, and he may never be remembered for his competence, tough-sounding rhetoric is no substitute for a realistic assessment of Obama's agenda and policies—nor is it a substitute for the facts. *Webster's* dictionary defines "failure" as a lack of success, but facts show that this president has been very successful in implementing his legislative agenda. It is this agenda, consisting of policies snipped from the Bolsheviks' past and resurrected from the garbage dump of history that is so deeply troubling.

Those who are bewildered by the President's agenda portray him as out of touch, incompetent, and misguided. The stark reality, and what most Americans have thus far failed to recognize as immutable fact, is that the President may be out of touch and incompetent, but he and his supporters are not misguided; they are directed by the ideology of Marxism-Leninism. As a result, his critics keep stressing the obvious over the important.

This president should be judged by what he does as well as by what he says—not by the promises he makes, but by the promises he keeps. The President who, during his 2008 election campaign, told Americans that he is capable of working across the aisle has been unable to find political common ground with anybody outside his Democrat base. Since the 2009 inauguration very few issues of importance have been resolved without a crisis. Obama's administration is in a permanent state of war with the Republicans about the future of this country; with the business community about taxes and regulations; with the states about health care, oil and gas drilling, border security, education, and voting rights; and with the Catholic Church about church policies on abortion and contraception.

> *There is a simple explanation for the President's actions: our president lives in a different world—the world of Marxist dialectical materialism, where change is the product of a constant conflict between opposites, arising from the internal contradictions inherent in all events, ideas, and movements.*

Consequently, Obama is acting in a predictable ethical and moral fashion, consistent with Marxist dialectical materialism. Karl Marx believed that the history of humankind is fundamentally the history of struggle between social classes. Therefore, most important political, economic, and cultural developments can be explained in terms of their relationship to what he called "class struggle." Since almost any event can be misconstrued and exploited as a "class struggle," the President finds himself in the midst of permanent warfare with everyone who may doubt his intellectual preeminence. As long as Obama could see the world as a conflict between opposing forces, he could seek conflict as the process leading to achieving his strategic objectives. It is important to understand that he is not just incapable of conflict resolution; *he is manufacturing conflicts* in order to shore up his political base, create confusion, and disparage political opponents.

In this respect, the President and his team relied on the experience of their infamous predecessors. Lenin was a master at taking advantage of chaos. He believed that crises create opportunities for change, or, in his mind, revolution. "Our task," wrote Lenin in 1902 in *What Is to Be Done*, *"is to utilize every manifestation of discontent, and to collect and utilize every grain of rudimentary protest."* Indeed, if you want to change a society, here is Lenin's script: cause the problem. Spread the misery. Send a cadre of professional community organizers to unite all of the angry and disinherited spirits to fuel an organized revolt. Entice chaos and violence. Exploit chaos for larger political objectives. Blame your political opponents, demonize and criminalize them. Move decisively to request a temporary suspension of civil liberties in exchange for the restoration of law and order. Usurp power before the deceived masses realize that there is nothing more permanent in politics than something temporary.

> *From Lenin to Obama the political landscape changed, but the scheme remains assertively consistent.*

Taking advantage of a crisis has always been a strategy for extremists to make fundamental changes in society. In recent history, the Bolsheviks skillfully used the First World War and the economic downturn in Russia to overthrow the Democratic Provisional Government in 1917 and impose a dictatorship of the proletariat. In the 1930 Reichstag election, the Nazis took advantage of Germany's economic and political crisis to gain 143 seats—a vast improvement over their previous showing—which led to the demise of the Weimar Republic. A senior Nazi official, Gregor Strasser, claimed that what was a disaster for the Republic was "good, very good for us."

"Never allow a crisis to go to waste," former White House Chief of Staff Rahm Emanuel told the *New York Times*, echoing Lenin and Strasser. *"There are opportunities to do big things,"* he concluded. Self-proclaimed radical socialists Luke Cooper and Simon Hardy, in their book *Beyond Capitalism: The Future of Capitalist Politics*, validated the administration's strategy when they wrote in 2012, "For

the left it is no problem to reimagine, to re-conceive, the economic crisis as an opportunity for radical politics."[8] They still sound like Lenin, don't they?

In 2008, Obama's campaign was shamelessly excited about an opportunity to exploit a national emergency to push for "CHANGE" and there was no reason to alter this winning strategy for the 2012 election other than to replace "CHANGE" with the communist slogan "FORWARD." It is hard to believe that the American public took seriously a slogan which had been painted on the placards and walls all over the USSR for seventy years. Remarkably, they did so with self-destructive ignorance.

This governing by crisis has been exacerbated by the fact that in the mind of a Marxist, anything less than 100 percent support is betrayal. Indeed, unable to persuade his opponents of the merits of his case, Obama treats political discourse as warfare and resorts to insults rather than intellectual arguments. He views politics not as a contest between competing ideologies or policy visions, but as an attack on his personal definition of right and wrong. Political pundits who express concern that permanent confrontation may jeopardize the President's strategy simply do not understand the President's strategy. The state of permanent confrontation *is* the strategy. Confrontation is the source of his strength; lack of confrontation [*contradiction*] quashes his confidence and drains intellectual energy.

In classic Marxist style, Obama uses bullying tactics and issues direct threats to his political opponents and even tried to, and arguably did, cow the Supreme Court in order to secure a favorable outcome for his health care legislation. In October 2010, before the November midterm elections, Obama spoke with Eddie Sotelo, a host of Univision, and issued a warning:

> *"We're gonna punish our enemies and we're gonna reward our friends who stand with us on issues that are important to us."* And then, referring to the

---

[8] *Luke Cooper and Simon Hardy,* Beyond Capitalism: The Future of Capitalist Politics, p. 18.

> Republicans, he added, *"Those aren't the kind of folks who represent our core American values."*

To those who do not believe Karl Marx's "History repeats itself, first as tragedy, second as farce," ponder Lenin, who declared during the Russian civil war, *"Who is not with us is against us."* Marxists are monopolists in the fields of politics and power. They tolerate no rivals, no competition of ideas. Obama's intolerable attitude toward dissent created the environment of enduring conflagration that inevitably diverts the efforts and intellectual energies from defining the national interests. This method of governing challenges a political order constructed over 250 years of existence of the United States and can be incurably damaging. The drama of infighting has gradually raised awareness of the electorate and the November 2010 and 2014 elections exposed the President's ideological vulnerability and strategic weakness. After a staggering defeat in 2010 the President promised, and after even greater defeat in 2014 reiterated, his intent for cooperation "across the aisle" and a willingness to compromise. But this opportunistic approach encountered an irreconcilable ideological dilemma: revolutionary Marxism has not been known for its spirit of cooperation or compromise. Indeed, Marxists accept compromise only as ephemeral expediency, a temporary respite, which would ultimately lead to the destruction of opposition and seizure of ultimate power. In this manner, Marxism-Leninism defines compromise as "a solution equally unacceptable for all parties involved." It is considered a temporary necessity, to be abolished as circumstances permit. This state of affairs is not negotiable—Marxism is not a policy, it is a cause. In the relentless pursuit of his aim, the President—failing to build moral consensus—went back to doing what he does best.

Everything about Obama is absolute. Passionately convinced of his rightness, Obama continues seeking domination in the way of a totalitarian ruler, never missing an opportunity to enhance his eminence by denigrating his political opponents. Victory at any cost becomes the only acceptable outcome of political discourse. We remember too well his arrogant pronouncement, *"I won."* The man should have learned from Lloyd George[9], who remarked, *"Injustice, arrogance, displayed in the hour of triumph will never be forgotten or forgiven."* Obama was setting up an adversarial posture from the outset. In this hostile atmosphere there is no room for statesmanship, cooperation, or compromise. The Republicans who have been trying to work with the President to find a meaningful compromise on issues concerning the nation have been deluded, outwitted, and proven to be hopelessly naïve or politically shortsighted.

> *Unable to find a middle ground between total victory and total defeat, Obama, in too many instances, has purposely worked America into a deadlock.*

Motivated by political imperatives, the President continues to emulate Marxist tactics and rhetoric by exploiting class warfare, civil disobedience, and riots, reaching out to minorities and intellectuals, and dividing the nation along racial lines and income brackets to implement his programs. Impelled by conviction and devoured by ambition, Obama disastrously divided the nation into "those who are with us" and "those who are against us." That tactic was condemned by another former Senator from Illinois, Abraham Lincoln, who famously said, *"A house divided against itself cannot stand."* It was true for Lincoln—and it is true for Obama.

As the leader of the nation, the President is expected to govern by constitutional principles and political consensus. Obama, however, unable and unwilling to secure hegemony through consent, has been acting as a Marxist guerrilla leader who hates political opponents and seeks imposition of his agenda by a combination of force, coercion, and emotional mass appeal. As a consequence, instead of being a symbol of national unity, he has fostered a condition of civil upheaval.

So let's meet the real Barack Hussein Obama—Marxist theorist, Bolshevik revolutionary, and President of the United States. Let's also meet his so-called Democratic (in name only) Party.

---

[9] *British liberal politician and statesman (1863–1945).*

CHAPTER 4
American Liberal Bolshevik

If it looks like a duck and walks like a duck...you know the answer. But if it speaks like a Bolshevik, acts like a Bolshevik, and thinks like a Bolshevik, then what is it?

Historical Inevitability

I've often been asked, "Who are the Bolsheviks?"
The Bolsheviks (Bolshevik means "majority" in Russian) were a radical faction of the Marxist Russian Social Democratic Labor Party (RSDLP), a revolutionary party aimed at establishing a socialist state in Russia, which split from the Menshevik (minority) faction at the Second Party Congress in 1903. Although the dispute erupted ostensibly over minor issues of party organization, the two branches of the RSDLP were ideologically apart about the strategy of replacing the existing economic and political order with a socialist state. The necessity of replacing the existing order with a new system emanated from RSDLP's theoretical basis—Marxist dialectical materialism. For those unacquainted with Marxism, dialectical materialism, in a nutshell, is the amalgamation of two philosophical theories: dialectics and materialism.

Marxist dialectics is the philosophy of permanent evolution of the natural world applied to society. It purports to explain the perennial progression from primitive forms of human organization to the concept of state, from slavery to feudalism, from feudalism to capitalism, and so forth. The main postulate of Marxist dialectics is that capitalism, the evil system based on "exploitation of working people," is not eternal and will eventually be replaced with a more advanced form of society. At this point Marxism makes a giant philosophical leap and declares that this advanced society is "communism," with an intermediate step called "socialism."

Materialism argues that the reality of the surrounding world determines the way people think and what they believe. "It is not the consciousness of men that determines their existence, but their social existence that determines their consciousness," wrote Karl Marx. The logical conclusion is that since we know that capitalism will eventually be replaced with communism via socialism, why wait? By changing social existence we change people's consciousness and subsequently craft a new humanity. Dialectical materialism is the science of man-made societal change.

As stated earlier, the two fractions differed on the methods of the implementation of change, not the ultimate objective. The Bolsheviks rejected permanent evolution in favor of permanent revolution. Their strategy and tactics, originating from the political and economic theories of German economist Karl Marx and further developed by Russian professional revolutionary Vladimir Lenin, called for the imposition of a new world order by force via "dictatorship of the proletariat."[10]

The Mensheviks, led by Julius Martov and Pavel Axelrod, although supporting a revolutionary approach in principle, were more inclined to use democratic institutions and trade unions to accomplish the transition to socialism. The Bolsheviks, led by Vladimir Lenin, would have none of that. They had always had deeply rooted contempt for what they considered bourgeois democratic institutions and would not wait for the peaceful transition to socialism that could take an unforeseen period of time. They wanted "Socialism Now" and would happily use violence to achieve their objectives. The Bolsheviks ultimately won, became the Communist Party of the Soviet Union, and eventually liquidated their comrades in arms in accordance with Marxist comradeship ritual. This breed

---

[10] *Proletariat: lowest social class of people, unskilled laborers.*

of Marxist Socialists believed that they were the intellectual elite destined and capable of changing the tempo of history at their discretion and had never been secretive about the methods of accomplishing their objectives. Prominent Bolshevik and Marxist theoretician Nikolai Bukharin[11] described them with proletarian frankness:

> "*From the point of view of...historic proportions, proletarian enforcement in all its forms ranging from firing squads to forced labor is, as paradoxical as it may sound, the method of generating communist humanity out of the human material of the capitalist era.*" [12]

This brutish combination of a political movement and a terrorist organization embodied the ultimate expression of Marxism. To the Bolsheviks, Marxism was not just another political and economic theory; it was the supreme gospel, an infallible truth that prophesied universal social justice. Bolshevism was not just a moral cause of justice; it was a geopolitical endeavor that was supposed to end up in global conquest. Therefore, hereinafter the author uses "socialism," "communism," and "Bolshevism" interchangeably.

The Bolsheviks' unshakable conviction was augmented by Marx's theory of "historical inevitability." In 1814 French astronomer Pierre-Simon Laplace came up with a theory of how to predict the future. He theorized that if you "know all forces that set nature in motion, and all positions of all items, of which nature is composed," together with all the laws of physics and chemistry, then "nothing would be uncertain and the future, just like the past, would be present before your eyes." Karl Marx applied this idea to society and history and developed a theory of "historical inevitability." The Bolsheviks believed that communism represents the vanguard of history, and its triumph over capitalism is inevitable. It is

---

[11] *Prominent Soviet politician, member of the Politburo and Central Committee, executed in March 1938 as an enemy of the people.*

[12] *Bukharin,* Economics of Transition, *Chapter X*

a "historical inevitability" and therefore should be forced upon a population incapable of appreciating its greatness or understanding the concept of economic equality and the fairness of wealth distribution. The concept was not new; it originated during the French Revolution in a decree, issued in December of 1792, declaring that the French nation would treat as enemies of the people those who refused to accept liberty and equality.[13]

As an ideologue of the French Revolution, Jean-Jacques Rousseau, put it, people would be "forced to be free."[14] "Forcing people to be free" was the underlying motivation for the 1917 October Revolution in Russia. Of course, for the leaders of the revolution this meant freeing the wealthy from their possessions. Unfortunately, at this writing, generations of Americans have grown up with no memory of Bolshevism. American schools barely mention this tragic period in world history. But for someone who has personal experience and memories of this era, the situation could not be clearer—the so-called progressives have set a course to force America to "be free" and the leadership of the Democratic Party is acquiescing in the abandonment of the core principles of the Republic. Just as with his predecessors, Obama's convictions are based on Marxist dialectical materialism and the theory of "historical inevitability."

There is no way of sidestepping this comparison: both the objectives and the techniques coincide too closely. Incontrovertibly, just like the Russian Bolsheviks, they want Marxist-Leninist socialism, and they want it now. There is no need for a messy democratic process when the outcome is preordained. In the absence of an ideological counterweight, Obama and the leadership of the Democratic Party emulate the strategy and tactics used by the Bolsheviks to seize power in Russia in 1917 with remarkable subtlety.

Yet despite the conceptual similarities between the Russian Bolsheviks' methods and strategy and Obama's approach, there is

---

[13] *Source: Thomas C. Mendenhall et al.,* Quest for a Principle of Authority in Europe, 1715 to Present *(New York: Holt, Rinehart and Winston, 1948), pp. 82–83.*

[14] *The Social Contract, Chapters 6–9.*

one fundamental difference. In contradistinction to their viciously murderous predecessors, who paved the road to their "bright socialist future" with the bonds and bloodshed of their victims, Obama's ideological paradigm involves a benevolent approach. This eunuch version of Bolshevism adapted to contemporary America's economic and social realities is no longer the terrifying Bolshevik monster that shook the world with terror; this crossbred critter exploits indifference, complacency, and acquiescence. It replaces the dictatorship of the proletariat with the dictatorship of government bureaucracy, and the expropriation of private property with statism—i.e., government control of the economy and supremacy of the values of the state that result in domination of the economic and political life of the citizenry. Although it is also led by intellectual elites committed to changing humanity and influencing the tempo of history, the driving force behind this socialist model is bondage: *"The hand that feeds you controls you."*

Liberal Bolshevism is "Bolshevism with kid gloves," and it is founded on dependence.

Liberal Bolshevism's slow-roll strategy is designed to do to the United States incrementally what Russian Bolshevism did to Russia in 1917 abruptly. Notwithstanding its heavy Russian accent, Liberal Bolshevism is bringing under one roof all the true believers and intellectuals disheartened and disillusioned by the ugliness of Stalinism, Maoism, and other socialist "isms" but still yearning for equality, fairness, and righteousness. It is also intended to ascertain ideological cohesion among pseudo-patriot advocates of strong governmental authority and left-wing lunatics, to whom capitalism is a common enemy.

Obama shall be given credit where credit is due. The scheme is resourceful; under the guise of the common good, the Democratic Party has engaged in social engineering of the most radical kind. An unemotional logician and imaginative tactician, Obama, while preserving the theoretical significance of Marxism, trashed those nineteenth-century Marxist orthodox theories and Lenin's principles that applied to an impoverished country and stood in the way of twenty-first-century American capitalism, and replaced them with his own pragmatic Marxism.

It shall be emphasized that, although based on different premises, this pragmatic Marxism is not a fundamental revision of the "Marxism of Marx" in any shape or form; it is simply a method of achieving Marxist objectives, which serve both the ideological and the utopian ends of egalitarianism. The ideology remains as a guide to the Marxist future, albeit adapted to the objective factors as a pragmatic imperative, consistent with Marxist dialectics.

This American version of Marxism, dug out of mothballs and tailored for the twenty-first century, promotes the same false ideals and pseudo-liberal values. It is still characterized by its belligerent atheism, collectivism, unscrupulousness, falsehood, demagoguery, and ruthless treatment of ideological opponents. In not so elegant terms, it can be said that the brutal Russian version of Marxism ruled by lies and indiscriminant terror, while the "gentle" American variety rules through lies and coercion. The goals are the same; only the methods differ.

As Marx himself stated, *"Men make their own history, but they do not make it as they please; they do not make it under circumstances chosen by themselves, but under circumstances directly encountered, given and transmitted to them from the past."*

Obama's Marxist professors and the scholars who shaped his ideas may find the roots of Obama's pragmatic Marxism in Reformism, Gramsci's Marxist doctrine and Fabian Marxism, or even Russian Bolshevism, for which the so-called revolutionary pragmatism with no morality was a central tenet of the failed "scientific socialism" they advanced in the immediate aftermath of the October Revolution. It is not the purpose of this book to delve into how, and in collaboration with whom, Obama has developed his progressive version of Marxism, or whether Socrates and Aristotle had any influence on his thinking. We may be curious, but in the final analysis it is not important.

What is important is that by imaginatively commingling the Mensheviks' strategy of a nonviolent transition to socialism with potent Bolshevik tactics, and using his own theoretical platform for developing consistent socialist programs, Obama has accomplished what generations of American radicals tried and failed to do—unite Marxism and pragmatism. In doing so, Obama showed the face of a crafty politician with the underpinnings of a philosophical intellect who, by adroitly maneuvering among the passions of liberals, the mistrust of conservatives, the clumsy forcefulness of the Republicans, the inevitable opposition of free-marketers, and the idealism of Americans, has been successfully transforming the USA into the USSA, the United Socialist States of America. It's been said that nothing is more creative—or more destructive—than a brilliant mind with a purpose.

Given the political reality, Lenin would have emphatically acknowledged the strategic brilliance of Obama's ideological model of Marxism, which, despite its benevolence, manages to preserve the spirit and heritage of Bolshevism with all its witchery and majesty.

Against this background, it would be fair to call President Barack Hussein Obama the American Liberal Bolshevik and his political party the American Social Democratic Party. It is from here on I venture to present Obama and his party's philosophy, motifs, the principles of their morals, their ethics, and their strategy. In doing so, I will validate this alarming indictment beyond a reasonable doubt, in harmony with the historical facts, and by letting the facts speak for themselves.

Philosophy of Poverty

During the 2008 presidential election, John McCain said about Obama, "I am not questioning his patriotism, I am questioning his judgment." Should McCain read Trevor Loudon's book *Barack Obama and the Enemies Within*, published in early 2008, he might understand how profoundly wrong he was. Obama is blessed with sound analytical judgment, but his ideology and agenda raise doubts about his commitment to American idealism and, therefore, must be questioned.

While McCain did not question the future president's ideology, the mainstream press, offering euphoric support for a black presidential candidate, failed to vet him and also actively suppressed critics challenging his associations and background. Media bias became even more blatant after Obama's 2009 inauguration. Since the inauguration, the preponderance of the media have been enamored with the President, comparing him to John Adams, Thomas Jefferson, and Abraham Lincoln. *Newsweek* veteran Evan Thomas, who inherited ideological zeal from his avowed socialist grandfather, Norman Thomas,[15] while in a state of extreme excitement went even further, attributing to Obama God-like qualities when he said on MSNBC, "In a way, Obama's standing above the country, above—above the world. He's sort of God." Mr. Thomas demonstrated the fullest extent of his liberal journalistic bias by disgracefully imitating the Holy Bible at Acts 12–21, 22:

And upon a set day Herod, arrayed in royal apparel, sat upon his throne, and made an oration unto them. And the people gave a shout, [saying, It is] the voice of a god, and not of a man. Hallelujah!!!

In that moment any doubts about the President's birthplace were put to rest; he was treated as if he had been born in Bethlehem. This atavism, a "cult of personality" reminiscent of Joseph Stalin's, was shamelessly and arrogantly reincarnated in the United States by the liberal press in revealing its intense commitment to Barack Obama. In contrast, even Joseph Stalin's cult of personality never elevated him to the status of God; he had to settle for the modest title of "Father of All Nations." The liberal press's frantic worshipping of Obama that began before his first inauguration continued unabated. In 2012 the *Newsweek* cover had a side shot of Obama's head, and the "Inauguration 2013" cover story announced "The Second Coming."

---

[15] *Norman Mattoon Thomas (November 20, 1884–December 19, 1968) was a leading American socialist, pacifist, and six-time presidential candidate of the Socialist Party of America.*

The role of championing a cult of personality assumed by the liberal media should come as no surprise; the media have consistently supported this model of governing that has been the epitome of every Marxist regime that ever existed. The naïve crowds euphorically bought into a cult of personality, and Marxists have universally used the media to proliferate the brainwashing seduction, hypnotizing the ignorant masses to await with religious piety the rise of the Star of Captivating Happiness. That would explain how a false prophet who offered nothing beyond facile "Hope and Change" and meaningless "Yes We Can" has such an enormous following of worshippers.

Adhering to the cult-of-personality pattern, James T. Kloppenberg has gone so far as to call Obama a philosopher president. The philosophy that has guided President Obama, according to Mr. Kloppenberg, is pragmatism. So, what is pragmatism? How does it relate to the average observer? Pragmatism is a philosophical movement that claims that an ideology is true and a proposition is to be found to implement the ideology by adopting ideas and convictions to the circumstances. There should be no mistake. Pragmatism is not a movement of new ideas; it is rather an instrument of implementing ideas and policies. But Mr. Kloppenberg, despite wide elaboration, stopped conspicuously short of defining the nature of Obama's pragmatism. The reason this is significant is because pragmatism could be a weapon of pragmatic thinkers seeking practical accommodation with opposing views, or it could be a philosophy of political chameleons that lack principles and instead are linked to cynicism and political expediency. Or it could simply be a tool of an imposter who uses elusive and disingenuous rhetoric to conceal his real objectives and win the support of the electorate. Hence, we should not fall in with this vague description of the President's pragmatism on strictly philosophical terms without first defining the vision, the programs, and the policies.

Given the litany of the President's socialist policies, Mr. Kloppenberg perfunctorily provided an eloquent affirmation that the philosopher President's pragmatism intended to disguise the implementation of Karl Marx's exhumed "Philosophy of Poverty" (which is how nineteenth-century French politician, philosopher, and socialist Pierre-Joseph Proudhon described Marx's theories).[16] The indictment becomes even more evident if we strip away the cult of personality, the media drumbeat, and the theatrical performance before the teleprompter. We are then forced to recognize that

> *Obama's agenda and principles of governance read as if they came straight out of the University of Marxism-Leninism. There is nothing new here but the striking parallels between the Russian Bolsheviks and Obama's administration: both utterly convinced of their own uncompromising righteousness and both equally obsessed with power and control, and both share fanatic belief in economic equality.*

The President, having disdain for the democratic process, exhibits the attributes of Bolshevism. His administration displays a plethora of distinctly Bolshevik traits, and the intellectual heritage of Marxism-Leninism is profoundly entrenched in this president's administration. Machiavelli once noted that we can know a leader by the people he surrounds himself with. Obama created a shadow government inundated by thirty left-wing radicals—self-professed communists such as Van Jones, Mao Tse-Tung admirers such as Anita Dunn, anti–free marketers, constitutional revisionists, anti-business and anti-gun activists, First Amendment opponents, and supporters of big government and a welfare state (although some of them are no longer with the administration).

Those hand-picked appointments of incompetent but loyal "czars" were intended to overtake our elected form of government and circumvent Congress's approval and scrutiny. Although Obama called them czars, in reality they are more akin to Lenin's commissars, overseeing their respective departments and making sure the President's destructive socialist policies are implemented

---

[16] *In 1846, Proudhon criticized Karl Marx's theories in his book* System of Economical Contradictions: or, The Philosophy of Poverty. *In the next year Karl Marx responded to the criticism with his own book,* The Poverty of Philosophy.

to the letter. As is the case in all Marxist governments, this one is ideologically driven and prizes fidelity to the cause rather than competence. Competence has never been Obama's trademark, and after two terms the superficiality of his administration is so appalling that it may stand out as the most inept in American history. The amalgamation of ideology and ineptitude feels like the reincarnation of Bolshevism in its ugly form and substance.

Speaking of substance, if there were still any uncertainty about President Obama's political pedigree, his eulogistic orations saturated with Marxist ideology alleviated any doubt of his intention to remake the country by his own authority that he sees no limits to. The panegyrics revile the commissar's spirit of autocracy and offer us a glimpse of his agenda and strategy, making him the best witness against himself. Very often the witness unwittingly expresses his intended predation, and it behooves all of us to pay attention to what he says. The conundrum is that most Americans, unfamiliar with the language of ideology, continuously fail to connect the dots. Some listen but do not hear, others hear but do not listen; unfortunately only a few listen *and* hear what their President is saying. From the outset, Obama and the members of his administration were never secretive about how they intended to govern. Regrettably, even those of us who do listen and hear, hear the obvious and very often do not hear the important. Hereinafter, I shall endeavor to translate the language of Marxism into English. In his address to the nation in January 2010, Obama proclaimed:

> *"These disagreements, about the role of government in our lives, about our national priorities and our national security, they've been taking place for over two hundred years. They're the very essence of democracy."*

Here he stated the obvious, and then came the important, which erased the obvious: *"But we still need to govern."* Obama is not the first head of state for which pluralism and democracy are an impediment to omnipotence and governing. And how he intended to govern was later explained by his longtime political consigliere and his chief of staff at the time, Rahm Emanuel, who confirmed the application of Bolshevik practice when he promised that Obama would govern "through executive orders and directives to get the job done across a front of issues." In his interview on the television program *60 Minutes* that aired on December 11, 2011, Obama confirmed how he intended to resolve *"these disagreements"* when he emphatically declared:

> *"What I'm not gonna do is wait for Congress. So wherever we have an opportunity and I have the executive authority to go ahead and get some things done, we're just gonna go ahead and do 'em."*

With arrogant self-confidence Obama was saying that he could not wait for democracy to work. He clearly relished the position of power and it was going to his head. In January 2012, frustrated with the GOP Congress's refusal to rubber-stamp his destructive agenda, Obama reacted with immense and visceral hostility to the democratic process:

> *"But when Congress refused to act, and as a result, hurts our economy and puts our people at risk, then I have an obligation as president to do what I can without them. I've got an obligation to act on behalf of the American people. And I'm not going to stand by while a minority in the Senate puts party ideology ahead of the people that we were elected to serve."*

One caveat: the President is not the only one elected. "WE" means the House and the Senate, consisting of five hundred thirty-five representatives, as well. But the President, consumed with power and inspired by the Democrats applauding the pattern of lawlessness, did not slow down. On July 24, 2013, speaking before Knox College in Galesburg, Illinois, Obama confirmed once again his disregard for the Constitution:

> *"So, yes, Congress is tough right now, but that's not going to stop me. We're going to do everything we can, wherever we can, <u>with or without Congress</u>, to make things happen [emphasis added]."*

This time, in order to justify his authoritarian political practices, he took a page from Bolshevik Yakov Sverdlov,[17] who praised the efficiency of Bolshevik rule:

> *"It is very good that legislative and executive powers [in Soviet Russia] are not divided by a thick wall as they are in the West. All problems can be decided quickly."*

It is worth remembering that every time the world is driven by the brazen conviction that power can accomplish anything, the world ends up in lies, tyranny, and blood.

Lacking intellectual rigor, governing by executive orders, and using power instead of achieving consensus have become the mode of operation of the President and his Social Democrats. This dictatorial style of governing should surprise no one. Supporters of this form of "one-man-rule" philosophy try to justify it as being routine because previous presidents, both Democrats and Republicans, were not shy about using executive power to advance their agendas. But the issue here is quality, not quantity. Some of Obama's executive orders have bluntly violated the Constitution and the rule of law.

For instance, the unilateral decisions to relieve work requirements for welfare recipients and to block deportation of some young illegal immigrants are in clear violation of U.S. immigration law and existing legislation.

Further, the President is not embarrassed to contradict himself when he believes it is politically expedient. From July 2010 through November 2014, Obama had been telling the American people in explicit terms that he had no power under the Constitution to defer

---

[17] *Yakov Mikhailovich Sverdlov was a Bolshevik party leader and chairman of the All-Russian Central Executive Committee.*

the deportation of and provide legal status to illegal emigrants. Although the Constitution was not amended during this period, on November 20, 2014, Obama issued an executive order that blocked the deportation of 4.3 million illegal immigrants. Numerous waivers and unilateral changes to Obamacare, refusal to defend the Defense of Marriage Act in court, and blatant attempts by the Environmental Protection Agency to regulate carbon emissions after Congress refused to pass global-warming legislation are just a few of the most outrageous examples of the progressives' and social democrats' ideas of autocratic governance.

When the President can ignore the law, replacing the legislative process with executive orders, we are no longer governed by the rule of law and will then be no better than a communist regime or a banana republic. The President is using his authority to challenge and sacrifice the guiding principles of our nation with outlandish arrogance. American idealism embraces the national debate on both sides of the issues. Although the process may seem a messy and long-drawn-out affair, it is itself an expression of the vitality of American democracy—not the weakness the President and his soul mates perceive it to be. The separation of powers outlined in the Constitution imposes constraints that are permanent features of our system of governing and that characterize a mature democratic process.

The Liberal Bolshevik's impatience with and scant respect for the democratic process gave Obama and his party no impetus to work on legislation and move it through Congress. Bolstered by "historical inevitability," they have no motivation to build consensus. When unable to pass legislation through the democratic system of governing, they instead prefer to take an "easy pass" through the highway of American democracy. They treat the Constitution like a traffic light with all three colors on at once. So they choose the one they like best. Why? Because what they are trying to accomplish is "the right thing to do." "The right thing to do, the right thing to do," joyously declares the President over and over again. It is as if Obama and only Obama has a monopoly on virtue and the ultimate knowledge of what "right" really is, or there is a common meaning to it, self-importantly demonstrating a cynical disregard for one of the most fundamental aspects of American democracy:

The American people do have the constitutional right to be wrong, but the President does not have the right to define for them what is right.

In our representative system of government, which has not yet been abdicated, what is "right" is determined by the people's duly elected representatives in Congress. Perhaps the media and Democrats who unequivocally support the President's actions think that the Founding Fathers could not envision a genius like Obama in the White House and failed to address this extraordinary circumstance in the Constitution—something like a constitutional "force majeure" clause. Thus, this "minor" imperfection of the U.S. Constitution shall not be an impediment to "do the right thing." Harvard historian James T. Kloppenberg, reflecting on the newly found convoluted democratic principles of the left, explicitly agreed with Obama's attitude toward governing. In his book *Reading Obama*, Mr. Kloppenberg explained that Obama brings to the White House "a refreshing new way of thinking about the role of democracy." This president's "refreshing new way of thinking" can be summed up in a single word: contempt. Contempt for the office and for democratic institutions *is at the root of the Democrats' political tactic.*

The question we should ask ourselves is this: Haven't we been in this dance before? Some of us remember that when the concept of "the right thing to do" was applied in the Soviet Union by the Bolsheviks, it resulted in twenty million Soviet citizens being murdered in labor camps and prisons by Lenin and Stalin. Millions were starved to death building the so-called "great construction projects of communism" and even more died in the Gulag's mines, spitting out bloody chunks of their lungs. The screams of the victims of those who did "the right thing" have been heard all over Europe.

Disastrously, there was bloody reasoning behind the Bolsheviks' terror. The reasoning was, and still is, that we Marxist-Leninists are right, we know that we are. The most advanced theory in social science, Marxism-Leninism, tells us that what we are set to do is a "historical inevitability"; it is going to happen regardless. The Marxist doctrine is by itself sufficient to determine the proper strategy for any given situation and warrants our intellectual preeminence. Forget "we the people." That should explain why the President never admits mistakes. He cannot be wrong; *he is following the teachings of Karl Marx*, and those who are following him cannot be wrong either. It's always someone else's fault.

A popular Moscow joke colorfully depicts the clutter; President Obama held a cabinet meeting with leading Democrats to discuss a host of disasters facing his administration. Obama, as usual, blamed George Bush, Joe Biden blamed the Republicans, John Kerry blamed Vladimir Putin, Nancy Pelosi blamed global warming, Eric Holder blamed racism, Barbara Boxer blamed the rich, Harry Reid blamed the Koch brothers, Dianne Feinstein blamed the Tea Party, Michelle Obama blamed obesity, and Hillary Clinton was screaming, "What difference does it make?"

But back to my original point. "The Marxist doctrine is omnipotent because it is true," Lenin said. This is a Marxist truism. Those who disagree with Bolsheviks are enemies of the people; they prevent Bolsheviks from realizing the bright future. If enemies do not surrender, they need to be destroyed. Thus, the followers of Marx and Lenin have no reason to conceal their deep distrust of and intolerance for the democratic process. We should see their logic. The Democrats feel justified in subverting those democratic principles which prevent them from achieving the speedy implementation of their agenda.

This conviction of self-righteousness alleviates the sense of reality and rejects the concept of morality. Reasoning, sound judgment, and logic are being replaced by mystical obscurantism. Just like their political tutors, our Liberal Bolsheviks, once launched on a course, will not abandon it; they will pursue their illusory dreams with maniacal determination regardless of the efforts or the sacrifice, using all means at their disposal, irrespective of any ethical or moral consideration. These zealots exhibit boundless devotion to their leaders and share unwavering faith that the future belongs to them. The mystical obscurantists easily discard the tragic lessons of their ideological predecessors as mistakes made in the process of implementing progressive ideas. This time they will get "the right thing" right.

Fear and Hope

Bolshevik orthodoxy teaches that in order to control the masses the leader should instill fear and hope. The president expressed plenty of hope in his book *The Audacity of Hope* and has been peddling plenty of fear in his speeches and actions. Fearmongering, intimidation, demagoguery, and lies are potent weapons of regimes having a hidden agenda. The President has been frightening this country by manufacturing threats from such Obama-declared enemies as Wall Street, decrying the undue influence of big corporations, special-interest groups, and the so-called extremists of the Tea Party. The President uses scare tactics constantly to support his agenda. He warned us: If we do not bail out the banks, the economy will collapse; if there is no stimulus package, unemployment will be above 8 percent; if we do not bail out GM and Chrysler, the automobile industry will cease to exist. We were told the economy would sink into a deep recession if the "Jobs Bill" was not approved by Congress and money was not handed out to "too big to fail" corporate cronies. The list goes on: If the debt ceiling is not increased, Social Security recipients, military and federal retirees, and those on disability will not get their government checks. If Congress does not increase the debt ceiling, the U.S. will default on its payments. And if the U.S. defaults on its payments, Dante's Inferno will materialize with all its horror and suffering. This pathetic ritual, a mixture of determination and foreboding, is repeated over and over again. The artful manipulator always projects a sense of drama—or farce, depending on one's perception.

"Scaring the American people is exactly what President Obama is doing," Sarah Palin said. "The president is getting pretty good at this fearmongering and trying to cram down the public's throat this idea of bigger government, more spending." Scaring is one thing, governing is quite another. Faced with the reality of governing, Obama is attempting to camouflage his lack of leadership and inability to do any productive work with an overabundance of passionate speeches, but his passion and eloquence can only obscure reality, not change it. There is not a shred of evidence that any of the calamities that he is predicting will ever occur. When a "minuscule"

$100 billion per year spending cut known as the sequester went into effect in March 2013, President Obama predicted the economy would tank. It didn't. Environmental Armageddon never happened and we have not run out of oil.

There is no evidence that the "Jobs Bill" the president promulgated would ever stimulate the economy and produce a meaningful reduction in unemployment; actually, evidence points to the contrary. In light of the existing regulations and constraints imposed by the EPA, the President and Democrats should have known that their cheerful promises cannot be fulfilled—just getting permits for a substantial infrastructure project will take years. Notwithstanding the dubious feasibility of the President's legislative agenda, all problems genuine or spurious have one common remedy: spend more money. Why? We will examine that question in the following chapters.

Effluence and Affluence

Declining confidence in the future is weighing heavily on Americans nowadays, and less than a third believes the country is heading in the right direction. And for good reasons. As the largest debtor in the world, with a straggling economy, widespread poverty, a poorly educated population, crime ridden and cocaine addicted, with no borders and selective application of the law, the United States is in turmoil domestically and disrespected abroad. Conventional wisdom would suggest that the President should get off his socialist donkey and offer a comprehensive agenda that would secure the support of both Republicans and Democrats. But neither politics nor experience nor temperament prepared this president to deal with the intractable issues of the economy, business, finance, and domestic politics, compounded by foreign policy. None of this is a concern for the president, though.

As previously noted, Obama does not follow conventional wisdom. He is following the Bolsheviks' ideology that *great ideas can be realized in one grand ideological assault.* He believes that by the sheer application of political power and the suppression of dissent he can impose economic equality and universal happiness.

Wrapping himself in a cloak of morality, the President is skillfully transforming the socialist effluence into political affluence. When Obama outlined his second-term agenda, he insisted that the unequal distribution of wealth was a major economic issue before the American people. In his 2012 State of the Union address the President called it *"the defining issue of our time.... No challenge is more urgent. No debate is more important."*

Passed over by the public and barely debated in the media, this critical proclamation by the President of the United States was in fact his mission statement declaring his strategic imperative: *distribution of wealth.*

Inquiring minds would beg the question: What are the *unimportant* issues of our time? Could they be economic stagnation, high unemployment, and a skyrocketing national debt? Obama's statement strips off the pretense and discloses his priorities, and explains the lack of progress on the other issues. The President has admitted in unambiguous terms that his objectives, to misquote James Carville, have nothing to do with the economy, stupid. The economy simply is not "the defining issue of our time." Got it? The defining issue is the transformation of the "opportunity society," or whatever is left of it, to a welfare or pauperized society, which is a society not able to sustain itself and relying on handouts. Obama learned, probably from his Marxist professors, that the side controlling the language of the argument controls the argument.

It is becoming remarkably evident that Obama is attempting to frame the terms of the debate away from the state of the economy and the socialization of the country. The Democrats like to talk about gay marriage, contraceptives, student loans, inequality—anything to distract attention away from the economy and the national debt. It may be shrewd politics, but the President is having a difficult time hiding his true agenda from the American people. Obama's attempts to express his concerns about the economy are unpersuasive. The more the American people try to digest his ideas of stimulating the economy and getting the country out of recession, the more mystifying and contradictory they appear. Obama said in Florida in April 2010:

> *"What drags our entire economy down [is when] the gap between those at the very, very top and everybody else keeps growing wider and wider and wider and wider."*

Mr. President, you didn't build that utopia; Karl Marx did. Marx, unable to deny the obvious—that capitalism offers upward mobility for all segments of the population—invented the theory of "relative poverty" to substantiate the notion of capitalist exploitation of working people. The crux of the theory is that, although the overall society is getting richer and the income of all classes and quality of life improve as a result of ever rising productivity and subsequent availability of items of mass consumption, rich people accumulate wealth faster than people in lower-income brackets. Therefore, working people are not getting their fair share of prosperity. And, with time, people in lower-income brackets, despite their growing income, are getting poorer and poorer. Not actually, of course, but relatively. A classic Karl Marx acrimonious contradiction: the more capitalism succeeds, the more it fails.

Never mind that since Marx's *Das Kapital* saw the light of day 150 years ago, there has been no shred of credible evidence to suggest that income disparity has anything to do with economic growth. But according to the Democrats, in order to get the economy going we have to close the gap—take from the rich and give to everybody else. It is that simple. Unfortunately, historical memories seem to have already forgotten the lessons of their defunct Soviet predecessors. How did this simple economic formula work out for them?

Although this phenomenon has been evident to everyone since the Greeks invented mathematics, the Democrats have embraced it with alacrity and used income disparity as a propaganda tool against the capitalist system. For those few of us who never went to school, or perhaps did but now are having a senior moment, consider this: if you have a million dollars invested at a 10 percent annual return, at the end of the year you get $100,000. If you have invested only $10,000, you get only $1,000. That is a simple explanation for income disparity. Clearly, it is good to be rich—that is why we all aspire to shoot for the moon.

This president, either unable or unwilling to differentiate the truth from spin, exhibits the virtuoso's gift to say whatever suits his needs at the time, no matter how exaggerated, fanciful, or ridiculous it sounds. Perhaps Mr. Kloppenberg may attribute it to Obama's vulgar pragmatism, which abandons the notion of objectivity and truth in order to push the country into the socialist gutter.

More Power to the Poor

One thing is exceedingly evident. President Obama was very passionate about raising taxes on the rich, regardless of the impact on the economy. Why? His arguments are inconsistent and poorly constructed. He has never articulated whether he feels it is necessary on economic grounds as a road to prosperity or on moral grounds as a road to socialist virtue. The President declared:

> *"We cannot afford a trillion dollars' worth of tax cuts for every millionaire and billionaire in our society. We can't afford it. And I refuse to renew them again. In the end, that's what this election is about. Do we participate in a politics of cynicism or a politics of hope?"*

The answer should be: neither. We have not elected a spiritual leader to offer us hope. Hope is neither a plan nor a strategy nor a solution. Hope has no connection to intelligence; it is an act of self-delusion or desperation. The President's job is to provide leadership, to offer a coherent strategy for getting our country out of an economic slump, and to project a vision for the future.

If at the time of his speech raising taxes was an economic issue and the purpose of raising taxes was a reduction of the deficit, the remedy couldn't work. The proposed tax increase on the rich could raise around $70 billion per year. We had and, unfortunately, still have a trillion-dollar annual shortfall, so $70 billion is 7 percent of the deficit, making it irrelevant.

As we should have learned from experience, there is no correlation between the taxes we pay and the money we spend. Every time the administration tells us that taxes will pay for the deficit, it never happens. When Ronald Reagan took office, the deficit was $1 trillion. Taxes have been raised a number of times since, and the current deficit exceeds $19 trillion. Furthermore, when the President said that raising taxes during a recession would put businesses into a deeper hole, he made it clear that raising taxes is not an economic issue. Therefore, we have to assume it is a moral issue.

Without challenging the morality of raising taxes, we could all agree with the President that raising taxes during a recession is the wrong approach. Then it is fair to ask: Why were the Democrats prepared to risk an economic downturn and why was the President spending so much of his time and political capital on this incendiary issue, particularly if there was no imperative to seek its resolution as long as the economy was in a recession? The president would be better served raising taxes once we were out of the recession; it certainly would increase his credibility and eliminate the argument that doing so sucks money out of the economy.

Perhaps it is hard to the untrained eye to see the logic and purpose of this presidential gambit. However, if the American people could wear my magic red communist glasses they would see a clear picture of the President's well-coordinated efforts, summarized in the following two quotes:

> *This is the moment when we must build on the wealth that open markets [capitalism] have created, and share its benefits more equitably.*

and

> *I think when you spread the wealth around, it's good for everybody.*

It is refreshing to hear the president admit that this country's wealth was created by the free market, not a socialist economy. But how could it be good for those whose wealth will be spread around? Pot recently became legal in D.C. If anyone needs evidence that it causes cognitive impairments in the brain, here it is. What's more, the President did not elaborate on who will be on the receiving end of this generosity. The President didn't, but I will:

> *Being a Marxist, the President believes that wealth is produced by the exploitation of the working class and it does not belong to individuals, it belongs to the nation. Therefore, it must be redeemed by society in the form of taxes and welfare.*

Taxation is one of the elements of the Liberal Bolshevik strategy, the importance of which cannot be understated. In 1819, Chief Justice John Marshall famously observed that

> *"An unlimited power to tax involves, necessarily, a power to destroy; because there is a limit beyond which no institution and no property can bear taxation."*

Never before in American history has this enormous power reaffirmed by the Supreme Court been used to lead the assault on liberty and self-reliance. The Democrats' determination to raise taxes confirms, once again, what should be clear from the start: the economy, the deficit, and unemployment are just a smoke screen to divert the country's attention from their one consuming passion—their egalitarian dream.

So, within this context, when the President does not participate in security briefings, does not adequately address the deteriorating international situation, or fails to attend a security meeting in the White House Situation Room during the attack on our consulate in Benghazi, it should be understood that, to the President, compared to the scale of the "big thing," those issues are peripheral.

Iran developing nuclear weapons and threatening Israel with a nuclear holocaust, or military losses in Afghanistan, or tragedies in Libya and Egypt, or the humiliating Syrian fiasco, or the VA scandal, or any other domestic or international debacle are just "bumps in the road," as Obama's administration has expressed on numerous occasions. This thinking sets the President's priorities; notice he never missed a vacation and hardly let a fundraiser go to waste for any domestic or international "bump in the road."

Disturbingly, the President and his supporters are determined to achieve their "historic" objective at any cost. Just as the Russian Bolsheviks did not care whether Russia would be defeated in the war with Germany or the Russian economy would be ruined, or whether millions of people would perish in the civil war and famine as long as they achieved the communist dream, the President does not care about the economy, domestic scandals, and world turmoil as long as he is getting closer to addressing, in his words, *"the defining issue of our time."*

A rising economy provides employment, boosts self-reliance, deflates the possibility of discontent, and subsequently precludes the socialization of the nation. Ambiguity allows Obama and the Democrats to conceal their ideological motivations and pretend that they are working hard to solve the nation's problems, fighting the enemies sabotaging the government's efforts to protect the middle class and save Social Security, etc. Maintaining poverty ensures dependency and provides the votes to fashion the perception of legitimacy. The Democratic Party is resolute in providing its constituency with food stamps, subsidized apartments, free medical care, free cell phones, and other free stuff, and enough money to ensure their support for "progressive" policies, ignoring any abuse of power and criticism from the opposition.

The great worry facing the country is that there are too many people perfectly content to turn a blind eye to the perpetrated chaos, waste, fraud, and destructive policies of the administration, including government intrusion into their lives and the assault on democratic institutions. As George Orwell observed, "The choice for mankind lies between freedom and happiness and for the great bulk of mankind, happiness is better." Americans have been offered the heroin of bondage wrapped in happiness and too many of them, foremost among them the so-called minorities, have happily accepted it. The objective of this process is making sure that the socialist gains are "locked in" and even if the Republicans one day regain the presidency in addition to control of the House and Senate, they will be impossible to reverse. This passé ideology has been seeping into the Democratic Party, raising radical passions among the rank and file and finding support among the leadership of the party such as Senators Harry Reid, Chuck Schumer, and Nancy Pelosi. Democratic Party presidential candidates Hillary Clinton and Bernie Sanders, and the potential aspirant for the office, Senator Elizabeth Warren of Massachusetts, are leading the ideological offensive. Although the first one is still probing for her socialist—excuse me, progressive—bearings, being fully aware of the perils of ideological openness, the latter two are openly enthusiastic socialists, throwbacks to the Soviet Union who have fully adopted Marxist ideological tenets and proudly flaunt their convictions with exceptional skill and consistency.

In search of an effective sale mechanism, the Democrats are focused on public impact with the awareness that there are two different Americas. They are not black and white; they are not rich and poor. They are the one who has failed to learn from history, convinced that socialism is too extreme to the American psyche to merit serious attention, and the other who clandestinely believes that socialism, in fact, has already arrived and is making sure that America can no longer live without it.

Visiting Florence recently, I was stunned by a sculpture by Vincenzo de'Rossi, a sixteenth-century Italian sculptor, who seemed to have been communicating the divine premonition of this lethal American predicament in a statue of two heroes of Greek mythology, Hercules and Diomedes. Hercules (the American people) is holding Diomedes (Obama) upside down, preparing to throw him, while Diomedes tightly grips Hercules' penis, as if to say, "Are you sure, America, you want to throw me out? Who is going to pay for socialism, for all the entitlements you have become so addicted to?"

> *In a democracy the poor will have more power than the rich, because there are more of them, and the will of the majority is supreme.*

So said Aristotle[18] about 2400 years ago.

---

[18] *Ancient Greek philosopher, scientist, and physician (384–322 BC).*

And to stay in power and implement their agenda, the Democrats need to keep it this way.

The statue of Hercules and Diomedes in the Hall of the Five Hundred

CHAPTER 5
Building Socialism

"The problem with socialism is that eventually you run out of other people's money."
—Margaret Thatcher

God has distributed nothing as fairly as brains—nobody complains that he did not get enough; and God distributed nothing as unfairly as money—nobody has enough.

Socialism and the Socialists

Viva socialism. Viva equality, universal happiness, brotherhood… you know. Despite its popularity and wide appeal, socialism remains one of the most misunderstood concepts of political science. What is socialism? What socialists are actually fighting for? Herein I will attempt to raise the curtain of the misconception and dispel much of the misunderstanding and ignorance about socialism.

Socialism is a political philosophy and economic system that promotes egalitarianism—a theory of economic equality. Modern socialism originated in the eighteenth century as a working-class economic and political movement that opposed private property and criticized the effects of industrialization on society. It is usually defined as "common ownership of the means of production." In the early nineteenth century, "socialism" became a panacea for all the ills of society: economic, social, and political. By the early twentieth century the Soviet model of Marxist-Leninist socialism, which included the creation of a centrally planned command-and-control economy, became a classic model for the socialists of the world to follow. They became strong advocates of this system for Western Europe and the United States. These socialists formed communist parties in their respective countries to pursue building socialism around the world.

Lenin defined socialism as society organized on the principle *"from each according to his abilities and to each according to his work* [contribution]." "To each according to his contribution" sounds like capitalism, doesn't it? If you work hard, if you are smart or entrepreneurial or have been blessed with talent, you make a greater contribution to society and you subsequently get a greater reward. So, what is the difference? The difference is in society's assessment of the intrinsic value of an individual's work.

In the capitalist system, value is defined by free-market forces and therefore is objective and unlimited. As Ayn Rand pointed out in her book *For the New Intellectual*,

> "*The economic value of a man's work is determined, in a free market, by a single principle: by the voluntary consent of those who are willing to trade him their work or products in return. This is the moral meaning of the law of supply and demand.*"

The key word here is "*voluntary*"; nobody forces anybody to participate in trade and buy what he does not need. Capitalism offers an individual economic freedom to work, invent, succeed, and prosper without boundaries. Under socialism, on the other hand, the value of an individual's work is defined using Karl Marx's concept that the "universal measure for value, expressed in terms of money, corresponds to the amount of labor time that goes into the making of each commodity." This concept does not differentiate intellectual labor from physical labor, inventor from laborer, artist from house painter, and so on.

I have to admit that when I first read these words many years ago, I invoked Albert Einstein who said, "If you can't explain it simply, you don't understand it well enough." In plain English, the "value" is defined by government, which has the power and authority to delimit what is fair and adequate based on the amount of labor invested into development and production. The bottom line: the system is restrictive. In order for Marxism to work, those who have the greatest abilities and those who work the hardest must be satisfied with the same, or not substantially different, rewards as those with lesser abilities and those who don't work at all.

Unlike socialism, which defines the value of products by the amount of social labor expended on production, capitalism defines the value of products by their usefulness. At the time Alexander Graham Bell invented the telephone, the consensus was that it was not really needed—just like electricity, Xerox machines, Apple computers, and many other discoveries and inventions that were not fully appreciated by contemporaries but fundamentally changed our lives. Even the experts have had a hard time evaluating innovations and their impact on society. Thomas Watson, former chairman of IBM, announced in 1943, "I think there is a world market for maybe five computers," Fred Smith, founder of Federal Express, received a "C" grade from a Yale University professor for his idea for overnight delivery service because the professor deemed it unfeasible. And even Albert Einstein predicted in 1932, "There is not the slightest indication that nuclear energy will ever be obtainable. It would mean that the atom would have to be shattered at will." All were proved spectacularly wrong.

The point I am making is that if a committee of government bureaucrats were to assess the intrinsic value of those contributions, they would consider them insignificant and the contributions probably would never see the light of day. In fact, they did not see the light of day in the socialist world until the capitalist free market established their usefulness and values. That is the fundamental difference between capitalism and socialism.

According to Marxist orthodoxy, socialism is the lower stage of communism, which is based on the principle of "from each according to his ability, to each according to his needs." It implies that a person of limited ability may have unlimited needs. This is a fatal delusion of those who believe in communism. Lenin said in his book *To the Rural Poor* that in his "new and better" society there "must be neither rich nor poor"; the individual's need would be defined by the society (government). For example, in the Soviet Union, the eligibility threshold for a new apartment was limited to 100 square feet per person. Therefore, a family of four was eligible for 400 square feet of living space, which did not include kitchen, bathroom, and other non-living spaces. That is how "to each according to his need" works in a real working-people's paradise. According to Marxist teaching, the upper stage, communism, is only possible after the socialist stage achieves a level of productivity that ensures an abundance of goods and services sufficient to satisfy all available demand. Again, society (government) defines what is "sufficient."

State socialism, which employs the power of the government to create an egalitarian society via a government-planned command-and-control economy, ensures full employment, but in doing so de-incentivizes innovation and, in consequence, suppresses growth and productivity. Since all means of production belong to the government, all employees work for the government and cannot sell their labor on the open market; they are effectively property of the State. They are paid in accordance with their "needs," as defined by the government. This version of socialism is nothing less than a modern form of slavery or serfdom, and gives us a glimpse of how the Marxist Bolsheviks' "right to work" theory works in an actual socialist world. It also explains why there is no unemployment in a socialist state; slaves cannot be unemployed. This phenomenon was amply demonstrated in the Soviet Union and other "advanced" socialist countries.

The concept of a government-planned economy was the source of jokes in the Soviet Union. Here is one that illustrates the Soviet-planned economy.

Brezhnev was reviewing a military parade. The troops marched down Red Square; tanks rolled, followed by a squad of intercontinental ballistic missiles, and closing the parade was a crowd of people in mink coats walking casually and waving red flags. "What is that?" asked Brezhnev of one of his marshals, who responded, "Comrade Brezhnev, those are people of the GosPlan [the agency responsible for planning the economy]; it is the most destructive force in our arsenal."

Regardless of which version of socialism has been tried, whether the dictatorship of the proletariat or democratic socialism Western-style, all have proven to be colossal failures. We are not here to debate the philosophical validity of socialism. History has issued its verdict. The lessons of the past century serve as a stark reminder that socialism and government control of the economy are not the answers for an ever-changing industrial society.

Contemporary exponents of "social justice," however, cannot be persuaded by the lessons of history. The ideas of these people—liberals, progressives, socialists, and communists—are not new; they have been tried many times, and history has attested to their sanity. What greatly exacerbated those outcomes was the fact that egalitarianism, the ideological basis for all the above labels, has been perverted over the last half century from a social science into deism with elaborate dogmas and inspired scriptures. It is not a theoretical abstraction; the difference between science and religion is that science requires proof, whether by experiment, knowledge gained through experience, or historical precedent. Religion, on the other hand, is the suspension of critical reasoning, requiring no proof; it is simply a set of beliefs. Modern-day liberals, progressives, democratic socialists, and communists (it is challenging to recognize distinctions and differences between the brands), for the most part, are ideological fanatics. There is no sacrifice too big and no price too high to pay for achieving their ultimate objective: the creation of an egalitarian society. These people will not relinquish ideas that have been disproved repeatedly by historical precedent, clinging to them as if they were divinely ordained prophecies, and no amount of reality can shake their convictions. For them, acceptance of reality equates to denial of faith.

They are convinced that their mission is bigger than life; therefore, they are emotionally immune to human suffering, and human life has little value when it comes to fulfilling their mission. Here is a partial list of mass murders committed in the name of building the bright socialist future: the communist revolution in China, the resulting civil war, and the Cultural Revolution cost between 50 and 80 million lives; the Russian revolution, civil war, and Stalin's purges killed between 20 and 30 million and enslaved millions more in labor camps; Cambodia had 2 million victims; and North Korea thus far has a "meager" 1.6 million. And these genocides have not deterred those with a deranged mind from trying it again.

Once, I had a particularly illuminating discussion with a KGB general I befriended during his long emigration ordeal from the former Soviet Union. I pointed out to him that the Great Russian Experiment with socialism had failed despite the heavy price tag—economic decline and 30 million victims executed during the process of building the new society. The man shrugged. "Yes, we made mistakes; we just executed the wrong people. As Lenin taught us," he added, "The path to paradise passes through hell." Although this damaged perpetrator of Stalin's terror was actually quoting Dante, he was making clear that he would not hesitate starting it over again, because this time he knew the "right" people to execute.

Americans fare no better. When I came to America, one wealthy businessman asked me, seriously, why I had left a paradise where citizens received free housing, free education, and free medical treatment. When I tried to describe to him the horrors and absurdities of socialism, my interlocutor just sighed and politely told me that Karl Marx's scientific ideas were right, but the experiment failed due to flawed implementation. To which I mockingly responded that if Marx's ideas were scientific, he should have experimented on animals first. Not surprisingly, the interlocutor remained unconvinced. "The goal was worthy; the execution was flawed. I could do it differently, I would know better," he said.

In 1976, in the Alastair Buchan Lecture, Henry Kissinger observed,

> "We have nothing to fear from competition…if there is an economic competition, we won it long time ago.… In no part of the world and under no other system do men live so well and in so much freedom. If performance is any criterion, the contest between freedom and Communism, of which so much was made three decades ago, has been won by the industrial democracies."

Unfortunately, performance is not a criterion, the dream is. You cannot defeat a dream, you cannot defeat religion, and you cannot defeat utopia. In the 1920 British writer Herbert George Wells visited Bolshevik Russia and interviewed Vladimir Lenin. During the interview in the Kremlin, Lenin shared his vision of the future of his country and socialism. In the aftermath of his visit Wells wrote an insightful book, *Russia in the Shadows*, in which he called Lenin "The Kremlin Dreamer." Almost one hundred years later another Kremlin Dreamer, Bernie Sanders, is recycling the familiar Marxist arguments against capitalism and pointedly spinning Lenin's fairy tales here in the United States. As this neo-socialist movement gathers momentum and the slogans of Bolshevik's revolution are being reverberated from coast to coast, millions of disaffected dupes and untutored casualties of the American education system, along with George Bernard Shaw-like[19] Hollywood progressives, are perfectly willing to set this country ablaze to fulfill Bernie's heady gospel of Marxism constructed on hopes, myths, and grandiose promises.

It is like smallpox, an infectious disease that everyone has to get and overcome in order to develop immunity. As Alexander Solzhenitsyn pointed out, *"For us in Russia, communism is a dead dog, while for many people in the West, it is still a living lion."*

This living lion feels so comfortable nowadays in the United States that we may even see a headline in the official "fully authorized" organ of the American Left, the *New York Times*, declaring, "America without Capitalism: For Most, a Better Life." If enough Americans become conditioned to abrogate their responsibilities to the government and prefer a secured life in poverty, we can truly say that America has seen better days.

We have to be mindful that every ism—communism, socialism, fascism, Obama-ism—has its supporters and benefactors. Thus, we should not be surprised by the populist support the Democrats are getting while selling Obama's version of Marxism. Those who imagine themselves on the receiving end have every reason to think they will be better off with socialism.

---

[19] *George Bernard Shaw was an Irish playwright and an ardent supporter of Stalinism.*

The illusory ideas of socialism transcend time and appeal to people of all colors and races. The magnetic appeal to an uneducated man of limited faculties (sorry, abilities) to fulfill his unlimited needs at the expense of the "exploiters of working people" is irresistible. Unlike other religions, this one promises paradise on *this* side of the grave. No matter how many books are written documenting the economic and political absurdities of socialism, no lessons of history will dampen the magic of socialist's divine providence.

The election of a socialist government in America in 2008 and the reelection of President Obama in 2012 are living testament to the ongoing vitality of Marxism. The specter of communism will haunt the world as long as there is capitalism. If socialism is allowed to take root and the malignant metastasis of Marxism spreads throughout the nation, it cannot be reversed. Voters who became accustomed to getting something for nothing cannot be deprived of those privileges. Therefore, if we continue down our current path, our future belongs to socialism. The only consolation is that this future will be short-lived.

All the socialist invocations about the superiority of socialism cannot override the reality: socialists may win, but socialism is doomed. As the record shows, despite its populist appeal, the system is fundamentally flawed and unsustainable, with a life expectancy of about seventy years. That is the historical span of time that it takes for wealth distribution to exceed wealth creation. As commitments to a welfare society become unattainable, the system ultimately self-destructs.

Few events in history rival the gap between exuberant optimism and tumultuous reality, great dreams and vain illusions as the spread of socialism. Its rise and fall created one of the most tragic episodes of the last century. It has created unparalleled violence, millions of innocent victims of terrorism, modern slavery, and environmental disasters of biblical proportions. The movement has gone from spectacular triumphs to humiliating defeats—from victory in Russia in 1917 and the conquest of Eastern Europe and China in the 1930s and 1940s, to what seemed an unstoppable march in Africa and Latin America in the 1960s and 1970s, and then to the spectacular implosion of the Soviet Union, the liberation of Eastern Europe, and the economic liberalization of China.

Intellectual decay and economic stagnation, coupled with political malaise, have befallen socialism during its historically short tenure. The archeologically short timeline of socialism confirms this claim. The Bolshevik revolution took place in Russia in 1917, and totalitarian socialism met its demise in 1986. Western Europe chose the democratic version of socialism in 1945, and seventy years later it is unraveling. North Korean and Cuban totalitarian versions are each in intensive care. For anyone who would like to educate their kids about socialism, I would recommend the 1948 "Make Mine Freedom" cartoon available on the Internet at *www.youtube.com/watch?v=Oz9fX_HfsXA*. The main character even resembles Obama. Seniors who have suppressed their memories or suffered historical amnesia and voted for socialism would enjoy it as well.

Marxism by Any Other Name

Socialism was not born as the result of Immaculate Conception. The venom of socialism was deposited into the American organism as early as the 1920s, and its offspring has been growing ever since. The unwavering commitment to American Liberalism, this country's philosophical foundation since its inception, has been slowly replaced with a set of morals foreign to American values.

Liberalism, an idealistic political philosophy born after the defeat of Napoleon, a philosophy of freedom, which epitomized individual liberty, freedom of the press, freedom of religion, and free elections, with the passage of time evolved into a broader vision of an ideal society, a brilliant future of economic equality. The concept of economic equality required a radical reconstruction of humanity and, like all utopian ideas, could not be implemented on a voluntary basis. It required the application of power, whether in the form of violence, coercion, subterfuge, or all of the above. Indeed, it was the point of no return; and like a fall that cannot be stopped halfway, it signified the evolution of the fruitful coexistence of liberalism and socialism in this country into an inevitable merger of the two ideologies. The process was facilitated because, despite some differences in interpretation of their respective faiths, they were branches of the same egalitarian tree that produced Marxism, Leninism, and Stalinism, and after the American liberals crossed the threshold of economic equality, which is incompatible with individual liberty, there was no longer a principal difference between the two ideological vistas. Therefore we shall not be confused by the ideological taxonomy.

Winston Churchill insightfully described the divergence: "Socialism seeks to pull down the wealth; liberalism seeks to rise up poverty." The implications of the de facto conversion of liberalism into socialism were profound; socialism acquired a pragmatic political cover that preserves its enduring appeal, found acceptance by the American Left, and was gradually incorporated into the policies of the Democratic Party. Henceforth, socialist principles, built on concepts originally advanced by liberals, became the guiding factors of the party's economic and social programs.

Back in 1927, an American socialist, Norman Thomas, made a stunning validation of the ideological link between liberalism and socialism, and inadvertently acknowledged the inherently fraudulent nature of liberalism when he clairvoyantly asserted that

> *The American people would never vote for socialism,... [but] under the name of liberalism [nowadays rebranded as progressivism], the American people would adopt every fragment of the socialist program until one day, America will be a socialist nation without even knowing how it happened.*

The Democratic Party has been slowly accomplishing the amalgamation since the 1930s, dismantling American Judeo-Christian values and fomenting the ideological transformation of this country via public education, endorsement of socialist policies, and the proliferation of the welfare state and polarization of racial relations. The progression gained force with Franklin Roosevelt's Economic Bill of Rights, which had its ideological roots in Russian Bolshevism.

Although in the main the American people have been unaware of the upsurge of this ideological evolution, it has not gone unnoticed to some contemporaries, and many renowned Americans have tried to raise the alarm, to no avail. In 1936, Al Smith[20], a prominent Democrat and a great American, left the Democratic Party and accused the Democrats of taking the party of Jefferson, Jackson, and Cleveland down the road to socialism under the banners of Marx, Lenin, and Stalin. Incidentally, this was a period of widespread infiltration of the U.S. government by communists, communist sympathizers, and KGB agents, to the extent that by 1940s, to some erudite observers, the American government looked like an extension of the Kremlin. Overzealous KGB agents, unable to contain their excitement, called FDR "the Kerensky of the American revolution,"[21] to be replaced by Lenin.

Just as Norman Thomas predicted in 1927, the socialization of the Democratic Party progressed to the point that in 1944 this unimpeachable authority on American socialism announced his resignation:

> *I no longer need to run as a Presidential candidate for the Socialist Party. The Democratic Party has adopted our platform.*

Sure enough, the socialist virus continued its growth, giving "small doses of socialism" to the American organism, as Nikita Khrushchev foretold back in 1959 during a meeting with then Secretary of Agriculture Ezra Benson, until it eventually poisoned the party. As the Russians say, if a baby snake is well fed it will grow

---

[20] *Alfred Emanuel "Al" Smith (December 30, 1873–October 4, 1944) was an American statesman who was elected governor of New York four times and was the Democratic U.S. presidential candidate in 1928.*

[21] *Alexander Fyodorovich Kerensky (May 1881–June 1970) was a Russian lawyer and politician who served as the Chairman of the Russian Provisional Government between July and November 1917. On the 7th of November, his government was overthrown by the Vladimir Lenin–led Bolshevik Revolution. He spent the remainder of his life in exile, in Paris and New York City, and was buried in London.*

into a dragon. Eighty years after Norman Thomas's stunning 1927 prediction, America was ready to deliver socialism, and the left has seized the moment, forcing the nation into ideological retreat. Without liberalism, which has served as an indispensable foundation block of socialism, socialism would have found neither temptation nor opportunity in this country.

Although Obama's ship is sailing into uncharted waters—the concept of Liberal Bolshevism has never been tried before, as an ardent Marxist, Barack Obama has every reason to believe that this time socialism will work. As expressed by Karl Marx in the preface to *Das Kapital*: "*The country that is more developed industrially shows to the less developed the image of their future.*" Since the nineteenth century the most economically developed country has been the United States, so according to Marx's dictum the bright future of socialism was supposed to materialize in the United States.

As Obama sees it, socialism was attempted in the most impoverished and economically backward countries. Whether it was Russia, or China, Cuba, Vietnam, or any other socialist country, they all skipped the capitalist phase, which according to Marx was pivotal in accumulating wealth, and slid straight from a pre-industrial and in many instances a feudal state into socialism. Subsequently, there was not much wealth to distribute, which is why socialism has always failed. This theory feeds into the contemporary Marxist narrative in defense of a feeble ideology. Real socialism is not deficient, contemporary Marxists say; the reason it has failed is because Lenin, Stalin, Mao, and other descendants of Karl Marx did not follow the teachings of the "thinker of the millennium"[22] and did not practice "pure," theoretically perfect socialism. In that spirit, this is the time to implement Marx's revolutionary ambition, this is the time to rediscover the virtues of socialism, this is the time for tantalizing possibility to retest the communist hypothesis, this is the time to do it right, this time is different. The inheritors have not forgotten history but haven't learned from it either. The maniacs are still pursuing an abstract theory of socialist obsessions and just like the

---

[22] *In a 1999 BBC poll, Karl Marx was voted the "thinker of the millennium" by the people of the world.*

"thinker of the millennium" 150 years ago; contemporary Marxists are pathetically misreading economic reality. Politically they find themselves between the bloody past, which they are trying not to repeat, and the future they cannot clearly define.

Although imperfect, U.S. capitalism is practical; it has accumulated a lot more wealth per capita than Russia or China. It also became global and it ignores borders. As a result capital is looking worldwide for places where risks are lower and profits are higher. Furthermore, movements of capital around the world are performed in milliseconds. As the drive to socialism intensifies, the United States is becoming less attractive to investments and capital is already drying up or moving out, resulting in a lack of sustained economic growth. Eventually our socialists will encounter the insoluble Marxist quandary: the system cannot survive without more wealth creation, but it is too hostile to wealth creators to have them around.

Thus far, as the United States shows the image of its future to the less-developed world, as Karl Marx observed, the future with socialism looks anything but bright. As the concept of socialism is being embraced in the United States, the central underpinning of socialism has been overlooked or misunderstood:

> *Unlike capitalism, which is a product of spontaneous evolution of an economic system extending over centuries, the building of socialism is an organized and disruptive artificial process associated with ideological polarization, cultural and political confrontations, and violation of the existing moral order. The construction of this unnatural social organization requires a deliberate approach and enforcement.*

Antagonistic to a social order at the apex of which stands freedom—the absence of government suppression of individual choice—socialism requires a form of behavior that cannot sustain itself and therefore necessitates enforcement. Since socialism cannot be implemented without enforcement, its very nature is contradictory to freedom. Although confirmation of this socialist phenomenon is evident in our daily life, for many Americans whose contemporary political thinking is more backward than that of the Russians or Chinese, and for too many of them living in a flat-earth, know-nothing, Jesse Watters[23] world, it is next to impossible to grasp the veracity of CHANGE and recognize that it is, in fact, tyranny. Hence, social conflicts are unavoidable, suppression of civil liberties is inevitable, and violence is probable.

The proponents of this new order may say that this is a tyranny for the common good. Of course it is. So were the French Revolution and the Bolshevik Revolution in Russia and the Cultural Revolution in China; so were the man-made Great Famine in the Soviet Union and the extermination of Jews in Nazi Germany. When the institution of tyranny is not restrained, the tyranny does not dissipate, it intensifies. It ultimately employs violence to sustain itself, and there is no limit to the violence perpetrated "for the common good."

But there is more to it. Alexander Solzhenitsyn, in his acceptance speech for the 1970 Nobel Prize in literature, colorfully described the quintessential component of this new moral order:

> *We should not forget that violence does not exist alone and cannot exist alone: it is inevitably interwoven with lie. Between them is the most virtual, the deepest of natural bonds: violence has no other cover but lie, and lie cannot be sustained without violence.*

Poignantly, the American socialist saga exhibits all the familiar socialist traits. The people have been constantly bombarded with lies and when the masses are subjected to lies long enough, they lose the ability to analyze and accept evidence to the contrary. It is not because the evidence isn't compelling enough, but because lies offer comfort, they play on our selfish emotions, they promise to relieve

---

[23] *Jesse B. Watters is a television producer and interviewer at Fox News. His "on the street" interviews with people became a reflection of Americans' political ignorance.*

us of our civil responsibilities; not to worry, everything will be taken care of.

It gets to the point that people become allergic to the truth; it is near impossible to admit that we are ignorant, stupid, and naïve. It is extremely painful to concede that we have been duped by an impostor who betrayed our trust and acquired power through quackery, lies, and intimidation. It feels, and for a good reason, as if no one in our government is telling the truth nowadays. Incessant lies have become so blatant and widespread that they cannot be treated as a moral category but rather as the essence of the government itself. The country is slowly getting used to swallowing distortions, falsehoods, and propaganda. Lies acquire the status of policies that have international and domestic implications. In many instances they are so far outside the realm of objective reality that it feels as if we have reached the threshold of forsaking common sense and reason. The most bizarre and ridiculous arguments are brought forward in support of insane policies and they are taken seriously while a brain X-ray or examination by a psychiatrist is in order: a wall would not protect our borders, Africa's regions infected by Ebola should not be isolated, voter IDs disenfranchise voters, businesses do not produce jobs, etc. I am sure that the reader is quite familiar with such absurdities; hence, I need say no more about them.

A combination of myths and fictions is the basis of socialist ideology. Myths represent the theological aspect of the socialist religion—the source of conviction for true believers. The process of creating "fictions" is to condition the masses to repel reason and accept a set of beliefs that the masses will regard as positive in support of an egalitarian hierarchy of values, and at the same time to undermine the resistance of many others who apprehend its nature and oppose it with all their might and fury. The multifaceted deception may take a form of scientific theory such as Keynesian economics, climate change, or actions taken presumably for the common good such as Obamacare or a budget deficit. All of those policies and actions have one thing in common: to abrogate the laws of nature and economics to implement the sweeping ideas of the Democratic Party's political and economic "CHANGE."

As the Soviet experience has amply shown, this kind of political CHANGE necessitates political statistics. Government data related to unemployment and the economy consistently show miraculous improvements right before elections, health care enrollment numbers are purposely skewed to make them better than expected, and even weather patterns are politically motivated in order to support government policies like global warming. As Paul Singer, a prominent American hedge fund manager, wrote in November 2014, "Nobody can predict how long governments can get away with fake growth, fake money, fake jobs, fake financial stability, fake inflation numbers, and fake income growth."

In an act of political sagacity, President Obama moved control of the census from the Commerce Department to the White House in early 2009. The U.S. census does not just count the population; it also affects redrawing of congressional districts and subsequently the composition of the Electoral College and allocation of funds. Moreover, the census is in charge of producing enrollment numbers for Obamacare. Do we need to say more? It is obvious that the party that controls the census is in a position to perpetuate its hold on political power. But the lies are not limited to statists, which are only one part of the White House propaganda machine; the socialist lies are profound and sinister. This is the most poisonous weapon in the Bolshevik's armory that covers all aspects of American life, transforming this country into the "Kingdom of Crooked Mirrors."[24]

Moreover, as Solzhenitsyn pointed out, *"lie cannot be sustained without violence."* The Liberal Bolshevik and his cohorts, unlike their Russian counterparts for whom mass murder was "the instrument of social hygiene," thus far have not used bloody violence to sustain falsehood; they have found instead a temporary refuge in tyranny and lawfulness.

In this American socialist paradigm, the President, politicians, and federal officials, with the full support of the media that continue pouring on the President's accolades, are permitted to lie with impunity to the American people to cover up government wrongdoing. The dictatorship of government bureaucracy replaces constitu-

---

[24] *The novel by the Russian writer Vitali Gubarev that describes distorted reality.*

tional principles and the rule of law with legal inequality by fraudulent concealment of government officials' misconduct and criminal activities. The IRS affair is a recent specimen of interdependency of lies and tyranny. The President used the power of the State, in this case the IRS, to suppress political opponents. When the scheme was exposed, the members of the administration offered preposterous stories riddled with lies, half-truths, and deception in order to protect the tyranny.

The tyranny reciprocated by providing legal protection to the liars, ensuring immunity from breaking the law. Although no reasonable person would believe this new version of "the dog ate my homework" (in this case the hard drives of six computers), the liars could afford to be arrogant, knowing perfectly well that the tyranny will protect them, allowing the conspirators to escape culpability and personal responsibility. This illicit version of "esprit de corps" protects and handsomely rewards those who are actively widening and fomenting the transition to the socialist paradise.

"The Voting Herd"

History did not begin with Barack Obama's advent. By the dawn of Obama's reign the Democratic Party had almost completed its evolution into the Social Democratic Party. For those who are not familiar with the terminology:

> *Social democracy is a political ideology that has as its goal the establishment of socialism through implementation of a policy regime that includes, but is not limited to, high taxation, government regulation of private enterprises, and establishment of a universal welfare state.*

At that historical juncture the Democratic Party had developed immense socialist programs and the apparatus to support them. The party leadership was searching for a leader ideologically aligned with the new programs, and not just any leader—the party needed a "Deliverer." The Democrats found him in Barack Obama, an unscrupulous, single-minded fighter who believes that any method is justified to serve a socialist purpose. He was perfectly suited for his time.

No modern president has enjoyed greater support, admiration, and sense of obligation from members of his party as Obama. Immortalized in life, he serves as the avatar of socialist dreams turned into reality. In the language of ideology Obama personifies "the mind, honor, and conscience of the party." His election energized his party to an exuberant faith in its ability to implement an American "perestroika." For those on the left, liberals, democrats, social justice supporters, a few remaining communists, and all of those troubled souls who passionately hated this world and did not know why this was a fantasy-dream coming true.

The genius of Barack Obama has been in his ability to hide the ideology behind a veneer of ambiguity—to rally for a cause he never defined. His populist pronouncements that almost perfectly imitate the Bolsheviks' demagoguery managed to create a mystical profusion of Play-Doh dreams to fulfill any aspiration: transparent governance, world peace, fraternity, clean air, equality, global justice, fairness, equal pay, human rights, women's rights, minority rights, gay rights; you can order any tray you want and it is free. Thanks to the fatuity of the American public, there has not been any effective comprehension of the totality of the assault nor its enervating effect upon national vigilance. The popularity of Bernie Sanders is proof that Obama has completed the job of transforming the Democratic Party and changing the country. Without Obama, Sanders would have remained a socialist quack from Vermont never taken seriously. We may surmise that the socialist dragon has come of age and socialism in America no longer looks like an exceedingly lofty ambition anymore.

Yet, despite Sanders' popular appeal, the Democrats are painfully aware that "socialism" is still a dirty word in the political vocabulary and liberalism has lost its former charm, and, indeed, using terms such as socialism and liberalism would be too forward leaning. So they masked the socialist ideology by not mentioning the world "socialism" without the prefix "democratic" and replaced the word "liberal" with "progressive." Whether liberal or progressive, or democratic in terms of the issues and, especially in terms of tactics, the party became a plagiarizing scum of Lenin's faction of the Russian Social Democratic Labor Party, or Bolsheviks, which coincidently also had "democratic" in the party name.

It is not a stretch to equate the Democratic Party with the ideas of socialism and the principles of the Bolsheviks' Democratic Centralism.[25] It requires uniformity of thought and action, exhibits the signs of Soviet obedience, and equates the will of the party with the will of the people.

The Democrats do not debate Obama's legislative proposals or question his agenda; they support unequivocally and unanimously every presidential initiative without even reading the proposed legislation before voting for it. Remember the infamous words of former Speaker of the House Nancy Pelosi: "We have to pass the bill so that you can find out what is in it." There is no reason to waste precious time when Democratic members of Congress and the President share the same sense of purpose and unity of objectives. Devotion to the President and the socialist cause has turned the Democrats in the House and Senate into what the Bolshevik Leon Trotsky called "the Voting Herd," acting much like the unthinking members of the Soviet Congress of People's Representatives, who for seventy years unanimously approved every one of the Communist Party's programs.

Just like the Soviet Politburo, a small group of ideologically driven Democrats in leadership positions formulates the policies while

---

[25] *Democratic Centralism is a set of organizational principles of Leninist political parties based on four governing principles:*
1. *All directing bodies of the Party, from top to bottom, shall be elected;*
2. *The Party bodies shall give periodic accounts of their activities to their respective Party organizations;*
3. *There shall be strict party discipline and the subordination of the minority to the majority;*
4. *The decisions of higher bodies shall be absolutely binding on lower bodies and on all Party members. Though the first two points seem to be natural for any organization perusing common objectives, the last two stand out. They have been commonly used by the leadership of the Marxist parties to suppress dissent and enforce complete obedience by extermination of critics within the Party.*

the majority, possessing limited understanding of the underlying ideology and not overburdened by convictions or moral virtues, is enmeshed in a philosophy which destroys individualism and self-reliance and fosters the blind following of leaders. There is no inner hesitation and no inner opposition. The psychopaths subordinated their responsibilities of elected representatives acting as political agents to the executive branch, applauding presidential executive orders and supporting the President, who contemptuously circumvents constitutionalism by passing coercive legislation. The people's representatives are idolizing the President, standing up with their souls and pants down.

These human cattle, prior to the elections, project the false image of disunity and passionately criticize the President's unpopular initiatives they have supported, voted for, and sold to the public with the same alacrity and missionary tenacity. To a political amateur it may appear that the defenders of the President's policies are falling out like the teeth in a comb. It may be hard to fathom, but this temporary adaptation to objective reality is fully consistent with the Democrats' *modus vivendi* and would not deprive the phony detractors of either presidential support or Democratic Party financial backing. It is a flexible and effective political organism comprising members united in devotion to their leader, sharing his ideological cause and trusting him to safeguard their re-elections.

Since the safeguarding does not always work, every time before the elections this crowd has a panic attack and desperately sniffs the political wind trying to ascend to a position popular with the voters and hopefully superior to political rivals. In the process they are exhibiting the combative spirit of earlier Bolshevism using all means available to suppress criticism and distort opponents' positions on the issues. The same people, who voted for Obamacare and, with straight faces, told the American people they could keep their insurance and their doctors are openly demanding that the President use the power of the Executive Branch to suppress freedom of speech and prosecute Republicans and the Tea Party for "lying" to the American people. In a brazen display of intellectual corruption, the Democrats have the audacity to accuse the opponents of their own sins.

This ideological conversion eroded democratic values, forced the Democrats to abandon their principles, and eventually led to the moral degeneration of the party. What is most troubling is that even the party's present-day godfather, Bill Clinton, supports the new party conversion. Incredibly, unembarrassed by his newfound convictions, Clinton is allying himself with the radical left, serving Obama to dismantle his own legacy.

Does ex-President Clinton now believe that he was wrong when he reduced government spending to the lowest level in three decades, or when he enacted comprehensive welfare reform, or achieved the largest deficit reduction in history, or cut the federal bureaucracy by more than 100,000 positions and reduced the White House staff by 25 percent? Clinton was not wrong; he has just surrendered his prestige and principles for political expediency. He missed the opportunity to act as a statesman and, in this critical moment for the country, he has avoided both doing the right thing and making praiseworthy history. There is no question that Clinton's position is cynical rather than substantive. The rank-and-file Democrats who voted for Clinton reflect this metamorphosis. They support the party without regard to the issues. Their unequivocal support of Obama's vision for America is so diametrically opposed to Clinton's legacy that it only confirms this contention.

It is almost inconceivable that in just twelve years, the Democrats have moved from conditional support of Clinton to unconditional support of Obama, a complete reversal of their values and vision for the country. These new Social Democrats do not represent the party of John F. Kennedy, Daniel Patrick Moynihan, or Bill Clinton—who has espoused the new persuasions and no longer even represents himself.

The Moral Decay

Socialism, a metamorphosis of liberalism, disguised in some corners as social justice, neoliberalism, and in others as progressive or "helper of the poor," is now both the "cause" of the Democratic Party and the "source" of its moral decay. In his utterly boring book *Thank the Liberals for Saving America*, eternal liberal Alan Colmes delineated a host of liberal accomplishments beginning with FDR, and proudly listed liberal legislation aimed at helping the poor. Whatever the validity of the liberal argument for helping the poor was, idealism and affinity have led to the destruction of self-reliance.

Back in 1965, highly intelligent and well-informed Senator Daniel Patrick Moynihan, in his eloquent testimony about the collapse of socialist policies, adumbrated the Democrats:

> *The steady expansion of welfare programs can be taken as a measure of the steady disintegration of the Negro family structure over the past generation in the United States. ("The Negro Family: The Case for National Action," March 1965)*

Moynihan's report also stated, "*The policy of the United States is to bring the Negro American to full and equal sharing in the responsibilities and rewards of citizenship.*" The Democratic Party, however, was marching to its own drummer and not to Senator Moynihan's foresight.

As the policies aimed at reduction of poverty gathered momentum and longevity, the reality Senator Moynihan foresaw fifty years ago materialized before our eyes to an extent not even the senator could have imagined. The effect of family disintegration engulfed all races in this country. It has become evident that the Democrats love the poor; they love them so much that they want more of them, and their programs have succeeded in accomplishing just that over the decades. The so-called War on Poverty was, in effect, a war on self-reliance.

Although the pursuit of the beloved liberal doctrine has been consistently producing results utterly different from those which were publicized, the Democrats continue deluding themselves with the offering of new ideas that are consistently more absurd than previous ones, to justify the failures. The latest offering is the pathetic White Privilege theory. Wikipedia defines White Privilege as "*a term for societal privileges that benefit white people beyond what is commonly experienced by non-white people in the same social, political, or economic circumstances."* That should explain why blacks and other minorities are falling behind in education and professional development. Factually, it proves exactly the opposite. Millions of immigrants come to this country every year; most of them are Chinese, Koreans, and Indians. With the exception of Indians, they do not even speak English. They all have their stories of poverty, suffering, humiliation, rejection, and despair, but their perseverance, determination, and hard work enable them to succeed in their American Dream. We forgot to mention that they are not whites.

While the Democrats are wailing about "the poor," the political elite of the Democratic Party would not deprive themselves of the luxuries of power. Never before in America was the gap between the imperial lifestyle of the professed defenders of the poor and working Americans so explicit. Never before in America was inequality of privileges so pronounced. The servants of the people divorced themselves from their masters, the American people, maintaining for themselves luxurious benefits such as generous pension plans, platinum health care, and a variety of perks unavailable to the average American. Just like their Bolshevik ancestors, they created their own world separate from "the people." The change in values was on full display during Obama's 2009 inauguration. The ostentation surrounding someone considered "sort of God" was not seen by Democrats as offensive or distasteful. Nor did they find the price tag of $150 million spent on inauguration festivities cynical and insulting to the millions of poor and unemployed Americans.

It is in this context (like the Bolsheviks, who parasitically plundered the wealth of Russia) that the American royal family travels in style, taking super-luxury vacations worldwide, fulfilling their most extravagant fantasies on the taxpayer's dime, including traveling with the kids to London for fish and chips, golfing at Martha's Vineyard, and taking an African safari at the cost of $100 million. The first-family lifestyle is reminiscent of African dictators and Arab sheikhs. The first lady alone has an unprecedented staff of twenty-two servants, at a cost of $1.5 million per year, while Americans suffer high unemployment and a rising cost of living

What a startling contrast with fellow Democratic President

Harry Truman. As president, Truman paid for all of his own travel expenses and food. When offered corporate positions at large salaries after his retirement, he declined, stating, "You don't want me. You want the office of the President, and that doesn't belong to me. It belongs to the American people, and it's not for sale." Today, politicians have found a way to cash in and become quite wealthy while enjoying the fruits of their offices. Good old Harry Truman was correct when he observed, "My choices early in life were to be either a piano player in a whorehouse or a politician. And to tell the truth, there's hardly any difference." As Baron Acton[26] informed us around 150 years ago, "Power tends to corrupt, and absolute power corrupts absolutely." The Democrats, while in control of the House and Senate, brought corruption to a new and shameless level when representatives openly accepted bribes to vote for the health care bill. The list of those bribed is so long that it would take a chapter to list them all, but a couple stand out.

Senator Ben Nelson, Democrat of Nebraska, accepted a bribe to vote for the bill but requested a waiver for his state. If this bill is good for the country, then why not for Nebraska? Conversely, if it is not good for the people of Nebraska, why is it good for the rest of the country? The so-called "Louisiana purchase" is another example. Senator Mary Landrieu bargained $300 million for her vote, camouflaged as government assistance to Hurricane Katrina victims. The Republicans' apparent incorruptibility was refreshing to see. No Republican accepted a bribe, but not for the President's lack of trying.

The integrity of Senate Democrats was tested in 2008 when Illinois Governor Rod Blagojevich was poised to make a Senate appointment to replace the seat of President-elect Barack Obama as junior senator from Illinois. Senate Democrats made it clear weeks prior that they wouldn't accept an appointment made by a governor accused of selling this very Senate seat. "I agree with their decision," President-elect Obama said. Blagojevich, however, made a capping play with a knight's move: he appointed his friend Roland

---

[26] *Baron Acton, prominent historian and liberal member of British Parliament (1834–1920).*

Wallace Burris, who happened to be black, to the Senate seat. The President and Democrats immediately accepted Mr. Burris. The reaction of the President and the Democratic Senate mirrors the story of Roman emperor Caligula, who once made his favorite horse a senator. It seems that, had Blagojevich appointed a horse to the United States Senate, the President and Democratic senators would have supported it, as long as it was…a black horse.

Evidently, the prerequisites of being Obama's Social Democrat are political expediency and knavery supplemented by a congenital lack of integrity and common decency. There are hardly any thinkers or mavericks left in the Party, but rather a gathering of pedestrian opportunists who, unlike their Bolshevik precursors who clearly professed their egalitarian vision and prophetic absolutism, are hiding behind ambiguous "fundamental change," unable or unwilling to define their political ambitions. Indifferent to common principles of constitutional legitimacy, they vehemently support Obama's enshrined socialist agenda through deceptive legislation and coercion, thereby imposing a new moral ascendancy that seemed inconceivable just two decades ago.

Dreams and Reality

How does one build a socialist society? How to apply the ideas of Liberal Bolshevism to real life with all of its incalculable political complications and economic hazards? How to force the submission of the people and industries to government control?

As discussed earlier, the transition to socialism can be accomplished either by violent revolution with the imposition of a dictatorship of the proletariat, where the proletariat is used as a revolutionary force, or by the gradual transition from free markets to wealth distribution via government regulation of the economy and taxation. Obama and the Democrats have chosen a two-track strategy.

The first track emulates Lenin's revolutionary blueprint—the prerequisites of which are the revolutionary environment creating upheaval and needing the availability of a revolutionary force.

But there was a problem. In the United States the proletariat—organized masses of working people, who, according to Marx, had "nothing to lose but their chains"—ceased to exist decades ago. There was an effort to organize non-working people who had "nothing to lose" to stoke street violence and resurrect an appearance of proletarians with the Occupy Wall Street movement. Predictably, this premeditated unrest akin to Mao's Red Guards of the Cultural Revolution failed miserably.

Unfortunately for the Democrats and their allies, those people who "had nothing to lose" had nothing to gain either. Instead of storming the bulwarks of bourgeois institutions of power such as banks and corporations, as real revolutionaries would be expected to do, they were more interested in drugs and easy sex than presidential politics. After urinating on the streets of American cities and creating riots accompanied by vandalism and confrontations with police, the militant movement became an embarrassment for the Democrats. Subsequently, after spending a great deal of money on police overtime, cleaning the streets, and restoring damaged property, this organized banditry had to be quietly shut down.

The failure of the movement to create a virtuous dynamic that would lead to the socialist revolution in the United Sates became a source of contention among Marxists and socialists. Since 2011, a sizeable body of socialist and communist literature has been published to explore and analyze the failure of the movement from a Marxist-Leninist perspective. The most notable is the work of prominent Marxist Paul Mason, *Why It's Still Kicking Off Everywhere: The New Global Revolution* (Verso, 2013). Additionally, the book of radical socialists Luke Cooper and Simon Hardy, *Beyond Capitalism: The Future of Capitalist Politics*, published by Zero Books in 2012, attributed the failure of the movement to the organizers' disregarding Lenin's conception of the vanguard party as the inspirer and organizer of the proletarian revolution.

The following excerpts from the book, albeit for the most part blissfully delusional, nevertheless are indicative of the left's perception of the movement.

> *Occupy has challenged the specific form of liberal "representative"...has opened up an avenue for a more far-reaching socialist vision.*

> Occupy serves as a continual reminder of how important democracy and participation is to the renewal of a healthy socialist project.
>
> Activists from Occupy, the student movement, and the new grassroots campaigns in the unions, will often not have a 'conscious program' in the way that the left understands the terms, but they have proven able to build vibrant and exiting campaigns from which we need to learn.
>
> We need to take advantage of the antagonisms of the current social crisis to build and renew forms of dynamics of struggle that can deepen the cracks in the capitalist order.

The authors transparently point out that Occupy had "*the immediate inability to lead the resistance necessary to turn the tables on austerity and provide the working class with confidence and belief in the socialist project.*" Inadvertently, the socialists confirmed what we knew all along: the socialist project will—if allowed—grab power through violence and destruction. As the French political thinker Alexis de Tocqueville pointed out, "History is a gallery of pictures in which there are few originals and many copies." The foregoing is a copy of Lenin's original: "*The struggle must be organized, according to 'all the rules of the art,' by people who are professionally engaged in revolutionary activity. The fact that the masses are spontaneously being drawn into the movement does not make the organization of this struggle less necessary. On the contrary, it makes it more necessary.*"[27]

The White House took notice and endorsed socialists' thesis and when an opportunity presented itself through the killing of a black teenager by police in Ferguson, Missouri, in August 2014, the President and his party decided to take direct control of events. They

---

[27] *Lenin, "The Primitiveness of the Economists and the Organization of the Revolutionaries,"* Part IV of What Is to Be Done?, 1901

mobilized professional organizer Al Sharpton, a sympathetic media, the Department of Justice, and the prestige of the Oval Office to organize a nationwide revolt under the banner of "victims of racism." In the process the administration embraced a system of justice ruled by staged mass demonstrations and introduced its distinct concept of legitimacy based on racial chauvinism. This combination of mob justice and peculiar legitimacy redefines the limits of permissible; it offers the mob a relief from self-imposed misery in hatred and vengeance. Bonded by the credo of freeloaders—"we are entitled to more"—this segment of the population under the encouragement, or at least toleration, of Washington is allowed to riot, loot, assault, burn down buildings, and otherwise destroy property, and provide false and misleading testimony to a grand jury with impunity. Those "programmed to fail" products of America's failing public education system, in the name of defending human rights, viciously disregard the rights of humans.

Whether the ongoing revolt is labeled "Occupy Wall Street," "Hands up, don't shoot," or "Black lives matter," the "near" objective of this campaign is to weaken law enforcement, forcing it to choose between security and political posturing. Should law enforcement get overwhelmed, the radical turmoil could gain momentum and expand liberal grievances—social, economic, racial, and gender—and turn them into a broader replay of the 1960s upheavals. The objective is to forge a revolutionary movement fanned by the discontents of temperamental or resentful segments of the population that increasingly regard the government as having an obligation to improve their well-being. Determined not to *"allow a crisis to go to waste,"* the Democratic administration is enticing violent rules of conduct and manipulating a multiplicity of divergent political interests, keeping them cohesive enough to support ideological conquest. This explosive ploy inevitably leads to a bloody outcome. Deadly attacks on New York City police officers and elsewhere is a prelude to what to expect.

> *The Democrats are either impervious to or undaunted by the prospect that the inflamed rhetoric of Al Sharpton and other provocateurs gives a false*

sense of purpose and an aura of heroism to disturbed souls looking for a motive to unleash their anger, which may result in catastrophic destruction and massive loss of life.

In any event, given the unwavering support the participants are getting from the Democrats, the administration is clearly comfortable with a greater level of anarchy if it can bring about its vision of CHANGE.

It is easy to forget that Obama had actually made an attempt to create a private army that would resemble the Bolsheviks' Sentinel of Revolution—NKVD, which later became KGB—or Hitler's SA (also known as Storm Troopers or Brownshirts), which could be used as a revolutionary force to safeguard "fundamental transformation" of the nation. In a speech delivered in Boulder, Colorado, on July 2, 2008, Obama called for the creation and establishment of a *"Civilian National Security Force"* that would be *"just as powerful, just as strong, just as well funded as the U.S. military."*

Providentially, the idea of having another armed force did not get much traction among the American people. Still, we should not misjudge the implication of Obama's "initiative" or revel prematurely. As Lenin taught, "First try with a bayonet; if hard, back off and try again until you find a soft spot." Obama tried and has found the soft spot. The administration is quietly proceeding with the militarization of federal agencies, expanding the role of Special Weapons and Tactics (SWAT) teams beyond the Secret Service and the Bureau of Prisons to the Department of Agriculture, the Railroad Retirement Board, the Tennessee Valley Authority, the Office of Personnel Management, the Consumer Product Safety Commission, and the U.S. Fish and Wildlife Service. It is not exactly a private army yet, but if one day it is put under one central command, it could be.

The standoff at the Bundy ranch in Nevada and the raid of federal agents on the Gibson Guitar factory give us a glimpse of what to expect from the all-powerful federal government. In the standoff at the Bundy ranch federal agents showed up with guns blazing against farmers and women in an attempt to seize Bundy's property.

Anti-Obama demonstration in Houston, 2010

In the incident with Gibson Guitars, whose owner is a Republican donor, the factory was raided by agents from the Homeland Security Swat Terrorism Unit, FBI, Border Patrol, IRS, EPA, OSHA, and the Department of Agriculture with automatic assault rifles drawn to prevent Gibson Guitars from using illegal wood that was perfectly legal for Gibson Guitars' competitor—Martin Guitars, owned by a Democratic donor. Although the case was thrown out of court, the government de facto prevailed by punishing Gibson Guitars by way of millions of dollars in legal fees and lost revenue. These two cases vividly demonstrate the tyrannical nature and intimidating power of the government and the extent to which it is prepared to be used against citizens. Just like his precursors, our Liberal Bolshevik does not find it distasteful to use force and practice arbitrary interpretation and selective application of the law to suppress dissent. While

Lenin's strategy of militant Bolshevism to transition America to socialism has been facing unsurmountable problems, due to the lack of a private army and the absence of a proletariat, the other track—Obama's strategy of embracing Liberal Bolshevism—although in constant flux and with some of its components at times beheld inconsistent and contradictory, nevertheless has been executed with formidable political skill and conviction.

In a quest to re-engineer the free-market economy and replace American self-reliance with government dependence, the Democrats have been employing the methodology developed by the Bolsheviks during the early stages of the Bolshevik revolution in Russia. The preponderance of the evidence and application of the theories of Marxism and Leninism make this conclusion irrefutable. Predominantly, Obama is following Lenin's path as it had been signposted, with the enhancements described earlier. In order to succeed, as the Bolsheviks' teaching goes, the government needs to take control of the economy and dominate everyday life by making its citizens dependent on the government. The Bolsheviks' promise of a social paradise was a lure to make Russia's citizens dependent on government handouts and fall into the grip of Communist Party. To accomplish this, Lenin declared, *"Debauch the currency to overturn the basis of society."* The destruction of currency was a main component of Bolshevik strategy.

In his interview with London's *Daily Chronicle* on April 22, 1919, Lenin's 50th birthday, and published in the *New York Times* on April 23, 1919, as "Talk with Bolshevist Head,"

(See Appendix I for the full text of the interview) Lenin outlined his strategy for the dismantling of capitalism. During the interview Lenin further elaborated on the implementation of his strategy at length:

> *Hundreds of thousands of ruble notes are being issued daily by our Treasury. This is done, not in order to fill the coffers of the State with practically worthless paper, but with the deliberate intention of destroying the value of money as a means of payment....*

New York Times, April 23, 1919. Interview with V. Lenin

> *Experience has taught us it is impossible to root out the evils of capitalism merely by confiscation and expropriation.... The simplest way to exterminate the very spirit of capitalism is, therefore, to flood the country with notes of a high face-value without financial guarantees of any sort....The great illusion of the value and power of money on which the capitalist state is based will have been definitely destroyed.*

In his book *The Economic Consequences of the Peace*, published in 1919, prominent British economist John Keynes [28], an admirer of the Russian Bolshevik revolution, whose ideas served as the basis for Keynesian economics, offered a lucid comment on Lenin's strategy for the destruction of capitalism:

---

[28] *John Maynard Keynes, British liberal economist (June 5, 1883–April 21, 1946) whose ideas have fundamentally affected the theory and practice of modern economics. His book* The Economic Consequences of the Peace *was a best seller throughout the world.*

> *Lenin is said to have declared that the best way to destroy the Capitalist System was to debauch the currency. By a continuing process of inflation, governments can confiscate, secretly and unobserved, an important part of the wealth of their citizens. By this method they not only confiscate, but they confiscate arbitrarily.... Lenin was certainly right, there is no subtler, no surer means of overturning the existing basis of society than to debauch the currency. The process engages all the hidden forces of economic law on the side of destruction, and does it in a manner which not one man in a million is able to diagnose.*

The Russian Bolsheviks' gambit succeeded: Russia's economy was paralyzed and the Bolshevik government was able to solidify its control over all aspects of Russian citizens' lives. Which led to Mr. Keynes' admission in his book *The End of Laissez-Faire*, published in 1926, that his socialist economic theories, which incorporated the Bolsheviks' economic experience, "can be much easier adapted to the conditions of a totalitarian state than...a large degree of *laissez-faire*." There should be little doubt about this. Keynes, whose theories are based on government control of the economy, was even more confused about economics than Karl Marx.

CHAPTER 6
The Three Planks of Liberal Bolshevism

The Democratic Party is in need of Great Change;
"we the people" are in need of Great America.

The Liberal Bolshevik's Strategy

Obama's war to end the laissez-faire involves a comprehensive multi-faceted strategy that rests on three planks: destruction of wealth, replacement of American self-reliance with government dependence, and replacement of a capitalist market economy with a government-controlled political economy. These planks are fundamentally interrelated and interdependent, and cover a vast theater of operations that includes the areas of health care, global warming, the war on oil, economic policies, taxation, inequality, fairness, and other components of the President's "fundamental change."

The strategy is augmented by a series of tactical legislative fiats and executive actions aimed at overwhelming the system and keeping it in a state of permanent crises, emulating the approach developed by radical socialists Saul Alinsky[29] and Cloward and Piven[30]. Alinsky's tactic, to no surprise, was a close analog to the Bolsheviks' methods in terms of form and substance. Cloward and Piven's

---

[29] *Saul David Alinsky (January 30, 1909–June 12, 1972) was an American community organizer and writer. He is known for his book* Rules for Radicals.

[30] *Richard Andrew Cloward and Frances Fox Piven, Colombia University political scientists, proposed a plan in 1966 to hasten the fall of capitalism by expanding welfare and bankrupting the country, causing economic collapse.*

approach was to overflow the welfare system with new applicants to the point of financial bankruptcy and therefore facilitate political turmoil that would hopefully lead to socialism.

Again, just as in the case with Marxism, Obama added a touché of his own pragmatism to modify and enhance the concepts. He is not running with a bomb like his buddy Bill Ayers or Lenin's brother Alexander Ulyanov, and unlike Alinsky and Cloward and Piven, who advocated subversion of the system from the outside by means of community organizing, expanding entitlements, and violent upheaval, Obama uses the power of the Oval Office to facilitate disruptions from the inside per Lenin's directive: *"Sometimes history needs a push."*

The "push" is to orchestrate and exploit a crisis; whether it is a financial crisis, economic crisis, border crisis, budget crisis, or immigration crisis is not important. We can see the application of this strategy in the enormous proliferation of entitlements, offering food stamps to illegal aliens, refusing to enforce the immigration laws, the recently orchestrated influx of children from Latin America, which has undertones of both Alinsky and Cloward-Piven, and of course Occupy Wall Street, Black Lives Matter, and other radical movements. To heed Lenin's words, *"Those who are engaged in the formidable task of overcoming capitalism must be prepared to try method after method until they find the one which answers their purpose best."*[31]

The state of permanent upheaval enables the Democratic Party to magnify, employ, and *"utilize every manifestation of discontent, and to collect and utilize every grain of rudimentary protest"* to replace the existing moral and economic order with new morals and economic relations. This is a familiar Marxist template that has been proven effective in seizing power in Russia, China, Eastern Europe, North Korea, and elsewhere.

---

[31] *Quoted in* Russia in the Shadows, *by Herbert George Wells, p. 157.*

Plank I. Destruction of Wealth

Barack Obama's administration, with the explicit support of House and Senate Democrats, is clearly replaying Lenin's strategy for the downfall of capitalism, spending and printing money at unprecedented levels. The staunchest supporters of the President's policies and disciples of Keynesian economics, Nobel Prize–winning economists Paul Krugman and former Chairman of the Federal Reserve Ben Bernanke, successfully emulated Lenin's know-how. The area doesn't matter: it could be bailouts, stimulus plans, health care, solar energy, manure management, tattoo removal, or condoms. Some of you might think I'm using hyperbole to make a dramatic statement. Regrettably not; it is all too true. The Stimulus Bill does include $200,000 for tattoo removal, $335 million for condoms and sexually explicit "STD prevention" programs, and, thanks to Tom Harkin, a former Senator from Iowa, almost $2 million for swine odor and manure management.

This is one part of the seemingly incomprehensible strategy for the destruction of wealth. Another part of this strategy is the dramatic acceleration of the growth of the country's national debt during the last seven years. From 1977 to the end of President Bush's term in January 2009, the debt reached $10.6 trillion. For the last seven years President Obama has been traveling around the country promising to reduce the national debt. During his tenure, however, the debt has grown by 100 percent and amounts to nearly 100 percent of the projected gross domestic product. Indisputably, the President needs and wants to spend more, much more, to accomplish his objective. His administration demonstrates a high level of creativity when it comes to spending. The newest ideas are a "jobs bank" with a $1.5 billion budget, relaxation of student loan repayment rules to allow many students not to repay their loans, very generous foreign aid, advertisements to recruit welfare recipients, and even welfare checks to illegal aliens. Obama's mastery of spending has no boundaries. After widely publicized fiascoes of government investments in alternative energies, the Obama administration engaged the Pentagon in the development of wind and solar energies. According to a recent report from Pike Research, annual spending on renewable energy by the Department of Defense will reach $10 billion by 2030. "The DOD is positioned to become the single most important driver of the clean-tech revolution in the United States," says Pike Research president Clint Wheelock. In his 2009 Inaugural Address the President told the American people:

> *Those of us who manage the public dollars will be held to account, to spend wisely, reform bad habits, and do our business in the light of day, because only then [do] we restore the vital trust between a people and their government.*

In retrospect, it was another "bait and switch." Obama never loses his power to astonish Americans and to perform a grand sleight of hand, continuing to nurture and maintain an unprecedented gap between his rhetoric and actions, or lack thereof. The government is running up mountains of debt with increasing speed. In relative terms, Obama's predecessor, George W. Bush, sometimes referred to as "The Great Spender," looks like a fiscally responsible president. It is becoming exceedingly evident that the Democrats' objective is to spend, spend, and spend until the overwhelming debt results in a state of hyperinflation that will destroy our currency. The U.S. government will then flood the market with cheap dollars, devaluing the net worth of productive citizens, successful enterprises, and dollar-denominated assets around the world.

This may explain why this president and his Democratic allies in Congress did not pass a budget during Obama's first term in office. The budget is a controlling document designed to identify and manage expenditures. If there is no budget, there are no restrictions on spending; the gates are wide open. The issue here is not whether we are talking about a Republican-proposed budget or Democrat budget; by law, the President of the United States must propose a budget and the legislature's job is to debate, amend, and pass it. But no budget is the only acceptable option for this president. When the President finally proposed a budget in 2011, it did nothing to restore fiscal prudence; to the contrary, it was aimed to accelerate our nation toward bankruptcy. It was so ridiculous that even Obama's

Democratic exponents rejected it. The Senate vote on the presidential budget was 97 to 0 against it. The Republicans in the House did not wait for the President to offer leadership on the issue; they passed Chairman of the House Budget Committee Paul Ryan's budget and sent it to the Senate. The President and Democrats then attacked the budget like a pack of sharks. The media unmercifully denounced the budget as radical and ideological, exercising their prerogative to select the data supporting their ideological preference.

Despite all the criticism and ridicule of the Republican budget, Senate Majority Leader Harry Reid refused to bring it to the floor for a vote. Why? Because the Democrats' voting herd after the 2010 congressional elections got the message and it was not as coherent as it was in 2008. There was the distinct possibility that some renegades might cross the ideological barricade and work with the Republicans to develop a pragmatic and realistic approach to the budget that both sides could vote for. Barack Obama and Harry Reid could not take this risk.

So, instead, here's how it goes: the government spends more than it takes in and later requests raising the debt ceiling so it can borrow more. The president insists that "we must increase our debt limit so that we can pay our bills." This argument is hardly commensurate with reality; if we have to borrow money to pay our bills, we are not paying our bills. Congress, facing U.S. government default on its obligations, has no other option but to approve additional borrowing, because the money has already been spent. To those Republicans who expect concessions from the President to reduce future spending and make plans to shrink the deficit, Obama has stated publicly many times that it was not to be yesterday, it is not to be today, and it will not be tomorrow. The Republicans who refuse to conform to the rhythm of inevitable economic disaster find themselves disillusioned, disappointed, and frustrated. The lack of understanding of the President's objectives and motives leads to a series of political blunders.

If Obama's plans for "fundamental change" are to be implemented, he has to maintain spending. Anything short of it, even temporary freezing, would be a step backward. Apparently, at the time of Obama's reelection campaign nobody recognized the dire significance of the President's reelection slogan, "FORWARD." This is one reelection promise the President intends to keep. And so it goes, with the national debt at the time of this writing exceeding $19 trillion and getting us ever closer to economic calamity.

> *There are two ways to conquer and enslave a nation.... One is by sword.... The other is by debt.*
> John Adams said that.

When Republican presidential candidate Rick Perry accused Chairman of the Federal Reserve Ben Bernanke of treachery for unrestrained printing of U.S. dollars, he was maliciously attacked by the press. But Perry was literally right on the money for accusing the chairman of undermining U.S. currency and the stability of the country's economic system. It would be ludicrous to assume that the chairman, who is a Nobel laureate in economics, did not understand the improvident aloofness of his policies. It is hard to believe that the chairman and the President did not realize that the combination of an increased deficit and a flood of dollars would lead to inflation and de facto devaluation of the currency.

The reason we have not experienced hyperinflation yet is the simple fact that the U.S. dollar is the world's "reserve currency." As such, the U.S. dollar forms the basis of the global financial system. That's why the administration has been able to print and borrow trillions of dollars with no visible negative impact. We have the luxury to rack up enormous debts and then print more money. The rest of the world is beginning to realize the glooming reality of the U.S. dollar and is looking for a new world reserve currency. Should they succeed, the United States will no longer be able to print dollars without consequences, the country will go bankrupt, and all of us will have to learn to live in poverty.

Moreover, anytime the Fed inflates the money supply, it steals buying power from people who hold dollar-denominated accounts, including savings and pensions. Stealing under any other circumstances would be criminal, but since the government is doing it, I doubt that Obama's current attorney general, Loretta E. Lynch, will take the case. In personal terms, if you have $500,000 in your 401(k) or savings account or U.S. Treasury bills, you may have been looking forward to an independent and relatively secure retirement. But if the currency is devalued, you will lose purchasing power and eventually may need to seek government assistance.

Henry Ford once said, "Money makes a man free." Alternatively, the more money the government takes from its citizens, the less freedom they have. Unless interrupted, this process will continue until the complete submission of the nation.

Plank II, Replacement of American Self-reliance with Government Dependence

The Democrats and their allies on the left understand that getting Americans to accept socialism would be like putting a saddle on a cow. The United States, being a country founded by immigrants looking for freedom from the oppressive political regimes of Europe, is a nation with a strong commitment to the values of individual responsibility, personal freedom, and belief in limited government. The acceptance of socialism would require a massive cultural transformation and major adjustment in the American DNA—the moral lapse from self-reliance to government dependence. The legislative and philosophical foundations for this transition have been built by previous administrations, beginning with FDR's New Deal with its generous Social Security system, then strengthened by the development of a massive publicly financed education system, and later heavily reinforced by Lyndon Johnson's War on Poverty.

But *every* previous administration, Republican and Democrat, has contributed its share to the culture of dependency. The acid of dependency has been eating away the fabric of American society, creating an ideological Grand Canyon between the vision of the Founding Fathers, of self-government and personal responsibility, and our current heavily regulated society with reliance on government handouts, bailouts, entitlements, and racial and other preferences.

Americans are being corrupted by the concept of shifting the burden of personal responsibility to society. Crimes, drug abuse, teenage pregnancies, obesity, illiteracy, business failures, personal bankruptcies, and all other adversities are blamed on society. We have stopped celebrating winners and success, and more often glorify and celebrate mediocrity and failure. Celebrities are proudly broadcasting their drug addictions and joyfully announcing their entrance into rehabilitation clinics.

Social engineering and cultural diversity have become more important than merit standards, resulting in the dumbing down of our learning institutions to embarrassing levels globally.

Dependence plays a major role in the Democratic strategy of fundamentally changing America; independence is to be replaced with obedience, self-reliance with submissiveness, and eventually submissiveness will lead to bondage. The more the American people are indebted to the government, the more they will turn to the government to save them, assuring Democratic one-party rule for the future. Newt Gingrich made an important observation in his dazzling book *To Renew America*: "By definition, any civilization goes only a generation deep. If the next generation fails to learn what makes America tick, then our country could change decisively overnight."

I can confirm Gingrich's assertion with my own personal observations. Going back to Russia, where my company was building a few projects, and meeting with young Russians, I was shocked to learn not only how little they knew about their country's communist past but also how little they cared. It did take only one generation to change the country beyond recognition, although in this instance I would call it a positive development.

The Democrats are not far from achieving their objective, considering how much this country has changed since its inception and the apparent failure to pass the baton of freedom to a new generation. The Russian newspaper *Pravda* published an article in April 2009 titled "American capitalism gone with a whimper," which stated:

> It must be said that, like the breaking of a great dam, the American descent into Marxism is happening with breathtaking speed, against the backdrop of a

passive, hapless sheep; excuse me, dear reader, I meant people.

Although Obama lost the House, and after the 2014 elections lost the Senate as well, he still has the power of the executive office and will continue expansion of entitlements to trap more citizens in the welfare state, and the Federal Reserve will print more dollars until they become worthless. Although the journey to socialism suffered a setback with the 2010 and 2014 midterm elections, the President was reelected in 2012 and the Obama Express is moving FORWARD.

When I published the first in my series of articles "Anatomy of a Bolshevik" in November 2010, 47 percent of Americans did not pay any income tax. Recently, The Heritage Foundation estimated that 51 percent of Americans are not paying any income tax, and that number is growing. According to government statistics, more than 30 million Americans are getting welfare checks, 44 million are receiving food stamps, 8 million are getting SSI (Supplementary Security Income) payments, and millions enjoy subsidized housing.

It may be an eye-opener to some of us that a vast number of Americans have skipped the intermediate phase (socialism) and are already living in virtual communism, receiving government handouts in one form or another, "in accordance with their needs," from generation to generation. This cradle-to-grave welfare breed of new debased citizen-freeloaders, whose whole existence is contingent upon government generosity, constantly demands more and more largesse from its master. The Democrats are not going to disappoint their most dependent and dependable constituency. And their constituency will enthusiastically endorse these new and most grotesque kinds of freedom…freedom from work, freedom from responsibilities, and freedom from liberty.

More goodies in the administration pipeline include free health care, free tuition, more welfare, contraception pills, seemingly inexhaustible unemployment benefits, subsidized mortgages; and the list goes on and on. The Democrats know exactly how agreeably their promises fall on the ears of freeloaders who have been conditioned for decades to support the Democrats through increased financial dependence. What do you think Obama bought with the additional $5.8 trillion of debt we accumulated during the first term of his presidency? A better economy? Better schools? A safer environment? No, he bought more dependence. More government employees, more police officers, more teachers, more food stamps, more welfare; all these people in one way or another depend on the government. Furthermore, for many of them, due to their occupation or professional skills, the state is the sole employer. In the face of this objectivity, there are few salaries servants of the state will resist the temptation of safety at the price of freedom because, for those who are burdened by financial obligations, there is no freedom without economic security.

Benjamin Franklin famously said, "Those who would give up essential liberty to purchase a little temporary safety deserve neither liberty nor safety." Noble words, but we shall not allow deceiving ourselves that the choice is available. In many instances it is not. The Bolsheviks, as we know, enforced their form of communist freedom with terror, despotism, and dependence. We may skip the terror, but despotism and dependence are classical embodiments of Obama's Liberal Bolshevism.

In this connection it is important to understand—which, unfortunately, very few people, including many scholars of Marxism, do understand—that the prime purpose for the Bolsheviks' expropriation of the means of production was not the distribution of wealth, as is commonly understood, but first and foremost to ensure ubiquitous obedience. As Leon Trotsky put it, *"In a country where the sole employer is the state, opposition means death by slow starvation. The old principle, who does not work does not eat, has been replaced with a new one: who does not obey does not eat."*[32]

Fatefully, the "new" in this principle was that it was applied to Leon Trotsky and his followers by Comrade Stalin. Under duress, Trotsky revealed the guiding principle of Bolshevism that Trotsky, Lenin's "enforcer," ardently had practiced himself since 1917: starv-

---

[32] *Leon Trotsky,* The Revolution Betrayed: What Is the Soviet Union and Where Is It Going?

ing millions of Ukrainian peasants and members of the anti-communist opposition.

In fact, Obama is gradually following Leon Trotsky; as long as the country is going through protracted economic stagnation, safety will prevail over freedom. *This hideous doctrine is at the core of the Democrats' fundamentally ruinous economic policy.*

The ABC report by Diane Sawyer, that aired September 23, 2011, offered considerable evidence of this policy. Sawyer reported on government-financed infrastructure projects in New York, Alaska, and California, with a total price tag of around $7.8 billion, that were awarded to Chinese construction firms, despite a high level of unemployment in the U.S. construction industry. Why? Because this administration values dependence over employment.

I am intimately familiar with the side effects of dependence. The Soviet system was built on dependence. It is a chronic disease that is difficult to cure. As Karl Marx observed, "social existence determines consciousness." Many of those who stay on welfare or other government programs lose, over time, the capacity to be productive. All they have is the delusion that it's the government's obligation to provide support for the less fortunate. It is not, after all, their fault; it is just a matter of misfortune.

When I look at my two beautiful cats, I see a parallel between them and this huge and ever-expanding segment of American society. Many hundreds, perhaps thousands, of years ago, the ancestors of my cats lived in the wilderness and provided for themselves and their offspring. But over time, they became domesticated and totally dependent on humans. They lost the capacity to hunt, to defend themselves from enemies, and to survive on their own. If one day I decided to throw them out on the street, they would die from starvation and disease. That is what dependence does to people—they became socialists.

Another way for the present administration to extend its dominion is to widen the membership of government-friendly trade unions by solidifying the union bosses' control over the rank and file. This is exactly the plan behind the "Employee Free Choice Act," legislation that actually *deprives* workers of free choice by replacing private union balloting with publicly signed cards in the presence of

Liberal Bolshevism

union bosses. Like most of the President's ideas, it is not original; this one was borrowed from the Kremlin's revolutionary library. The Bolsheviks called it "The Principle of Democratic Centralism." This "Democratic Centralism" had nothing to do with democracy and everything to do with subjugation and control of the labor movement by making it an extension of the Communist Party. In this country the administration would love nothing more than to use the forced expansion of labor unions as a vehicle to gain extraordinary powers and a reliable source of election financing.

And finally, last but not least in this category, the so-called Universal Health Care Act, officially the Affordable Care Act, which is neither affordable for the millions who have to pay for it, nor universal, nor healthy—"health" is not even mentioned in the official title. The legislation is aimed at tightening government control over the health care industry, which is a vital phase in the formation of a welfare state. Our Commissar-Elect recognizes that without addicting a middle-class majority to government subsidies he cannot fulfill his aspiration of putting the harness of socialism around the necks of the American people.

As Ronald Reagan observed, *"One of the traditional methods of imposing socialism on a people has been by way of medicine. It's very easy to disguise a medical program as a humanitarian project; most people are a little reluctant to oppose anything that suggests medical care for people who possibly can't afford it."*

We can all agree that the existing health care system is a disgrace. Critics point out the high cost, lack of transferability in case of an employer-provided option, pre-existing conditions that cause people to lose insurance when they lose employment or change jobs, and the millions of people who don't have access to health care, among many other issues. It is not the purpose of this book to debate these issues, nor offer any solution to the problem; I will leave that to the experts. However, I do want to point out the way in which the Democrats make political use of this issue.

The President's brashness and sense of unbridled power are shown by the lack of any attempt to develop a solution. In actuality, the Democrats are not interested in solving the problem. The health care bill is the cornerstone of the Democrats' bid to restructure

American society and it goes a long way in increasing dependence and facilitating government spending. The Liberal Bolshevik and his loyal Democratic base spent two years exploiting a crisis to advance a socialist agenda using the full range of their potent weapons, from demagoguery and lies, distortion, misrepresentation, and intimidation, to common bribery, in order to push the law down the throats of the American people. The president's quotes below show the depth of deception and the lengths to which he and his allies were willing to go to achieve their objectives. We will try to find the truth by comparing the lies.

> *And so our goal on health care is, if we can get, instead of health care costs going up 6 percent a year, it's going up at the level of inflation, maybe just slightly above inflation, we've made huge progress. And by the way, that is <u>the single most important thing we could do in terms of reducing our deficit</u>. [emphasis added]. That's why we did it.*

Later, when the disparity between what the President says and what he does became all too obvious, he was forced to admit the truth.

> *But if you—if what—the reports are true, what they're saying is, is that as a consequence of us getting 30 million additional people health care, at the margins that's going to increase our costs, we knew that.*

This time the President sounded less poetic and more realistic. It was also a unique occasion when Barack Obama did not use the imperial first-person pronoun "I" and conveniently replaced it with the more modest "we" for the obvious reason. The confession sounded like a tepid acknowledgement of the obvious. Of course he knew that. Suffice it to say that anyone with a brain larger than a Neanderthal's should understand that extending health care to an additional 30 million people cannot cost less, and therefore cannot be "the single most important thing we could do" to reduce the deficit. He knew that but continued to deliberately and repeatedly mislead the American people. Perhaps the President thought that the American people are ignorant fools and wouldn't check up on him.

Richard Nixon has described it this way: *"Voters quickly forget what a man says."* Since the legislation was implemented the government got control over 17 percent of the American economy. This created an enormous new bureaucracy that regulates and dictates how health care is delivered: who can provide it, to whom it is provided, at what cost, what medical devices and procedures can be used, etc. The corrupt IRS is empowered to manage it and have access to individuals' tax returns and bank accounts to ensure universal purchase of insurance.

It is hard to estimate the total bill for his agenda, but health care alone will cost this country $1.76 trillion over the next ten years, according to the Congressional Budget Office, which has been notorious in underestimating almost any expenditure by the federal government. The health care bill is also recognized as a major contributor to the deficit, which is exactly the opposite of what the President promised the American people. The main reason for the cost is that households with incomes below 400 percent and above 133 percent of the federal poverty line that are enrolled in insurance plans are eligible for premium assistance financed by the federal government. In other words, millions of people will get health insurance for free. Or so they were led to believe.

No one has described the enticement of getting something for free as well as renowned Russian writer Mikhail Bulgakov. To depict the soul of socialism in his famous novel, *The Master and Margarita*, he described Satan's visit to Moscow. During a show that Lucifer has arranged at a local theater, the audience is showered with banknotes falling from the ceiling. People start fighting each other to catch the money. Then Satan makes a clothing store appear on stage and people are invited to exchange their old clothes for luxurious outfits. Again, a brawl erupts but the winners look as if they just came from a Paris fashion show. Satan watches the crowd with amusement, saying, "For the last two thousand years they haven't changed a bit." As soon as the show ends, the money turns to useless paper and the luxurious clothes disappear, leaving the "lucky" people completely naked.

There is a deeper and more sinister plot being prepared by the liberal supporters of Obamacare. When the program fails to live up to the abundance of improbable promises, the Democrats will blame...Republicans, of course. The reason the program failed, they will say, is because Republicans did not accept a single-payer system. Obama is already on record as having stated emphatically, in a 2003 speech to the AFL-CIO, "I happen to be a proponent of a single-payer universal health care plan"—i.e., a government-run system.

The Democrats will not "allow a crisis to go to waste," and will perpetuate the fraud into an even bigger fraud. Remember the pronounced objective of Obamacare was to fix the existing system. When it became potently clear that Obamacare was not providing what had been advertised, the Democrats began offering a fix to a fix. The truth is that the fix was in from the outset; now they are advocating a perpetual fix until it gradually advances into a single-payer system. I will have more on that subject in the following chapters.

Plank III. Replacement of a Capitalist Market Economy with a Government-controlled Political Economy

Lenin said, *"The way to crush the bourgeoisie [in this context, the middle and upper classes] is to grind them between the millstones of taxation and inflation."*

Obama has taken the Lenin's concept of the destruction of capitalism a step further, adding to the millstones of taxation and inflation a huge national debt, the high cost of energy, and an enormous expansion of the federal government in size and power. The Democrats have also imposed a straitjacket of government regulations that greatly impair the ability of businesses to expand and innovate. Just as any living organism needs oxygen and water to sustain life, the capitalist economy needs capital and cheap energy in order to thrive. Therefore, it is not a coincidence that the financial and energy sectors became the Obama administration's first targets for new regulations. The Dodd-Frank Wall Street Reform and Consumer Protection Act and the cap-and-trade bill are each imposing much stricter regulations on these sectors, making them further dependent on government regulators. According to the government, the Dodd-Frank act is designed to address the increasing propensity of the financial sector to put the entire system at so great a risk that it eventually needs to be bailed out at taxpayers' expense. In plain English, it is supposed to take the risk out of the banking business. Talk about a contradiction in terms! The legislation brought the most significant changes to financial regulation in the United States since the regulatory reform that followed the Great Depression, affecting almost every facet of the nation's financial services industry. It will not, however, prevent another financial crisis or additional bailouts of financial institutions, much as its proponents would like us to believe. J. P. Morgan Chase CEO Jamie Dimon characterized the law as "the nail in the coffin of big American banks."

As we know, the government has been enacting new laws and regulations after each economic and financial meltdown for the last two hundred years. The outcome of this latest one has already been felt by businesses and consumers. It unduly restricts the ability of banks and other financial institutions to make loans. Dodd-Frank has created yet another huge bureaucracy to regulate the financial sector of the United States economy. The act rests on the assertion that government bureaucrats understand the financial sector better than the captains of the financial industry do. The absurdity of this assertion was demonstrated by the President himself after the announcement of the J. P. Morgan multibillion-dollar loss on a risky trade.

Once, President Obama called J. P. Morgan CEO Jamie Dimon "one of the smartest bankers we have got" and praised J. P. Morgan as "one of the best-managed banks there is." What could government bureaucrats possibly know that Dimon, one of the most respected bankers in the business, and his executives do not? The president and the Democrats who fought to pass the bill as a supreme "savoir faire" should be embarrassed to see how the bill failed in its first encounter with the unembellished reality of the marketplace. But the bill does what it is supposed to do: the battle of socialists to enhance the government's control over the banking industry and limit private profits is being won.

Defending financial reform, Obama said in Illinois on April 28, 2010,

> *We are not trying to push financial reform because we begrudge success that's fairly earned. I mean, I do think at a certain point you've made enough.*

How about our Marxist teaching! It works! To a Marxist, the notion that a capitalist is making money fairly is an oxymoron. And for Obama to accept that the word "enough" is not in the capitalist vocabulary is an abomination. To add to the confusion, President Obama did not reveal his definition of "enough." It also begs the question: If you have made "enough," then what? Become nonprofit and send money to the government, which never has enough? It is not difficult to figure out which way this stinking socialist wind is blowing. As Winston Churchill summed it up: *"It is a socialist idea that making profits is a vice. I consider the real vice is making losses."*

In October 2011, the President sang the same tune when he tried to justify the creation of a new government agency, the Consumer Financial Protection Bureau: *"You do not have some inherent right just to get a certain amount of profit if your customers are being mistreated."* The new agency was created to define "enough." This new bureau has been granted enormous power to decide not only whether banks have the right to make a profit but also how much someone, somewhere, was allegedly mistreated. In the real world, the agency was designed to restrict profits. No due process required.

The energy sector will not fare any better under the cap-and-trade bill. The cap-and-trade bill, otherwise known as the American Clean Energy and Security Act, seeks to impose significant limits on the amount of greenhouse gases that energy producers and manufacturers emit into the atmosphere each year. According to its proponents, the bill is designed to curb global warming and promote alternative energy production. In reality, it is a tax on U.S. energy producers and end users for the purpose of raising the cost of electricity, thereby making alternative energies competitive. It can also be used as an instrument of political pressure. As with any regulation enacted by this administration, some entities will be granted exceptions to the rules. Plans are in the works to include some form of rebates on water and power bills to offset the higher cost of green power. Who gets those rebates will be determined politically. To no one's surprise, the program has been enacted in California, where it has become a giant driver to socialize (subsidize one group at the expense of another) the extraordinarily high rates of electricity, natural gas, and water.

Besides energy and finance, which have been strangled by new regulations, the rest of the economy is to be controlled by Obama's newly created oligarchy. For centuries, oligarchs were viewed as ruling elite empowered by wealth. Obama's oligarchs are a special breed. There are many rich people in this country, but they would not qualify for Obama's oligarch status. Obama's oligarchy is, first of all, a binary (reciprocal) relationship between business and government. In exchange for supporting government policies the oligarch gets juicy government contracts, often on a single-source basis. The government further reciprocates in kind, pushing legislation that gives the oligarch a competitive advantage or puts a competitor out of business altogether. The government's almost unlimited power transforms competition into monopolism by protecting the oligarch with tax advantages and bailout protection. And there is more to it. Appreciative oligarchs funnel money back to the Democratic Party. Among Russian criminals this practice is called (откат) recoil. In this country the administration calls it public-private partnership. I guess it is an expression of cultural differences; each society gets the type of criminals it nourishes. Regardless of what we call it, the practice unavoidably produces parasitism, decay, and economic stagnation.

The honor of the most prominent American oligarch belongs to Warren Buffet of Berkshire Hathaway. Buffet has been making money with this administration "the old-fashioned way"—as the ultimate insider trader, who made billions during the financial crises by collaborating with the government. During the crises he made a few super lucrative deals, such as bailing out the Bank of America and Goldman Sachs. Mr. Buffett was not secretive about how he was making money. "If I didn't think the government was going to act, I would not be doing anything this week," he said, referring to the $700 billion bailout, which would buy troubled mortgage assets from banks. Since Buffett was dealing directly with Paulson and Geithner, he did not just "think" the government was going to act; he knew it would. In return, Mr. Buffett ardently supports Obama's policies, even offering support for the President's higher-tax policies with the so-called Buffett rule. And why not? Mr. Buffett's business model is not based on minimizing taxes; it is based on maximizing influence and preferences. Nowhere does the vestige of this influence manifest itself as clearly as in the delayed Keystone pipeline. Mr. Buffett is making hundreds of millions of dollars transporting Canadian oil via rail by his Burlington Northern Santa Fe railroad and manufacturing rail cars for oil shipping by Berkshire Hathaway–owned Union Tank Company.

Warren Buffet of Berkshire Hathaway with the President Obama in the White House in October 2009.

The next in line is Jeff Immelt, CEO of General Electric. Bought for the $139 billion bailout of GE capital, he is the most faithful of Obama's lackeys. Mr. Immelt, a registered Republican, famously proclaimed, "We're all Democrats now"—which narrowly lost out to "We're all socialists now" on the cover of the February 2009 Newsweek magazine. Nowadays, there's hardly any difference.

Following these two is an array of government contractors and developers of the alternative energy projects that cannot compete within the rules of the free market and owe their very existence to government regulatory protection and financing. In short, every time Obama praises the harmony of public-private partnerships and calls it "a win-win solution," we know who loses.

As it is usually the case with a political economy, there have been unintended consequences. The President is caught in conflicting currents. The higher cost of electricity will have a negative impact on the President's dream to replace internal combustion engines with electric cars. It will certainly raise unemployment in such states as Pennsylvania and Virginia, and coal miners will not be happy. Furthermore, the higher cost of energy will be reflected in manufactured goods, from food to airplanes, and as a result more businesses will choose to move overseas.

But even these reasons will not stop Obama from offering "imaginative" solutions to this country's so-called addiction to oil. The President's efforts to power the twenty-trillion-dollar economy with windmills and solar panels have proven to be a colossal fiasco. His proposal to reduce American dependence on oil by manufacturing fuel from algae, though a far cry from the discovery of electricity or the invention of the internal combustion engine, is a vast improvement over his earlier proposal to reduce American oil usage by inflating tires and tuning up engines.

Conclusion

In Imperial China there was a particularly cruel form of execution called lingchi, which means slow slicing. In this form of execution, a knife was used to methodically remove portions of the condemned person's body over a prolonged period of time, producing a slow and painful death.

Liberal Bolshevism's destructive effect on our economy could be called economic lingchi; it is eroding the core principles of free enterprise one slice at a time. Notwithstanding that socialist principles have had difficulty implanting themselves into a free-market capitalist economy, and despite criticism and militant opposition by the Republicans, Phase I of Obama's Grand Plan, called "CHANGE," was successfully completed by the 2012 elections via increased spending, enactment of the Affordable Care Act, the Dodd-Frank Wall Street Reform and Consumer Protection Act, and tons of environmental and financial regulations.

Phase II, called "FORWARD," began with the rollout of the Affordable Care Act and the raising of the debt ceiling to ensure continued spending. The impact of the unsuccessful launch of Obamacare on Phase II should not be exaggerated. Although it seemed like a public relations disaster at the time, damaging his credibility and delaying some of the President's legislation, in the end it did not have a material impact on Phase II. The president is confident that people will get used to the high cost of health care, just as they got used to $4-a-gallon gasoline at one time. Opponents loudly criticize numerous deficiencies of the legislation and its implementation—as usual, emphasizing the obvious over the important. The important is that the President is correct when he says that Republicans "can't bring themselves to admit that [it's] working." The unvarnished fact is that Republicans can't bring themselves to admit that vital components of Obamacare are designed to subdue the health care industry, increase dependence, and spend money. The money has already been spent, and a lot more will be spent on subsidizing millions of people who did not have insurance and those who lost their existing insurance due to the new regulations. In this sense it is working. Furthermore, the existing health care structure, if not destroyed, has been irreparably damaged. As what has become the constant rehearsal of a familiar play, Obama will not let this crisis go to waste and much more money will be spent on "getting things right."

> *Destruction of the currency, widespread dependence, underemployment, combined with hyperinflation, will result in the most significant economic instability since, and perhaps including, the Great Depression. It will cause the breakdown of democratic institutions and the disintegration of moral order that should allow the Social Democrats to consolidate power, just as the Bolsheviks did in Russia a century ago.*

Apart from unexpected serious political problems, the President's Grand Socialist Plan is progressing satisfactorily so far. Americans inhabit a new world, but they seem to be oblivious to what is in store.

CHAPTER 7
Capitalism: The Known Ideal

No other society conceived itself as a product of exceptional entrepreneurship in pursuit of excellence—rewarded when it succeeds and punished when it fails.

Preview

The American free-enterprise system is the foundation of our economic freedom and is at the core of our industrial democracy. It is called an industrial democracy because economic freedom and our democracy are deeply *intertwined* and mutually inclusive. They epitomize the ultimate expression of our rights of *"Life, Liberty and the pursuit of Happiness"* as written in the United States Declaration of Independence. Democracy cannot exist without economic freedom and economic freedom cannot exist without the guarantee of property rights and an enforceable legal framework that, among other things, imposes limitations on governmental power.

This interrelation between the free market and democracy was even recognized by the arch-foe of capitalism, Karl Marx, who admitted that the development of capitalism with its free market had been a precondition for the evolution of all our democratic freedoms. If we take this admission to its logical conclusion we would have to recognize that the abolition of capitalism, which Karl Marx so fervently dreamed of, would unavoidably lead to the abolition of our democratic institutions. This ultimate interrelation has not been lost on the forces committed to converting this country into an egalitarian "paradise."

The conceptual problem with the conversion is that the government can't control people's lives without controlling the economy. Therefore, discrediting capitalism became a critical part of the American Social Democrats' strategy of converting free markets into a government-controlled political economy, sometimes referred to as a "moral economy."

Since its inception critics of capitalism have been divided into two principal camps—constructive and destructive. Constructive critics aim at restraining corporate influence on the political process, limiting the environmental impact of industrial activities, and preventing system fraud and abuse. The destructive camp, which consists of socialists, liberals, progressives, and communists, is expressing disagreement with the principles of capitalism in its entirety, advocating complete or partial dismantling of the system, and replacing it with a "fair" socialist economy. Proponents of this philosophy want to subjugate economic activities to government regulations, limiting profits and expanding corporate welfare.

The latest economic crisis provided fuel to the Democratic leadership, which launched a massive and vicious political attack on capitalism. They selectively employ destructive and constructive criticism of capitalism that best serves their propaganda purposes and peddle it to the public as an inherent flaw of the system, very often replicating the official Soviet template of grievances and metaphors such as exploitation, inequality, system abuse, pyramid schemes, and environmental Armageddon.

The Democrats want us to believe in socialism and its virtues. As a socialist Democratic presidential candidate, Bernie Sanders professed in his campaign slogan, this is "A Future to Believe In." But this is the thing; nobody has to believe in capitalism; it is here, it exists, and it works. In the following chapters we will analyze free-market capitalism, its values, its spirit, and its impact on our lives. We will expose the fraudulent nature of economic stimulus, global warming, the war on oil, and health care legislation.

We will talk about capitalism—its accomplishments and the opportunity it offers for universal prosperity and advancement in the basic elements and services that we take for granted every day of our lives. From soup and cotton to passenger jets and iPods, from polio vaccines to heart transplants, capitalism has done it all. From companies started in family garages to giant corporations, industrial plants, and laboratories around the world, no other system in the history of humankind has produced such innovation and such positive results for individuals, as well as for humanity at large.

The truth is that Karl Marx would never recognize modern capitalism. The striking irony is that what Marx and his followers were dreaming to accomplish through violent struggle has been accomplished through a peaceful evolution of the free-enterprise system that proved to be the most powerful engine for prosperity in the history of humankind.

Did Karl Marx Have It Right?

Although one could argue that Karl Marx has been completely discredited, even in the eyes of hard-core liberals, the Democratic Party used the 2008 economic crisis to actively promulgate socialist ideas. Despite the serious perils of socialism, which some of them do admit, they argue nonetheless that capitalism has not worked well and government involvement is necessary to alleviate what they perceive as deficiencies in the free-enterprise system. The financial crisis and following recession re-ignited the debate about the sustainability of capitalism. The economic slump created a panic among economists and politicians of both parties and opened the floodgates to new—or, in most instances, old and forgotten—ideas. There is no shortage of publications, opinions, and proclamations that the American Dream is slipping away, that the middle class is under pressure, and that it is more difficult than ever to reach middle-class status. The ill-starred Al Gore had this to say:

> *While we believe that capitalism is fundamentally superior to any other system for organizing economic activity, it is also clear that some of the ways in which it is now practiced do not incorporate sufficient regard for its impact on people, society, and the planet.*

The former CEO of Goldman Sachs Asset Management, David Blood, said capitalism has been blighted with "short-termism" and an obsession with instant investment results, which have ramped up market volatility, widened the gap between rich and poor, and deflected attention from the deepening climate crisis. Even such a respected American economist as Nouriel Roubini, who anticipated the collapse of the U.S. housing market and the worldwide recession that started in 2008, told the *Wall Street Journal* in August 2012:

> *Karl Marx had it right. At some point, capitalism can destroy itself. You cannot keep on shifting income from labor to capital without having an excess capacity and a lack of aggregate demand. That's what has happened. We thought that markets worked. They're not working. The individual can be rational. The firm, to survive and thrive, can push labor costs more and more down, but labor costs are someone else's income and consumption. That's why it's a destructive process.*

Roubini argued that the U.S. economy is flagging because businesses are hoarding cash—more than four trillion dollars by some estimates—rather than investing it in factories, new equipment, and more workers. As he put it,

> *If you're not hiring workers, there's not enough labor income, enough consumer confidence, enough consumption, not enough final demand. In the last two or three years, we've actually had a worsening, because we've had a massive redistribution of income from labor to capital, from wages to profits. Markets aren't working.*

Roubini is not alone in his assertions. Paul Krugman, a Nobel laureate in economics and supporter of Keynesian economics, believes that government involvement in the current economic crisis has been insufficient and advocates broad government participation in the economy. Robert Reich, political economist and secretary of labor under President Clinton, believes that government spending, high taxes, and big government are actually good for the economy. He contends that from the end of World War II until 1981, the richest Americans faced a top marginal tax rate of 70 percent or above. Under Dwight Eisenhower it was 91 percent. Even after all deductions and credits, the top taxes on the very rich were far higher than they've ever been. Yet the economy grew faster during those years, he claims, than it has since.

The problem is that this claim is based on an erroneous interpretation of the facts. In order to advance his ideological cause, just like his colleagues, Mr. Reich completely ignored the "causal link." A cat producing a kitten or a dog producing a puppy is a causal link. In Mr. Reich's case his cat produced a puppy. During the Eisenhower era, we had completely different economic relations with the rest of the world. After World War II the world was devastated and the United States completely dominated the world economy. American companies had no competition and enjoyed unlimited pricing power. Anything produced could be sold regardless of quality and production costs. Today we are competing in the world economy, and high taxes make our products less competitive. We all see the impact of high taxes on the economies of Western Europe. Therefore, we did not have a good economy because we have high taxes, but exactly the reverse is true—we could afford high taxes because we had a good economy.

Those who are ignorant of history or who have a short memory are proposing a new economic idea—the planned capitalist economy. Some are going even further and offering a political economy. Some favor a mix of some capitalist principles and government regulations to prevent crises and recessions and to ensure more adequate distribution of wealth.

Haven't we heard this before? To enhance the credibility of their arguments, some economists on the left have been touting their Nobel laureate status, but that speaks more about the agenda of the Nobel Committee than the quality of their ideas. If Karl Marx were alive today, he would be a Nobel laureate in economics many times over.

During the years since Marx's *Das Kapital* was published in 1867, there have been no shortage of critics of capitalism. With their continuing cacophony, the generations of supporters of socialism have grown up to fight both literally and figuratively for the utopian promised land of a social paradise and economic justice. So, Mssrs. Roubini, Krugman, Reich, Blood, and Gore are in good company. The opponents of capitalism are using the current crisis to rail against alleged flaws of the free market. They are blowing out of proportion certain flaws as symptoms of serious deficiencies that can be addressed only by government control and regulation. They are looking for villains in incompetent CEO's, greedy bankers, unscrupulous fund managers, market speculators, and crooks like Bernie Madoff, portraying those cases as an inherent flaw of the system. The truth, however, is that criminality is not an inherent flaw of the system; it is an inherent flaw of the legal enforcement agencies constantly failing to oversee their respective fields of law enforcement. Unable to enforce the existing laws, the government is trying to compensate for ineptitude with new legislation. After each crisis Congress gets busy making new laws and regulations intended to prevent abuses, protect average investors, and improve capitalism.

The idea that the capitalist system can be improved by the government, or by any other single entity, is pure fantasy. The unique feature of capitalism is the collective genius of millions of entrepreneurs, managers, traders, scientists, engineers, technicians, and laborers making billions of decisions every second around the globe with one purpose and one purpose only: to make money. To believe that anyone has the capacity to understand the intricacies of the movements of capital, can positively affect those movements, and is also able to distribute the proceeds of trades and profits fairly (whatever that means), without distorting the markets and creating economic and social chaos, is a veritable absurdity. Even Alan Greenspan, one of the most renowned economists of our time, referring to the 2008 economic disaster admitted, "I still do not understand why it happened."

Capitalism is an intricate economic system that does not result from a single event, but rather has evolved over the centuries. Thus far, it has demonstrated an extraordinary fortitude and resilience in overcoming a host of crises, economic downturns, the Great Depression, world wars, natural disasters, and many other calamities, while improving and transforming itself into a more productive system, resulting in the most impressive upward surge of wealth in history. Along with this wealth, the lifestyle of all Americans has been lifted dramatically upward as we all enjoy the incredible products and services of a successful economy.

Capitalism established its overwhelming superiority after World War II. The defeated countries of Germany and Japan, which were completely obliterated and whose economies were destroyed, adopted the free-market economic model. Twenty years later, those countries were rebuilt and prosperous. By contrast, the Soviet Union, which was victorious in the war, proceeded with a socialist economy, as did its Eastern European satellites, including East Germany. Twenty years later, they were still floundering in the ruins of economic stagnation. These annals provide a stunning demonstration of economic realities and an objective assessment of the respective economic systems.

So, was Karl Marx right? Are markets not working? Why do economic crises occur, and can they be avoided? What is the role of government in avoiding economic downturns or in stimulating the economy to alleviate a crisis once it develops?

The Centuries of Emancipation

If one searches online for "capitalism," eventually the description by Rosemary Peavler, a professor at Morehead State University, pops up:

> *Capitalism is an economic system that emphasizes private ownership of the means of production or a privately controlled economy. In a capitalist society, you have a free market and companies live by the profit motive. They exist to make money and maximize the wealth of their owners or shareholders, whether they have one shareholder or thousands. Prices, production, and the distribution of goods are*

determined by competition in a free market. There is supposed to be a limited regulatory framework. It is envisioned that legislation defines and enforces the basic rules of the free market. The government does provide some public goods and services as well as support.

Unfortunately, Rosemary's fundamental postulate, [*a limited regulatory framework*], seems to be long forgotten. So, what is wrong, if anything, with this system; and why do some people believe that capitalism has not worked well lately?

First, what is meant by "lately"? Are we talking about the last two years, twenty years, or two hundred years? Speaking in Kansas in December 2013, the President outlined his own time frame when he ridiculed advocates of a smaller government and fewer regulations.

"Now, it's a simple theory," he said. *"And we have to admit, it's one that speaks to our rugged individualism and our healthy skepticism of too much government. That's in America's DNA. And that theory fits well on a bumper sticker. But here's the problem: It doesn't work. It has never worked. It didn't work when it was tried in the decade before the Great Depression. It's not what led to the incredible post-war booms of the fifties and sixties. And it didn't work when we tried it during the last decade. I mean, understand, it's not as if we haven't tried this theory."*

Passing from fact to fancy, Obama showed that he does not know much about capitalism and detests what he knows. He is constantly attempting to disparage the free-enterprise system, distorting the record and, as usual, offering no program of his own. If the President thinks that the government is an engine of progress, the historical record does not support this contention. On the contrary, if government were the solution, the country I was born in would still be around. But the statement is so ludicrous that even Karl Marx disagreed. And Karl Marx did not just disagree, he wrote it in *The Communist Manifesto*:

> *The bourgeoisie [capitalists] has been the first to show what man's activity can bring about. It has accomplished wonders far surpassing Egyptian pyramids, Roman aqueducts, or Gothic cathedrals. The bourgeoisie draws all nations into civilization. It has created enormous cities and thus rescued a considerable part of the population from the idiocy of rural life. The bourgeoisie, during its rule of scarcely one hundred years, has created more massive and more colossal productive forces than have all preceding generations together.*[33]

Listening to Obama's rhetoric, one may seriously doubt that Barack Obama has lived in the U.S. rather than on some other planet. If American DNA did not work, as he declared, how did this country become the envy of the world, building the most vibrant economy and the most prosperous society the world has ever known? Something *did* work and has been proven to work, but our president obviously is not aware of it. The President and his supporters should replace Karl Marx's *Das Kapital* and Lenin's *What Is to Be Done* in their briefcases with Adam Smith's *The Wealth of Nations* and Ayn Rand's somewhat-easy-to-read *Capitalism: The Unknown Ideal*. Those books might help them to understand capitalism and its requisites. In the meantime, we suggest that readers take a brief trip through the annals of capitalism and its history to dispel the notion that we need Barack Obama to make it work.

We have to realize that capitalism is an economic system in perpetual evolution. Over the centuries it has evolved from the era of slavery, which continued for thousands of years, and the breakup of feudalism into a free-market capitalism—a high point of the private-enterprise system that created more overall wealth during the last

---

[33] The Communist Manifesto, Part I.

two hundred years than was created over the preceding seven thousand years of human civilization. If we invoke empirical evidence, past precedents, and economic prudence, we must conclude that capitalism has, overall, worked very well.

All major shifts in productivity, and the subsequent creation of wealth, have been associated with capitalism. Capitalism was the driving force behind the Industrial Revolution, the computer revolution, and the information revolution that have produced telephone communications, computers, the commercial Internet, nuclear energy, aviation, incredible advances in medicine, and many more breakthroughs. If not for capitalism, we would still be riding in carriages, sailing oceans in wooden ships, and using an abacus. For thousands of years, handicrafts were the only method of production known to man. One-thing-made-at-a-time was a slow and labor-intensive process. With the Industrial Revolution and the invention of steam- and electric-powered machines, productivity increased exponentially, and mass production of goods and services became possible. Mass production allowed the easy expansion of manufacturing, creating an economy of scale that provided supplies at a lower cost to meet demand. As efficiency rose, the economy began producing more and more goods and services and doing so at ever diminishing costs. Unlimited supplies of goods and services at lower prices contributed to a higher standard of living.

In an effort to further reduce costs, more and more sophisticated machinery and methods of manufacturing were employed, resulting in a continuing rise in productivity. At the same time, mass production required skilled labor, engineering, and technical support. As the cost of production was going down, the cost of labor was going up. Higher wages translated into greater consumer purchasing power. The society of mass productivity and mass production was born, which had an enormous impact on the economy, society, and our way of life.

At every step of the way in the development of capitalism we have seen the evolution of the relationship between labor and capital. The labor-intensive enterprises of the Industrial Revolution required huge labor resources that European cities could not supply until thousands of illiterate peasants migrated to the cities. Seeking opportunity, they were willing to accept any working conditions in exchange for what they saw as a secure income. This created a new class of labor that Karl Marx called the "lumpen proletariat" (poor underclass laborers), who, according to Marx, had "nothing to lose but their chains."

The last two hundred years of economic expansion has been characterized by an enormous rise in productivity and wealth. The initial phase of this period of mass production and mass productivity was marked by a concentration of wealth among the upper economic echelon of society—i.e., capitalists, the owners of the means of production. It was also characterized by the ruthless exploitation of workers: twelve-hour workdays, no health insurance, no safety regulations, and no vacations. The concentration of wealth at the top and miserable living conditions at the bottom inevitably led to a conflict. Mass production requires mass consumption to maintain balance, so when commerce produces more goods than can be consumed, an economic crisis will surely follow. Resolution of every crisis was followed by further expansion, innovation, and a rise in productivity. Higher productivity resulted in higher income and lower production costs, thus making goods and services increasingly more affordable. Mass production and high incomes stimulated the development of a society of mass consumption. As long as productivity was rising faster than wages, material prosperity was ensured. A key to the rise of productivity is innovation. The strength of the underlying economic and social forces of free enterprise ensures everlasting technological progress.

With the introduction of assembly lines and Taylor's management techniques, Henry Ford managed to greatly increase production and subsequently lower the cost of his Model T to the astonishing price of $290 per car. As the result of increased productivity, Ford was able to raise the pay for his employees, so his workers and thousands like them could afford to own a car. Sales went through the roof, and so did the profits of Ford Motor Company. It was later called "the cycle of prosperity." The affordable automobile changed America; it put the country on wheels. The automobile erased boundaries between cities and suburbs, improved distribution and deliveries of goods and services, and created a host of new industries. But that was just the beginning.

Over time, lumpen proletariat became organized into labor unions. The unions contributed to improving working conditions, further increasing productivity, and helped create more financial security among working people. Continued increase of wealth elevated the "lumpen proletariat," who had "nothing to lose but their chains," into a wealthy social order that had property and means of production. A new class of citizenry—the modern bourgeoisie, or middle class, the economic backbone of this country—was born, and new wealth meant having a lot to lose.

Contrary to Marx's prediction that the proletarians would have to rise in violent struggle to be liberated from poverty, the emancipation of working people has been accomplished through the peaceful evolution of the capitalist system as an ECONOMIC NECESSITY.

> *It is important to make abundantly clear that all these transformations of society took place without government mandates, involvement, or even encouragement.*

Upward mobility was not a result of FDR's New Deal, it has not emanated from LBJ's War on Poverty, it did not arise from Clinton's insane NINJA (No income, No job, No assets) loans for inner-city poor neighborhoods, or the artificial raise of the minimum wage, or the food stamps program or universal welfare, or any other government initiative or legislative actions aimed at the redistribution of wealth.

> *America's abundance was created not by public sacrifices to the common good, but by the productive genius of free men who pursued their own personal interests and the making of their own private fortunes. They did not starve the people to pay for America's industrialization. They gave the people better jobs, higher wages, and cheaper goods with every new machine they invented, with every scien-*

tific discovery or technological advance—and thus the whole country was moving forward and profiting, not suffering, every step of the way.

Thus wrote the Russian immigrant, novelist-philosopher Ayn Rand almost fifty years ago in her splendid book, *Capitalism: The Unknown Ideal.*

This period also marked humanity's most rapid and sustainable advances in living standards and life opportunities. To drive this point home, examine the following statistics. Just over 100 years ago, in 1913, in the United States:

- The average life expectancy for men was 47 years.
- Only 14 percent of homes had a bathtub.
- Only 8 percent of homes had a telephone.
- Only 6 percent of all Americans had graduated from high school.
- There were only 8,000 cars and 144 miles of paved roads.
- The maximum speed limit in most cities was 10 mph.
- A three-minute call from Denver to New York City cost 11 dollars, while the average wage in the U.S. was 22 cents per hour.
- The four leading causes of death were:
  1. Tuberculosis
  2. Diarrhea
  3. Heart disease
  4. Stroke
- The American flag had 45 stars, and
- The population of Las Vegas, Nevada, was only 30!!!

It boggles the mind to imagine what "didn't work," if left to continue not to work, may be like in another 100 years.

The Spiral of Evolution

The role of government in the development of capitalism resembles the story about three kinds of people. First are those who make things happen; second are those who watch things happen; and third are those who look at events and wonder, "What the hell is happening?"

Government, which had nothing to do with the rise of capitalism, noticed after a while that something was happening, that a great deal of wealth was being created and the government was not getting its "unfair share." What did it do? "Let's regulate it, tax it, improve it, and distribute it fairly." At that point Henry David Thoreau's maxim that *"the government is best which governs least"* was sent to collect dust on the shelves of history.

Unlike a planned socialist political economy, or what some economists call a "command and control economy," that is based on underproduction and inventory control to ensure constant demand for goods and services regardless of quality and price, the free-market capitalist economy is unregulated and based on overproduction. Overproduction creates competition and operates on the assumption that products and services of the best quality and lowest cost will outperform those of lesser quality or higher cost, or both.

Regardless of what triggers a recession, the underlying fundamental is overproduction, which is the result of excess inventories and excess capacity. Until the excess inventories are worked out and excess capacity is eliminated or absorbed, the recession will continue. If inventory cannot be sold within a reasonable period of time, production has to slow down and the labor force must be cut to reduce output. Reduction in the labor force results in diminishing purchasing power for consumers. This cycle feeds itself: diminished consumer purchasing power leads to further cuts in economic output, which leads to further reductions in the labor force, which leads to still further dwindled purchasing power and thus to an additional reduction in consumption…and so on until available capacity and production are balanced with demand. This vicious circle will continue until inventory excess is sufficiently reduced to create new demand. Then a new cycle kicks in: produce, employ, prosper, and overproduce until the next crisis. As long as the "survival of the fittest" is in place, weak enterprises perish while the strong, more productive, and better capitalized grow stronger. Old and outdated industries die and new businesses and industries, offering new goods and services, are born. Though painful to endure, economic crises serve as a self-cleansing mechanism to rid the marketplace of fat and inefficiency, making enterprises that survive the downturn leaner and more productive. Some call the process "creative destruction."

A new economic structure will rise from the ashes, with new industries offering products and services that most of us could not even envision beforehand. The private-enterprise system, like anything alive, can fall ill from time to time; yet in the process of recovery it can transform itself into a more vibrant and more productive system by eliminating waste and improving its business model. During the recovery, the system develops immunity against that particular "bacterium" and grows stronger and more resilient with each new "bug" it fights off. As long as the capitalist system is alive, it will advance from crisis to crisis, constantly improving its efficacy and unhindered prospects of making unlimited profits, ensuring perpetual progress and ultimately increasing wealth and prosperity for all.

Does the recent economic crisis redefine the capitalist economic model and signal the necessity for its replacement with a system that incorporates so-called economic justice and fair and equitable distribution of wealth, as the Democrats and the left want us to believe? Does it require fundamental and systemic change that can come only from the government, as the critics of capitalism insist?

> *It is essential to understand that the 2008 economic crisis was not a deviation from the established order or from the quintessential principles of capitalism, but rather a temporary disturbance in the economic equilibrium and a product of the evolution emanating from successes and failures.*

The Chinese word for crisis consists of two hieroglyphs; one means danger and the other opportunity. No matter how deep a crisis is, the opportunities are always there. The free market is a perpetual wealth generator, and its never-ending quest for perfection did not stop in 2008. New opportunities and a new form of capitalism are already emerging. One of the elements of this new form is the "built-to-order" concept that has spread like wildfire. Far superior to any previous incarnation, it does not require inventory, warehouses, offices, or even stores. Products and services are sold in virtual stores via the Internet as the march of capitalism continues around the planet, evolving into new forms and new business models offering new products and services at a lower cost.

As stated earlier, the most essential source of upward mobility for millions of workers is the inherent conflict between labor and capital. A constant source of conflict is the struggle for a greater share of profits generated by the rise in productivity. This relationship has evolved from employment-at-will to partnerships; from proletarians without means of production to the self-employed and to employees having a stake in enterprises. In any case, the conflict is always there. During a downturn, the conflict is exacerbated by hardship and reduction in employment, and must be addressed so that the spiral of evolution can continue. The most current economic crisis is no exception.

Labor unions are a prime example of the constant transformation of our economic system. They are also at the root of the current economic crisis. In this instance, labor unions, which contributed enormously to shaping the capitalist economic system—ending exploitation of children, protecting workers from industrial hazards, improving productivity, and raising wages—over time became more and more acquisitive, and have eventually priced themselves out of the market. At that point they become an impediment to progress and further improvement in productivity. When labor unions exhaust their usefulness, they become a drag on the economy, bankrupting cities, states, and industries. Teachers unions prevented meaningful educational reform, thus contaminating the American labor pool with illiterates. Manufacturers unions demanded wages and benefits that made American products uncompetitive with non-union foreign enterprises. American companies, in order to survive, are now compelled to move their operations outside the United States, causing a further decline in American manufacturing jobs.

Excessive governmental regulation contributes to downturns as well. There should be no doubt about the necessity of government regulations, especially covering product safety, rational protection of the environment, child labor, etc. However, we must be mindful that all regulations do have side effects, with the unintended consequences becoming evident only after a regulation is fully implemented. The problem is that government bureaucracies have no boundaries and no sense of proportion and are incapable of evaluating the ramifications of government regulations on efficiency and competitiveness, and then adjusting appropriately. Many regulations are intended to regulate past abuses already addressed by capitalism through crises. For instance, individuals who commit unethical business practices are not likely to be able to repeat scams that have already been exposed. The U.S. government, poorly equipped to understand economic and financial innovations, keeps piling on regulations, especially on the banking sector, without understanding that new financial instruments are constantly being developed to address the evolution of capitalism and promote economic growth, and with it, new schemes are invented to evade existing laws and regulations. Regulations created to address past abuses, for the most part, are ineffective and counterproductive, resulting in increased cost of doing business and in many instances greatly restrict the ability of businesses to continue operations.

For instance, several utility companies, including American Electric Power, Duke Energy, and Southern Company, recently announced they are closing coal-fired power plants. The closures are due to new EPA regulations that would add excessive costs to meet the new standards. The results: layoffs, higher electricity prices, and the possibility of power outages. Businesses that manufacture motor fuel will pay about $6.8 million in penalties to the U.S. Treasury because they failed to mix a cellulosic biofuel into their gasoline and diesel as required by law. The problem is that cellulosic biofuel is not commercially available. The list of U.S. government regulations that impede business and complicate the lives of American citizens is unending.

The counter-productiveness of government regulations is not limited to the United States. On the other side of the Atlantic, where socialist governments have been in power for decades, government regulations have reached the point of ultimate absurdity. In Spain, agricultural regions have been turned into deserts because farmers are paid for not producing crops. In Italy, fields that used to grow crops are covered with solar panels that do not generate power because there are no buyers—yet the land owners still collect lease payments. In Germany, the power utilities are obligated to buy electricity from individuals who generate power from solar panels at a premium over the cost of electricity. Russian immigrants there, who have a great deal of experience with socialism, supplement their incomes by using electric lights to light the solar panels at night, then sell the produced energy back to the power companies and collect the difference.

A fallacy widely held by economists and politicians is that during recessions small businesses are the key to recovery, and so they are showered with still more targeted programs. The role of small business in overall employment and the economy is greatly misunderstood. While statistically, small businesses create most of the jobs during a recovery, it is big business that moves a big economy. Only when big business starts increasing capacity, making investments in new buildings, equipment, and facilities, and subcontracting jobs to small enterprises, does the wealth subsequently begin trickling down to service industries, leading to significant increases in employment and the creation of new small businesses. It is said that "a rising tide lifts all boats." Small businesses do not make tides, but when companies such as Boeing, ExxonMobil, Chevron, and Caterpillar start making waves, their subcontractors will be taken along for the ride and get their piece of the action. They will increase staff, and more people will join the ride. The pizza parlor on the corner and the dry cleaner in the shopping center will get their share, and so on.

Another myth supported by some Nobel Prize economists on the left and subscribed to by the administrations of both parties is that government can create productive jobs that are associated with making profits. The supporters insist that the government should be operated as a business. The dichotomy here is that business is all about making money, while governments are all about spending money. Government, by its nature, is a "not for profit" enterprise and is supposed to invest in goods and services that are necessary for the public good but, because they are not productive, private enterprise would not invest in—such as national defense and law enforcement. During a recession, politicians talk a lot about legislating incentives for job creation. This is another case of emphasizing the obvious over the important.

> *The purpose of capitalism is not job creation. The purpose of the capitalist economy is to create wealth. Employment and the subsequent distribution of the spoils of an economy are by-products of capitalism.*

Hence, when Obama says that "we've got to build an economy that works for everyone," he misses the point. We've got to build an economy that works, period. Because when a capitalist economy works, it does work for everyone—everyone who wants to work.

Economic growth creates the need for more workers. The job of the government is not to ensure full employment or to reduce unemployment; the government's job is to provide legislative and regulatory conditions conducive to economic expansion. The rest will be taken care of by the free market. The conventional thinking of some modern economists is that the economy could be re-ignited by the government investing in infrastructure—building roads, dams, airports, etc.—and education. The evidence does not support this theory. As stated earlier, the Obama administration spent $862 billion of public money on a stimulus package. Was anything built with this money? The "shovel-ready" projects, as we already know, were not ready, and American education shows no improvement after receiving billions of dollars. Not a scintilla of improvement. But we did hire a lot more government employees whose salaries and pensions last long after the stimulus dollars are gone.

It is hard to disagree with Obama that without the stimulus the unemployment numbers would be even worse and the economy would look even grimmer. It is also true that putting more people on the government payroll to reduce unemployment numbers may be a good political ploy of smoke and mirrors for the short term, but it does not solve the long-term economic problems. Actually, it could make them worse. As stimulus money runs out, local governments will be forced to scramble to find new sources of revenue to keep everyone on the payroll. The government will then have little choice but to raise taxes, which will take more money from the economy, thereby exacerbating the ongoing crisis.

Someone forgot to highlight two basic economic verities: first, socialism creates jobs but fails to create wealth, and second, the only way to get a capitalist economy going and create wealth-producing jobs is to incentivize private investment. In summary, the stimulus-spending package perhaps made the President look better than he would look without it, but it has done nothing to stimulate the economy. It seems that George Orwell envisioned the current American socialist government when he observed that

> *Nearly all creators of Utopia have resembled the man who has a toothache and, therefore, thinks happiness consists in not having a toothache. They wanted to produce a perfect society by an endless continuation of something that had only been valuable because it was temporary.*

If our world's past history is any guide, government's ability to create productive jobs outside of labor camps is extremely limited. Accordingly, the argument can be made that, in most cases, the government is an impediment to job creation. If history has taught us anything, it's that government intervention in the economy has consistently produced negative results. There is an abundance of evidence of government interference producing catastrophic or near-catastrophic consequences. During the Great Depression, government interference only increased the pain, deepened the impact, and prolonged the suffering. During the Arab oil embargo of the 1970s, government interference into the oil market by imposing price controls only exacerbated the situation. Similarly, government intervention into the current recession, including the bailouts, economic stimulants, mortgage discounts, and quantitative easing, distorted the marketplace and prolonged the crisis, putting this country on the verge of bankruptcy. The policy of bailing out the "too big to fail" firms helps enshrine unprofitable firms in a manner that only hides inefficiencies and delays the inevitable. The record of government intervention into economy brilliantly confirms Ayn Rand's reflection:

> *Government "help" to business is just as disastrous as government persecution.... [T]he only way a government can be of service to national prosperity is by keeping its hands off.*

The Agony of Impotence

The following questions must be considered. What is the role of government? Is there anything government can do to prevent a recession? Is there anything the government can do to get us out a recession? Shall government promote, subsidize, or finance business ventures or projects it believes may stimulate the economy or do public good?

The question about the role of government has been debated in this country since the writing of the Declaration of Independence. No one pretends to know all the answers, but there are certain truths that will always be valid.

First, let the record show that governments cannot prevent a recession. Since 1807 the United States has had at least ten significant recessions, some, like the Great Depression, very serious. With each downturn government involvement in the economy has grown, and the numbers of laws and regulations have expanded exponentially. But the recessions continue, on average, every twenty years.

Following World War II, the federal government passed legislation that essentially said "it's the policy of the federal government to try to prevent recessions." Obviously the lessons of the previous century failed to make an imprint on the thinking of liberal economists and politicians—that the evolutionary nature of ever-changing industrial society cannot be controlled or pre-planned. Based on the statistics just given, the government was trying, figuratively speaking, to repeal the law of gravity. Market forces are too complex and a lot stronger than any government's ability to control them. For all the matter-of-factness, it is beyond anybody's ability to do so. Recessions are an integral part of a free-market economy.

Regretfully, government ineptitude too often prevents the market self-cleansing mechanism from functioning properly. The point is worth making again that this last crisis is a perfect example. The enterprises that had engaged in unethical or illegal activity to gain a market edge and increase returns should have been sentenced to "capital punishment" by the markets and condemned to bankruptcy and extinction. Their officers failed to uphold their fiduciary duties and should have faced criminal and civil justice. While some admitted crooks, like Bernie Madoff, were sentenced to long-term incarceration, the really big crooks that the market was defining as "too bad to exist" were declared by the government "too big to fail" and got a new lease on life. The officers of Merrill Lynch, Bank of America, City Group, and even AIG, who violated their fiduciary responsibilities, instead of going to jail and having their property confiscated got multimillion-dollar bonuses or golden parachutes. The Obama administration, whose non-action had the effect of rewarding criminal behavior, then incredibly accused capitalism as being responsible for the housing crisis, the recession, decaying cities, unemployment, inequality, and the bailout of financial firms at the expense of the middle class. Second, demagoguery cannot disguise ignorance. The government has only a foggy understanding of economic fundamentals; otherwise, government officials would realize the hopelessness and absurdity of their intervention in the marketplace—unless, of course, that is a part of the plan.

In this respect the Democrats' approach to the economy can best be described as an "agony of impotence." The approach has thus far boiled down to saving incompetent, criminal, or just obsolete business models and "too big to fail" corporations with an infusion of taxpayer money collected from productive citizens and successful enterprises; in other words, to keep losers afloat. Politicians don't like unemployment and it certainly hurts their reelection prospects, but they can't prevent it. Regardless of bailouts, restructuring, loans, etc., government cannot stop the permanent evolution of capitalism. It cannot prevent the inevitable; it only extends the agony of impotence. Enterprises that cannot compete or have exhausted their useful life need to die—so that they can be replaced by new businesses that have adapted to the new business environment. It is the essence of life.

Over the last eight years, the administration and Congress have taken a number of actions aimed at restoring economic equilibrium. None of them have worked as intended and have arguably worsened the situation. The stimulus package, cash for clunkers, the release of strategic oil reserves in an attempt to manipulate the price of oil, quantitative easing, mortgage refinancing, tax credits for new home buyers, bailouts—these efforts have failed miserably. Furthermore, nobody can account for $862 billion of stimulus money that disappeared into a black hole of government ineptitude and corruption. It could hardly have been otherwise. The colossal failure is not just a persuasive manifestation of government incompetence and corruption but is also a result of attempting to accomplish the impossible.

In continuing the pursuit of the impossible, can things get any more Alice in Wonderland? Oh, yes they can. The administration's efforts have reached the point of veritable absurdity as their leaders now try to convince the American people that unemployment benefits and welfare checks are forms of economic stimulus.

The Apostle of Wickedness, former Speaker of the House Nancy Pelosi, who never misses an opportunity to be both "Dumb and Dumber," believes that "unemployment checks serve as a job creator, because it injects demand into the economy." She also tells us that "it creates jobs faster than almost any other initiative you can name." Unbelievably, a number of prominent economists support Ms. Pelosi's "progressive" economic theory of the positive effect of unemployment on the economy. Among them are Nobel laureate Joseph Stiglitz, Executive Director of the Center for Tax and Budget Accountability Ralph Martire, and former Vice Chairman of the Federal Reserve and Clinton economic adviser Alan Blinder, who declared, "Extending unemployment benefits is one of the best forms of stimulus we know"—which tells us how much they know. To sum up the argument, the higher the unemployment rate, the better the economy. In the real world, the only positive effect unemployment benefits might have on the economy would be if the progressive members of Congress started collecting them.

The agony of impotence does not stop there. The research firm Moody's Economy tracked the potential impact of each stimulus dollar, looking at tax rebates, tax incentives for business, food stamps, and expanding unemployment benefits, and concluded that food stamps provide "a lot of bang for the buck to the economy." Moody's economist Mark Zandi stated that "for every dollar spent on that program $1.73 is generated throughout the economy." Is this seriously all the Democrats could come up with? One doesn't need a more vivid demonstration of the absurdity of socialist economics. The Democrats take a dollar from Peter (taxes), give it in the form of food stamps to Paul, and when Paul spends it, they claim it generates $1.73. What if Peter spent his own dollar? Wouldn't it generate the same $1.73?

Again, is Paul's food-stamp dollar greener than Peter's hard-earned dollar? To advance their radical ideological beliefs, the Democrats are prepared to abolish reason and dismantle even the lowest form of intellect. The socialists absolutely refuse to understand that in making more slices of economic pizza they are not making the pizza any bigger. It is like a child who exchanges one five-dollar bill for five singles and thinks he has become five times richer. It would be comical if it were not so tragic.

I will let readers decide whether we are dealing with dismal stupidity or veritable insanity or both. Whether it is unemployment benefits or welfare, or food-stamps, this is the Democrats' plan to prosperity and this plan will do to America what it has done to Detroit, Philadelphia, and Chicago.

Meanwhile, the administration has made its mark on the history of capitalism: in addition to the economies of mass production and mass consumption, it has created the economy of mass welfare. As American historian Ralph Raico[34] observed, "The audacity of the

---

[34] *Ralph Raico, the author of* Great Wars and Great Leaders, *is an American libertarian historian of European liberalism.*

Marxists' dream was matched only by the depth of their economic ignorance." But the supporters of the Keynesian economic theory, led by Paul Krugman, remain undeterred; they are trying to convince the country that the reason the economy did not recover is that the previous $862 billion stimulus package was not big enough. Where is the evidence? He has been calling for another, even greater stimulus package. At this point it is appropriate to explain how the stimulus works.

I will make it so simple that even the Nobel laureates can understand. Perhaps you remember this math problem that we all studied in school: Water is pumped into a tank and at the same time water is drained from the tank. Depending on the rates of water pumped and drained, the level of water in the tank fluctuates and eventually establishes equilibrium. Capitalism should work the same way. However, if somebody punches a huge hole in the tank's bottom, the incoming water will not be able to balance the outgoing flow.

That's exactly what has happened with our economy. The president and Congress made a huge hole in the country's money tank, and the usual suspects were collecting the outflow from it. Thus revenues could not balance the spending flow and the financial tank went dry. Instead of closing the hole, we are hearing that if we pump more water into the tank (our money, which they persist in calling "stimulus packages"), there will be sufficient inflow to the tank to balance the outflow, and a level of stability and even prosperity will be restored. What they refuse to recognize is that even if we tax all the rich, as the President suggests, even up to 100 percent of their income, we will not get sufficient inflow to overcome the outflow. Also, the number of predator receptors of the outflow will rise. Making matters worse, the money must come from somewhere—in this case, the administration's money would be borrowed from the federal Treasury, adding a huge sum to the federal deficit. And that is in the face of extremely low interest rates and a private sector sitting on three trillion dollars of cash; there is obviously no lack of liquidity in the economy. There is something obscene in this picture.

Ironically, this socialist administration and the liberal economists who develop economic policies for the President suffer from conservatism—conservatism of thinking. The president and his advisers are all fixated on solving problems—the housing meltdown, the economic downturn, and unemployment—rather than understanding the source of the problems and focusing on new opportunities. In order to move forward, one has to look forward. I would not expect a socialist president to offer intellectual assessments and compelling diagnosis of the current state of the economy. However, adding to the confusion and obvious gridlock, the Republicans also are not offering any plausible scenarios for ensuring long-term economic expansion. The most disappointing fact is that Mitt Romney, whom even Bill Clinton described as a man with a stellar business career, a man who spent much of his adult life fixing failed businesses, failed to offer an intellectually coherent path forward for the free-enterprise economy during his unsuccessful presidential campaign. The problem is that the President, his advisers, and the Republicans are all looking in an economic rearview mirror at the economy of mass consumption, which is on its way out, to be replaced with a new form that is more advanced and more efficient. Subsequently, the economists and political pundits erroneously believe this economy can be stimulated by increased consumer spending.

The most recent period of economic growth in the United States was fueled by a massive expansion of credit, which temporarily took the economy beyond its limits. Through excessive borrowing, consumers have already spent more than they could afford and cannot spend any more despite the rock-bottom interest rates. At this point, the consumer is essentially broke, the government is broke, the country is broke, and therefore we cannot spend our way out of this crisis despite artificially low interest rates that have been maintained for the last seven years. And yet this administration continues to insist that since private enterprises are not investing, the government should invest in the country's infrastructure in order to stimulate the economy. That is a gross misconception of contemporary capitalism. As stated earlier, according to the government, American corporations have accumulated cash totaling about three trillion dollars on their balance sheets, and they are anxious to invest it.

However, instead of the continuous progress that we have come to expect, especially in view of the available liquidity, we find ourselves threatened by continuous economic stagnation. It has happened because the President has created an inconsistent and generally anti-business political atmosphere, compounded by uncertainties and the unpredictability of government tax, health care, and environmental regulations, has created an unacceptably high business risk environment. In parallel, the President is trying to impose government control over the economy and loading up even more regulations on businesses to make them more responsible to government regulators. As Isaac Newton discovered, "for every action there is an equal and opposite reaction."

> *What the Obama administration and its financial advisers have failed to understand is that private enterprises defy regulations and refuse to endure submission to government authority by withholding investment, thus impeding the expansion of the economy.*

The wider significance of this current politically economic reality is that some of the great American corporations, forty-eight of them as of August 2014, according to the Congressional Research Service, have chosen to leave this country altogether. Leading the exodus are Foster Wheeler, Tyco, Halliburton, Cooper Industries, Transocean, Ingersoll-Rand, Noble Drilling, Global Crossing, Nobous Industries, Seagate Technology, and Burger King, all of which are no longer American companies. Pfizer and Walgreen Co. are currently looking for opportunities to incorporate overseas. Businesses do not take unknown risks. It is as simple as that.

Let Capitalism Work

It is becoming exceedingly clear that the era of mass consumption is approaching its end and that America is witnessing the dawn of a new era in capitalism. The new form of capitalism will rise from the ashes of this recession like a phoenix, vibrant and strong, igniting another economic boom that will last until the next bust. Nobody is smart enough to predict what this new form might be, but a host of very significant developments in the capitalist system has occurred over the last twenty to thirty years that could shed some light on what is yet to come. I call this new era: *the Era of Mass Prosperity*.

What distinguishes this era from others is the enormous amount of money that has been accumulated by private investment funds and corporations. American corporations have the highest cash levels ever; Apple alone is sitting on around $200 billion in cash. This state of affairs has set up some interesting dynamics.

Until recently, only the government could handle projects on the scale of the Hoover Dam and the interstate highway system. At present, however, large corporations and investment funds have sufficient resources to build projects on any scale. Following their capitalist nature, they are looking for adequate returns on their investments, and there are only a few alternatives that offer reasonable margins with acceptable risk. In the current environment their options are limited mostly to dividend increases and buyouts of other companies. But consolidation has its limits, and dividend increases do little for economic growth.

One area where opportunities abound is the country's decaying infrastructure. It needs repair and expansion. That entire sector of the economy would provide a steady income and good margins and would offer growth with low risk. What a fabulous place to park your money. This is one area on which we all would agree with the Democrats, who have been consistently advocating rebuilding the country's infrastructure. Our disagreement is over who is going to pay for it. There is no imperative for the government—federal, local, or otherwise—to finance and maintain modern infrastructure when private capital is available. The challenge of our time is to lift the economy from stagnation and put this country onto the path of accelerating growth. It requires opening a new frontier for economic expansion.

Conservatives (and I, needless to say, belong to this school of thought) consistently advocate for small government, but that does not mean that small government cannot be bold and think big. Really big, on a massive scale. The United States government in the past has been very successful at exercising its power and authority to facilitate new frontiers for capitalism, to create long-term economic expansion of a colossal magnitude. The most prominent acts of legislation that left enduring marks on this country are the Pacific Railroad Act and the Homestead Act signed by President Lincoln, and the National Interstate and Defense Highways Act signed by President Dwight D. Eisenhower. The Homestead Act stimulated settlement of the West. The Pacific Railroad Act created a new industry and had a major impact on the development of capitalism in this country. The importance of building the interstate highway system cannot be overemphasized. It is now time to take a bold step into the future. American pragmatism will prevail; Democrats and Republicans must overcome their respective ideological zeal and work together to facilitate the opening of a new frontier of capitalism and unleash a new era of economic reform and prosperity. This task of rebuilding the country and the economy has the following three principal components, which are interconnected and interdependent.

1. **Privatize Government Assets**

Privatization of government assets would fall into the category of "massive," on the same scale as the above-mentioned initiatives, but would not require government funding. Privatization of the infrastructure would include, but not be limited to, roads, bridges, tunnels, water treatment facilities, and government land. Privatization would open a new frontier for investment and relieve federal and local governments from having to fund, construct, operate, and administer the infrastructure. This in turn would undoubtedly result in greater efficiency in project development, smaller government, and lower taxes. But most importantly, it would ignite a huge economic boom and offer long-term productive employment to millions of people. To ensure compliance with relevant laws and regulations, privately owned roads, bridges, treatment plants, and other parts of the infrastructure could be regulated the way public utilities are.

This new government–private enterprise relationship would also result in a reduction of the deficit. Attracting investments for infrastructure would require dispensing with regulations that impede investment and economic development in this country. Just as Conservatives advocate tax code simplification, abolishment or redesign of health care legislation, and restraint of the EPA, it would also require simplification of the process for obtaining permits, facilitation of the eminent domain process, and the new legislation to provide long-term certainty regarding environmental restrictions and taxation of the assets.

2. Regain Energy Independence

Those of us who have been educated in engineering, not in law or performance art (no offense intended), recognize the undeniable fact that we still live in the nuclear/hydrocarbon age and as of now there is no commercially viable energy alternative to power this $17 trillion economy (this issue is discussed at length in Chapter 8). The future of this nation demands that we reclaim our energy independence. As legendary Sheikh Yamani, former OPEC oil minister, said, "The Stone Age didn't end because we ran out of stones, and the Hydrocarbon Age will not end because we ran out of oil." There is no doubt that a time will come when these energies are obsolete. But until then we must regain control over our destiny. A long-term program is needed to drill for oil in the United States, including federal land, and to utilize all energy resources available, including nuclear energy.

America enjoys enormous energy resources along with the competence and development capabilities available through its energy companies. We should stop referring to ExxonMobil, Chevron, and the like as oil companies; they are diversified energy producers, and ensuring a sufficient energy supply is their business. They will develop and produce the most efficient type of energy for the nation's consumption just as they have done for the last hundred years.

> *Without a cheap and reliable energy supply, the country will face profound and insidious vulnerabilities, and a sense of impotence will be a prevailing factor in American industrial policies and international relations for years to come.*

3. Redefine Free Trade

The conventional wisdom is that prosperity is a function of globalization. However, when the process encounters the imperatives of geopolitical reality and becomes overly politicized, as has happened in this country, it works counter to its objectives. A popular fallacy promulgated by both Republican and Democratic administrations is so-called free trade. The utopia of the global free market has not been beneficial to the U.S. economy, as most economists want us to believe. Over the past three decades, it has led to the de-industrialization of this country and the loss of millions of well-paying jobs. But guess what? Contrary to what has been publicized, free trade is not an economic theory promulgating economic development and wealth creation in the developing world; it is an economic model that emanated from a decidedly pro-Marxist ideology of redistribution of wealth on a global scale and it has been accomplishing exactly what was intended.

As part of the trade policy, it should be recognized that there is no such thing as free, whether it is trade or anything else. In this new world economy, the United States does not have a competitive advantage by virtue of information and advanced technology. Nowadays, if you know what you want and have the money, practically anything can be bought. Project financing is available to anyone anywhere in the world, provided by multilateral lenders and syndication of investors worldwide. The technologies are available to anyone willing to pay for them, and information is available to anyone with a computer or iPhone. In this environment, America cannot compete with the world of developing nations. Saying that an American worker is "the most productive in the world" makes for good rhetoric but has little to do with reality. If Chinese enterprises employing modern technologies do not have to comply with U.S. environmental and health regulations and pay their workers in a day what their American counterparts make in an hour, this country cannot possibly succeed. American industries are under military-style assault coordinated by the Chinese government that includes, but is not limited to, manipulating currency, dumping, stealing technologies and know-how, and counterfeiting American products.

The prevailing mood among the Democrats and liberal economists is that the imposition of taxes or tariffs on imports would make imported goods and services more expensive and subsequently hurt the American consumer. This populist argument based on neither economics nor history lessons. America needs to stop its job base from imploding and create a more dynamic economy to replace welfare checks with paychecks, welfare recipients with taxpayers. People who do not make much cannot consume much. This is an economic veracity. The history lesson emanates from the destiny of ancient Rome.

A millennium and a half before the United States was born, circa the second century CE, there was the Roman Empire. By that time it had begun to unravel from within. The agrarian economy that had been the foundation of the state was falling apart, unable to compete with cheap crops imported from North Africa. The consumers definitely benefited from the arrangement until North Africa's cheap crops destroyed Rome's economy, just as cheap imports are destroying America's industries. The situation is relevant and amenable to manipulation of trade by China, Japan, South Korea, and many other countries.

It is fine to compete with the countries that employ wages and regulations similar to those in this country, but the American trade partners should not expect to profit from a trade that takes advantage of American regulations and high wages and their artificially devalued currency. The United States still remains the world-dominant economic power, for which international trade, unlike for some of our more "backward" partners, is not a key building block of economic development. We are in a position to design an effective mechanism safeguarding American interests and enforcing a form of trade that reflects long-term strategic interests and restores the American role in the international balance of power. It can be applied in a manner that allows all the participants, including politically antagonistic entities, to enjoy the fruits of a global economic system. Those objectives should not be viewed as nostalgia for economic preeminence, but rather as an imperative for our economic survival.

None of the above three objectives can be achieved in isolation. We must succeed in all of them or we will not succeed at all.

4. What Is to Be Done

In previous chapters I have mentioned "laissez-faire" capitalism. It is worth reminding that the theory of "laissez-faire" capitalism was born sometime in the seventeenth century when a French businessman named Le Gendre, who, when asked by then-famous finance minister Jean-Baptiste Colbert how the government could help business, responded, "Laissez-nous faire"—literally, "Leave us be." Over the centuries this model has proven to be the best tool for unleashing human ingenuity. In the United States, where government oppression of private enterprise has historically been relatively feeble compared with the rest of the world, prosperity and human ingenuity flourished.

A few years ago I saw a big headline in the *London Times*: "Why don't we have our own Bill Gates?" The answer is obvious—in America, laissez-faire capitalism is not dead yet. To keep it alive, "the art of this deal," paraphrasing Donald Trump, is to achieve and maintain the delicate balance between capitalist entrepreneurship and government regulations, which are necessary to prevent abuses and uphold the law, and see that the regulations do not become an impediment to prosperity, especially during the hardship of economic downturns. This is, arguably, the most pressing problem before the regulators and legislators. In order to do that the government must do the following five things.

First, it must enforce bankruptcy laws to allow failed enterprises to exit the marketplace in an orderly manner. There is no reason to prop up the deadwood of our economy.

Second, it must reduce taxes to stimulate investment by big business and increase public purchasing power so the supply-demand inventory balance can be worked out, sooner rather than later. To do that, it needs to create real budgets—with stated and planned-for contingencies, as well as performance- and budget-based incentives.

Third, just as private enterprises cut out fat to become leaner and meaner during the recession, the government should use the opportunity to eliminate redundancies and reduce some of its bureaucracy. This is obviously politically vexing for any government, since it would increase unemployment.

Fourth, we need to create a new government agency, the Department of Deregulation. This department would review existing regulations every ten years or so for the purpose of simplifying or deleting outdated regulations or regulations that are ineffective or detrimental to the economy. And abolish those government agencies that have outlived their usefulness.

Fifth, we must stop building the economies of other nations. Saudi Arabia, Kuwait, the United Arab Emirates were all built with American oil money. China's economy has become a manufacturing plant for American corporations. Profits from the manufactured goods sold on the American market have built China's economy.

The solution to our problems is simple: "Laissez-nous faire." Just let capitalism work.

CHAPTER 8

The President's Socialist Economic Policy— Theater of the Absurd

"A great deal of intelligence can be invested in ignorance when the need for illusion is deep."
— *Saul Bellow*

Very often, government policies and actions look stupid and illogical to the common man. The government's first line of defense is secrecy: "You the people do not have sufficient information to render a judgment." However, when the full story comes to light, it is usually a lot dumber than we originally suspected.

The Biggest Economic Recovery Plan in History or the Biggest Economic Fraud in History?

Speaking in Philadelphia on January 30, 2015, Vice President Joe Biden, in a spirit of detachment from the facts, sent a new directive to the Democrats. "Democrats have to stand up; you've got to explain what we did," he said to loud applause. "Be proud of it.... We can't let the Republican Party rewrite history." The new Democratic message on the economy: We told you so! Referring to the 2009 stimulus, Obama said, "The record shows we were right." A skeptic may ask, What did the administration tell us in 2009 and what will the record show seven years later?

The American Recovery and Reinvestment Act of 2009 was hailed by the administration and the Democrats as one of the most significant pieces of economic policymaking in generations. Five years later, speaking in Kansas City, the President said, "The unemployment rate is at the lowest point since September 2008. It's dropping faster than any time in thirty years.... So the decisions that we made—to rescue the economy, to rescue the auto industry, to rebuild the economy on a new foundation, to invest in research and infrastructure, education—all those things are starting to pay off." This is one of the most uninhibited specimens of Obama's oratories and, as usual, is filled with patent overstatements. This self-congratulatory analysis has little relation to documented facts. Mark Twain observed that "Facts are stubborn things, but statistics are pliable." Here are the facts.

Obama's stimulus packages came in three basic types. In the first, the federal government puts money directly into the hands of consumers. The hope is that consumers will use the money to increase their purchases of goods and services. In the second, the federal government directly purchases goods and services, including infrastructure projects, equipment, software, law enforcement, and education, hoping this activity will increase jobs and spending. In the third, the federal government sends grants to state and local governments, in the hope that those governments will use the funds to purchase goods and services and hire more policemen, firefighters, teachers, and government employees.

The President said that if we passed his first stimulus package, which turned out to be $862 billion, we would keep unemployment no higher than 8 percent. One noteworthy caveat: in 2009 the official unemployment numbers reflected actual unemployment, but after prolonged periods of economic downturn, as people began exhausting their benefits and were no longer registered on federal rosters, the real number of unemployed was far greater than the official numbers. Experts estimate that the real unemployment rates were around 15–18 percent. The administration also promised to create (not save) between three and four million jobs by the end of 2010, 90 percent in the private sector. That would come at a cost of $215,000 to $287,000 per job.

"I'm absolutely convinced, and the vast majority of economists are convinced, that the steps we took in the Recovery Act saved millions of people their jobs or created a whole bunch of jobs," Obama declared at a press conference in July 2011. Or, to quote National Economic Council chair Gene Sperling from an interview in July 2011, *"There is no question that the evidence is showing that the type of things the President did to help state and local governments really mattered, were really helpful in pulling us from the brink of depression to a recovery."* Sounds great, but where are the facts? Opinions and wishful thinking are not evidence. As a university professor once said to his students, "If you can't express yourself in numbers, you know nothing about the subject." Here is a case in point.

> *This chart, borrowed from Libertyworks.com, was copied from Obama's report, published in January 2009 to persuade us that the "stimulus" or Recovery Plan would prevent millions of layoffs. Obama promised a maximum 8 percent unemployment rate if the recovery plan passed, or 9.1 percent without the recovery plan. Libertyworks.com added the bars showing actual unemployment rates.*

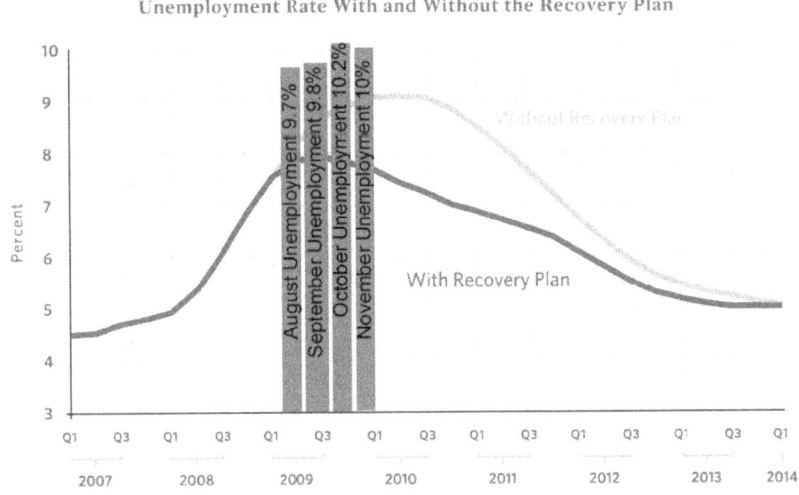

The chart from Libertyworks published in January 2009.

The recovery plan passed, the money was spent. The result: unemployment was above 8 percent during practically all of Obama's first term, the national debt skyrocketed, and the economy was still in a ditch. But even more to the point, as the President and his socialist supporters marked the five-year anniversary of the economic stimulus package, the unemployment rate as of February 2014 was said to be at 6.5 percent, and at the time of the President's speech in August 2014 was being touted at 6.7 percent. But the real unemployment numbers were significantly higher than the President promised they would be if we enacted the stimulus. As a matter of fact, according to the government's own chart, the unemployment rate should be a lot lower now without the stimulus, which points out the very opposite of what Obama and his economic team had predicted. The evidence does not support the President's claim. We must conclude that at best the stimulus had no effect on the economy and at worst it had a negative impact. The country got the worst of both worlds—enormous debt and nothing to show for it. If a strategy does not accomplish its stated objectives, a reasonable observer may conclude that the strategy has failed—but not with this president. He and the Democrats were just getting started.

Did the President tell the truth when he made those promises, or did he simply not know what he was talking about? The answer is in the January 9, 2009 report, "The Job Impact of the American Recovery and Reinvestment Plan," issued by the President's Council of Economic Advisers. The report stated:

> *It should be understood that all of the estimates presented in this memo are subject to significant margins of error. There is more fundamental uncertainty that comes with any estimate of the effects of a program. Our estimates of economic relationships and rules of thumb are derived from historical experience and so will not apply exactly in any given episode. Furthermore, the uncertainty is surely higher than normal now because the current recession is unusual both in its fundamental causes and its severity.*

The accuracy of calculations reflects the accuracy of the assumptions. The administration had no clue what it was projecting and probably did not care. The probability of winning in roulette when betting on red or black is 50 percent (47.4 percent in American roulette because of the green 00). The probability of winning on the President's roulette wheel was even lower. The report was nothing more than an exercise in intellectual futility. Any discussion about whether the stimulus worked is strictly academic: as noted earlier, the main purpose for the stimulus was to spend money and grow the debt. In this sense it did work.

The Church of Global Warming

George Bernard Shaw so aptly wrote, "The reasonable man adapts himself to the world; the unreasonable one persists in trying to adapt the world to himself." There couldn't be a better description of our president, who proclaimed in Berlin in July 2008, "This is the moment when we must come together to save this planet. Let us resolve that we will not leave our children a world where the oceans rise and famine spreads and terrible storms devastate our lands."

The Vice President was not far behind, just as persuasive but less vivid. "I think it is man-made. I think it's clearly man-made. If you don't understand what the cause is, it's virtually impossible to come up with a solution. We know what the cause is." Actually, we do not know that, but the Vice President, feeling entitled to his own facts, continued, "The cause is man-made. That's the cause. That's why the polar ice cap is melting," thereby outlining the administration's position on global warming. Apparently, "Apocalypse Now" is threatening a host of calamities and there should be no more debate about it. It is settled. We should take it as gospel and blow trillions of dollars in an effort to save the planet. And according to those two delusional alarmists, we should not wait another moment. Must act now!!!

Haven't we heard this song before? I am old enough to remember that not so long ago, in the mid-1970s, the world debated global cooling with the same vigor and urgency as we are debating global warming today. The cover of the April 28, 1975 issue of *Newsweek* proclaimed "The Coming Ice Age." In the article "The Cooling

World," the magazine suggested that, among other disasters, cooling "may portend a drastic decline for food production." In the June 24, 1974 issue of *Time* magazine, the article "Another Ice Age" painted a bleak picture for the future of our planet: "When meteorologists take an average of temperatures around the globe, they find that the atmosphere has been growing gradually cooler for the past three decades. The trend shows no indication of reversing. Climatological Cassandras are becoming increasingly apprehensive, for the weather aberrations they are studying may be the harbinger of another ice age." The *New York Times* was not far behind; on May 21, 1975, it published an article, "Scientists Ponder Why World's Climate Is Changing; A Major Cooling Widely Considered to Be Inevitable," predicting the horrible consequences of global cooling.

However, what the majority of the climate scientists so authoritatively predicted, and the media so loudly blared, and the supporters of global cooling so vehemently promoted in the 1970s never came to pass. The planet did not freeze and global cooling proved to be a fake. Never mind; if not cooling, there must be warming. As long as there is a climate, there is a change; as long as there is a change, there must be a crisis. As long as there is a crisis and the public can be kept in a state of fear, the politicians will call for spending, and more dollars, euros, yens, etc., will be allocated to combat the dreadful consequences of global cooling…or warming…or… Not to let a crisis "go to waste," the same publications cited above now advocate global warming.

I recently raised this argument with a renowned defender of global warming. His response was that science is a lot better today than it was forty years ago. "Does that mean science was wrong when it predicted a new ice age?" I asked him sarcastically. He did not respond. It really does not matter what science says; we simply must believe in global warming. This and other "discussions" with the supporters of global warming convinced me of the futility of citing scientific and historical records to initiate an intellectually honest dialogue. We should also be aware that these people will never cede their convictions and will continue to find arguments to justify them—even if these new arguments are diametrically opposed to those they previously espoused.

Since Galileo's time, ideology has been trying to overtake science; and it often has. It may just be human nature to want to acquire wisdom from prophets rather than bother with facts and scientific analysis. It came to a point where I finally realized that the struggle over global warming had become a religion and the three elephants from the ancient Hindu myths holding the Earth are coming back. This religion teaches us that Mother Earth may soon crack under the weight of our environmental sins, but the three elephants of Al Gore, Barack Obama, and Joe Biden will keep the Earth from sinking into the abyss if we just follow them and don't ask questions.

And so, the Church of Global Warming was formed. As with any religion, it has spawned extremists demanding an Inquisition. The Inquisition is headed by former Representative Patrick Kennedy, who once announced that anybody who does not believe in global warming is a traitor and should be treated as such. As we all know, religious fanatics usually demand full and complete obedience from their followers. The followers, in turn, must demonstrate that they are "more Catholic than the Pope." As a result, stupid things are proclaimed true and billions of taxpayer dollars are spent on absurd projects.

Although this time it was well thought-out. The importance of the theology of global warming for the President's strategy of re-engineering America cannot be underrated. It provides the foundation for at least two of the three planks of his strategy: destroying wealth and replacing a capitalist market economy with a government-controlled political economy.

Global warming justifies unlimited expenditure, strangles oil and gas production, practically stops coal mining, and puts power generation under tight government control. It also puts a lot of money into the hands of Obama supporters. People like Al Gore, who is managing exchanges of greenhouse gas emissions, like medieval priests selling an indulgence that forgives your carbon sins. In the process they stand to make an enormous amount of money, literally out of thin air, by underwriting the sale of "carbon credits" that industries, utilities, and other entities must purchase for the "right" to operate facilities that produce industrial emissions. In addition, the containment of global warming justifies support for the alternative energy industry, which cannot exist without government subsidies. Those are the reasons the President of the United States lent his authority and the prestige of his office to beat the drum with unwavering resolve for the nonsense.

Covers of Time magazines.

Covers of Time and Newsweek magazines.

To sell his economy-destroying legislation to the public, the President, as usual, was promising "an ocean of tomorrows." In 2008, the Obama-Biden comprehensive "New Energy for America" plan (at a cost of $150 billion over the following ten years) promised, among other great things, to create five million new green jobs as well as to put one million plug-in electric cars, which can get an equivalent of up to 150 miles per gallon, on the road by 2015, which proved to be another wild, overly optimistic promise.

This "ocean of tomorrows" is not quite reaching the American beaches. According to a new report by Pike Research, a Boulder, Colorado–based clean-energy market research firm, given current trends in sales, the goal of one million plug-in electric cars will be not attained before 2018. CBS News counted twelve "clean energy" companies that collected billions of dollars in federal assistance and are now in trouble. Five have filed for bankruptcy: junk bond–rated Beacon Power, Evergreen Solar, SpectraWatt, AES subsidiary Eastern Energy, and crony-clogged Solyndra. But according to The Green Corruption Files blog, that is only scratching the surface. The blog counted thirty two Obama-backed environmental firms that went bankrupt as of February 2014. These include Abound Solar, at a cost to taxpayers of over $400 million; Fisker Auto, $529 million; A123, $250 million; ECO Tality, $100 million; and Ener1, $118.5 million. In addition, twenty-two other Obama green energy projects are on the verge of bankruptcy. Widely touted as one of the administration's success stories, Amonix, a solar-panel manufacturing plant in North Las Vegas, was heavily financed under an Obama administration energy initiative. It closed its 214,000-square-foot facility only fourteen months after it opened. Solar Trust filed for bankruptcy protection in April 2012. The company held rights to the 1,000-megawatt Blythe Solar Power Project in the Southern California desert, which won $2.1 billion of loan guarantees from the administration. And the list goes on...

None of these persistent facts would weaken the love of Obama's supporters for the marvelous alternative energies. Brian Keane, president of SmartPower, a non-profit marketing organization funded to help build the clean energy marketplace, declared with a straight face, "The solar success story is a huge one for this administration. And it's time to tell the story truthfully." Truthfully? If the current situation is Mr. Keane's definition of success, I would be curious to know this administration's definition of failure. The marketplace has issued its verdict.

The whole global warming affair and the romantic dream of alternative energies remind me of the famous scene from Moliere's *Le Bourgeois Gentilhomme* in which M. Jordan, the play's principle character, is trying to improve his intelligence by taking writing lessons. He requests his teacher to help him with a love note. The teacher asks whether he wants the note to be written in poetry or prose. M. Jordan replies that he doesn't want either. The teacher explains that it has to be one of the two because they are the only ways to write. M. Jordan admits to his teacher that he is quite surprised by the fact that he has used prose for forty years without knowing it.

The supporters of global warming and advocates of alternative energy recite the poetry of dreams without any awareness that there exists a prose of reality. The President and his supporters believe that the hydrocarbons we use emit carbon dioxide gas, CO_2, that causes global warming, and that we must make the transition to clean, alternative, renewable sources of energy. This is the *poetry of dreams*. The *prose of reality* is that these people do not even know what hydrocarbons and CO_2 are.

On August 24, 2008, appearing on NBC's *Meet the Press*, former Speaker of the House Nancy Pelosi demonstrated appalling ignorance when she suggested that natural gas—an energy source she favors—is not a fossil fuel. "I believe in natural gas as a clean, cheap alternative to fossil fuels," she said at one point. Natural gas "is cheap, abundant and clean compared to fossil fuels," she said at another, revealing the depth of strategic thinking of the Democratic Party. It is also indicative of what can be expected from leaders of our country whose level of intelligence does not exceed the eighth grade of American public school education; the less knowledge, the greater the conviction.

Alleviating any doubts, EPA Administrator Lisa Jackson further confirmed that the administration is not governed by knowledge. In December 2009, the politically astute EPA professed the denouement of common sense when it declared that "carbon dioxide (CO_2) and other greenhouse gases are harmful to people and the environment." Stated Ms. Jackson, vehemently, "The administration will not ignore science or the law any longer, nor will we avoid the responsibility we owe to our children and our grandchildren." If the Vice President knows exactly nothing, Lisa Jackson knows everything...but not exactly. In response to Mrs. Jackson's thoughtful announcement, Ian R. Plimer, Ph.D. Professor Emeritus of Earth Sciences, University of Melbourne, had the following to say:

> *To state in public that carbon dioxide is a pollutant is a public advertisement of a lack of basic school child science. Pollution kills, carbon dioxide leads to the thriving of life on Earth and increased biodiversity. Carbon dioxide is actually plant food.*

The Obama administration is not just ignoring science, it is deliberately misleading the nation in order to advance its political agenda. Richard S. Lindzen, Ph.D. Professor of Atmospheric Science at MIT, who obviously does not belong to the "scientific consensus," wrote:

> *CO_2 for different people has different attractions. After all, what is it?—it's not a pollutant, it's a product of every living creature's breathing, it's the product of all plant respiration, it is essential for plant life and photosynthesis, it's a product of all industrial burning, it's a product of driving—I mean, if you ever wanted a leverage point to control everything from exhalation to driving, this would be a dream. So it has a kind of fundamental attractiveness to bureaucratic mentality.*

Speaking of not ignoring science, Lisa Jackson might be amazed to learn that only 0.03 percent of Earth's atmosphere is carbon dioxide, which is part of the air we breathe. Plants make themselves from it and, as the professors pointed out, by way of photosynthesis they produce oxygen. Therefore, if not for CO_2 there would not be O_2 and subsequently No Life on Earth. For those who are concerned about the buildup of CO_2 in the atmosphere and want all of us to "go green," the ultimate scientific remedy is to plant more trees, which would be cost-effective and useful regardless of which side of this ideological fence you are on.

Not to be confused, as M. Jordan was, we decided that it might be time to sort out the poetry and prose of global warming and alternative energy. Since most of us lack the intelligence of Mr. Biden, let's do it step-by-step and answer the following questions.

First, is there global warming?

Second, is CO_2 a major greenhouse gas that has anything to do with global warming?

Third, if there is global warming, is it man-made, as Mr. Biden believes?

Fourth, is alternative energy a solution?

Contrary to this administration's pronouncements, the science of climate change is not settled. Although many scientists, supporters of the environmental movement, and most of the media are committed to the theology of global warming, the science does not validate its existence. The administration's strongest argument is that the majority of the scientific community—they call it "scientific consensus"—supports global warming. "If the majority believe it to be so, it is so." This is a fallacious argument that the Romans called *argumentum ad populum* (appeal to the people) or *argumentum ad numerum* (appeal to the number).

Either way, the argument is totally irrelevant because scientific disputes are not settled by majority consent. As Aristotle pointed out, "consensus is the enemy of knowledge." The majority, which once believed that the sun revolves around the Earth, has been proven wrong throughout history more times than not. Every scientific breakthrough has been made in opposition to consensus. Heretics such as Galileo Galilei, Nicolaus Copernicus, and Albert Einstein were not just in the minority, they stood alone against the men of their time and eventually were proven right. The most recent example of a flawed scientific theory, global cooling, was also supported by a majority of scientists. And, by the way, who remembers the "scientific" theory of "acid rain" propagated during the 1970s and 1980s that was supposed to be destroying the forests and poisoning our lakes and rivers unless we closed down coal-fired power plants? Acid rain was also blamed on CO_2. Sounds familiar? Aren't we happy that President Reagan was wise enough not to take that nonsense seriously?

There is no convincing evidence that global warming exists as a permanent phenomenon rather than being just a forty- to fifty-year cycle, as some scientists believe. The historic record indicates that climate change is not a unique phenomenon of our period. At a time when Nancy Pelosi is declaring Greenland a global warming disaster because the island's ice cap is melting due to rising temperatures, it is worth noting that the island was covered with forests when the Vikings settled the region and created a farming community six hundred years ago. Perhaps that is why they named it "Greenland"! Pelosi might also be surprised to learn that the Romans grew grapes in northern England. Obviously, temperatures on this planet—at least in those two places—were a lot higher then.

It has been well documented that the collapse of the Old Kingdom in Egypt and the Akkadian Empire in Mesopotamia around 2200 BC were brought about by a catastrophic rise in temperatures and subsequent droughts. At the same time, the European continent was being subjected to a prolonged ice age. Given the level of erudition of the advocates of global warming and some of our elected officials, we should wonder whether they are aware that neither the Bronze Age civilizations nor the Romans nor Vikings had cars, oil refineries, or coal-fired power plants.

Considering the mountains of scientific data, in many instances highly controversial, assembled by both the supporters and opponents of global warming, we should recognize that the precise constellation of forces that leads to climate change is unknown at this time. Since no modern scientific model can explain temperature changes (either then or now), science is just not reliable when it comes to the subject of temperature change on this planet.

In case nobody noticed, the disciples of global warming are not sure the planet is warming either. Since the appearance of some evidence lately that suggests the planet may be cooling, they have stopped calling it global warming and are now calling the phenomenon "climate change"—just in case. Although they are not sure what it is, the vagueness does not deter the ignoramuses from insisting that it is still man-made and that we have to spend money to save the planet.

There is no compelling evidence to suggest that the source of temperature change is CO_2; other persuasive causes such as the sun's activity and the earth's reflectivity, could affect temperatures on this planet. The only reason CO_2 is blamed for climate change is because it is emitted by motor vehicles and industrial production. The environmental fanatics want us to abandon economic progress, become vegetarians, and ride horses and bicycles. Once the dogmatists had decided that global warming must be man-made, CO_2 became the obvious culprit.

The absurdity of global warming does not stop there. Let's assume, for the sake of argument, that there is a long trend of this planet getting warmer. The believers' proposed solution is for the United States to replace internal combustion engines with electric trains and restrict emissions from industrial and coal-fired power plants. There is a reason we keep emphasizing the United States; other countries, especially the major polluters such as Russia, China, and Eastern Europe, have no intention of following this destructive path.

China is adding 100 gigawatts of coal-fired electrical capacity a year with no environmental controls. That's another whole United States' worth of coal consumption added every three years, with no stopping point in sight, subsequently contributing up to 30 percent of the air pollution in Los Angeles. Much of the rest of the developing world is on a similar path. We can't stop the world's 5 billion poor people from burning the couple trillion tons of cheap carbon that they have within easy reach. We can't unilaterally make any durable dent in global emissions—because the other 80 percent of humanity desperately needs cheap energy, and because we and they are now part of the same global economy.

By advocating a ban on coal in this country, the supporters of global warming have demonstrated that they selectively collect, analyze, and utilize scientific data to support their ideological position.

Otherwise, they might have found that the theory of global warming is full of holes and has not yet been proven.

Recent fires in Southern California demonstrated that Mother Nature can produce in several days an amount of greenhouse gases larger than that generated by all the cars in the region in a whole year. California's yearly fires have been known since the Spanish conquistadors first visited in 1542. If we add volcanoes spitting into the air millions of tons of CO_2 every year for millions of years, then according to the proponents' theory, we should already be living on small islands surrounded by an ocean of melted Arctic ice. Therefore, based on historical records, there is NO compelling scientific evidence implicating human activity in having an impact on the Earth's temperature one way or the other.

Science, logic, and common sense validate that any change in temperatures is not man-made, and no amount of falsehood can make it so.

What about alternative energies? The administration holds a dual position on the subject. It is trying to convince the American people that alternative energies will alleviate the danger of global warming while simultaneously reducing our dependence on foreign oil. The problem with the administration's pursuit of alternative energies is that solar power generation, where the administration has invested most of the taxpayers' money, simply does not work on a large commercial scale. It lacks "commercially proven" technology and, in its current form, is unreliable and expensive. It cannot compete with conventional sources of energy such as coal, oil, gas, nuclear, or even wood chips.

Although the President's policy amalgamated the theology of global warming with the dream of renewable energy, supporters don't know that for the foreseeable future there is no practical way for renewable forms of energy to replace oil, coal, gas, and other hydrocarbons, which now provide 86 percent of our energy supply. Nor do they care to know—which may lead us into a real man-made calamity. The administration's efforts to curtail production of hydrocarbons may lead to insufficient energy supply and send the economy into a tailspin, resulting in a protracted depression. Yet the President is ideologically a Marxist, and notwithstanding his imaginable approach to building socialism, like all Marxists, he is a dogmatist. Dogmatism is a form of philosophical idealism that makes conclusions first and then selects facts to support those conclusions. In Obama's case, it is not just the omission of relevant data; it is the refusal to accept underlying fundamentals as well. It should not surprise us that during a June 2013 speech in Virginia, Obama announced that he will "double down" on his green energy exertions. Since the President has accepted the postulate of global warming and that the phenomenon is man-made and the source of the problem is hydrocarbons, he cannot be persuaded to change course, regardless of the *prose of reality*.

To make the situation even worse, Obama is pursuing two mutually exclusive objectives. In his *poetry of dreams* the President dreams to put a million electric cars on the road—which will require an increase in power generation and transmission to support this additional consumption. The *prose of reality* was outlined in a June 9, 2011 press release by American Electric Power Company. Its chairman and CEO, Michael G. Morris, stated, "Because of compliance with the new EPA regulations, we will have to prematurely shut down hundreds of good power plants, nearly 25 percent of our current coal-fueled generating capacity." Based on the regulations as proposed, AEP's compliance plan would retire nearly 6,000 megawatts of coal-fueled power generation. The futures market took notice. Electric grid operator PJM recently held a capacity auction, and the price for 2015, according to *Investor's Business Daily*, is $136 per megawatt, eight times higher than what was paid in 2012. In the regions where coal-fired plants are being retired, such as in northern Ohio, the rates are as high as $357 per megawatt.

In a rare display of intellectual honesty, Barack Obama admitted in an interview with the *San Francisco Chronicle* conducted in April 2009 that *"Under my plan of a cap and trade system, electricity rates would necessarily skyrocket."* The high cost of electricity, no doubt, will go a long way in increasing manufacturing jobs and "Building a Competitive Edge Here at Home." Isn't that how it works nowadays? It will also demonstrate presidential leadership in the form of food and gasoline rationing, as Obama hinted at in a speech in Oregon in May 2008:

> *We can't drive our SUVs and eat as much as we want and keep our homes on 72 degrees at all times...and then just expect that other countries are going to say OK. That's not leadership. That's not going to happen.*

I am here to debate the President's peculiar definition of leadership, but it seems he just offered his alternative vision of America powered by alternative energy.

Back to my original point: instead of increasing the generation of electric power to support additional consumption, the administration is planning to dramatically reduce existing capacity. Without a realistic program to replace the retired generating capacities and to address additional demand, the administration is creating an artificial energy crisis in this country—an Obama-made energy crisis.

What we are witnessing is a worldwide conflict between emotion and common sense. On the side of emotion are overabundance of unattainable goals and coercion; on the side of common sense are true science and logic. Hence, not to be discouraged that in the land of the blind anyone would see the spark of light, we shall employ logic to summarize the arguments:

a. There is no evidence that global warming exists as a long-term trend.
b. If we assume it does exist and the climate is getting warmer, there is no evidence that it is man-made and that CO_2 has anything to do with it.
c. Even if it were man-made and CO_2 were the cause, there is no need for dramatic changes in our energy supply and alteration of our living standards; just planting more trees will reduce CO_2.
d. Even if we accept the existence of global warming and agree with the President's Apocalyptic scenario and outlaw hydrocarbons, stop using internal combustion engines, get back on

horses, and shut down the petrochemical-industrial complex, all that will at best contribute to a temporary 20 percent reduction of CO_2 in the atmosphere (the U.S. contribution to the world's emissions). Temporary, because in a matter of a few years China, Russia, and other countries that do not share our suicidal compulsion will gladly replace the lost U.S. industrial output. This is the prose of reality; with the export of industrial capabilities and associated employment, the United States would be exporting CO_2 emissions and, without U.S. environmental regulations, in much greater volume.

e. And finally, if we do nothing, no calamities the President and his supporters predict will take place, because the Earth's temperature has been a lot higher at certain points in history and, although famine did spread in some regions, the oceans did not rise and terrible storms did not devastate our lands.

Any way we look at this, the global warming hypothesis is a vile blend of misinformation, political hysteria, and poorly concealed fraud. This is a bogeyman designed to frighten the public. Among other things, as stated earlier, the scheme is intended to redistribute wealth from the taxpayers to the rich cronies of the President and his party in order to make them even richer. That is one way the President is planning to "share the benefits of open markets *more equitably*." It is exceedingly apparent that the administration is investing enormous resources to solve a problem that does not exist—although it would not alter our lives if it did exist—with a solution that does not work.

Some sophists might ask where the idea of climate change came from, what its purpose was, and who was going to benefit from it. I have the answer if you are ready. This is really sweet. The following is what I learned while in the University of Marxism-Leninism, where the theory of climate change was part of the curriculum. In the early 1960s, General Charles de Gaulle, then president of France, was concerned about the industrial domination of the United States; at the time, U.S. industry contributed almost 50 percent of

The President's Socialist Economic Policy–Theater of the Absurd

the world's output. France, obsessed with Napoleon's greatness and status of great power, was defeated and humiliated in the Second World War. The French could bear being defeated by Germany, but being liberated by Americans was more than they could stomach. American expansionism, as Europeans called it at the time, needed to be contained. So, when one of de Gaulle's ministers came up with the idea that the more a country produces, the more it contributes to the world's pollution, de Gaulle seized the moment. That was de Gaulle's eureka moment—France would compensate for its humiliation and indignities by asserting a greater role in international affairs. In 1968, France formed the French Federation of Nature Protection Societies (FFSPN).

The idea that industrialization has a detrimental impact on the planet was not new; it has been around since the Industrial Revolution. However, the possibility of turning this concept into a political movement and a set of international agreements that would not only alter American economic expansion but also diminish its political influence on Europe was appealing to de Gaulle. For de Gaulle, this was a low-risk endeavor: since France's economy was in shambles after the war, any environmental limitation on its industry would have a negligible effect.

The Soviets embraced the theory with a great deal of enthusiasm. They shared de Gaulle's concern, but for different reasons. The United States was the preeminent economic and military power at the time. The Soviet Union saw the United States as a formidable opponent in its quest to spread communism to Western Europe and other parts of the world. The U.S. was a military-industrial giant that had proved to be the decisive factor in winning the Second World War. It possessed nuclear weapons and, as the record showed, would not hesitate to use them. Accordingly, the Soviet Union was eager to support anything that would undermine the United States economically and politically. The potential impact of an environmental treaty on the Soviet economy was not a concern, since the Soviet Union, as a matter of policy, never let itself be bound by agreements. The Soviets loved the idea so much that they financed the environmental movement via Western European communist parties up to the early 1980s. Funding dried up after the demise of the Soviet Union, but by then there was a whole new generation of fanatics to do the Soviets' job. The 1960s industrial pollution scheme evolved into an even bigger scheme: the global cooling movement, which later evolved into global warming to keep pace with the up-to-date environmental trend. That is how the West has been had. Ironically, the Soviets are no longer around to enjoy the spoils of their investment.

Albert Einstein used to say, "The definition of insanity is doing the same thing over and over and expecting different results." The American people would like to know how many times President Obama must take the taxpayers' money and loan it out to clean energy companies and expect different results. Or perhaps he doesn't. Why would he? Our Liberal Bolshevik is succeeding in spite of the fact that his alternative-energy program is failing. As stated earlier, the first plank of Obama's strategy of "fundamentally changing America" necessitates him to spend money, and the second plank requires control over the energy sector. Those are the reasons the President of the United States lent his authority and the prestige of his office beating the drum with maniacal intensity for the global warming humbug.

Whether the continuation of government investment in alternative energies is a manifestation of the President's dogmatism or just a shrewd strategy to spend more money, or both, we will never know. But what we do know, and the President also knows, that alternative energies will not succeed as long as there is cheap oil.

The Immense Power of Oil

> We can't have an energy strategy for the last century that traps us in the past. We need an energy strategy for the future—an all-of-the-above strategy for the twenty-first century that develops every source of American-made energy.

> They would not have believed that the world was round. We've heard these folks in the past. They probably would have agreed with one of the pioneers of radio who said, "Television won't last. It's a flash

in the pan." One of Henry Ford's advisors was quoted as saying, "The horse is here to stay, but the automobile is only a fad."[35]

Unless anyone is in doubt, I am compelled to inform them that President Obama is not Galileo or Henry Ford, not even one of the inventors of television. If anybody wants to trap this country in the past, it is this president, whose socialist agenda and Marxist philosophy of a government-controlled economy epitomize the ugly Soviet past. Although the President succeeded in converting the fundamental concept of physics into political demagoguery, his speeches, which are big on platitudes and hopeless idealism, do not generate any substantive debate, because there is no substance in the President's oratory. Instead of offering a logical and factual explanation of his position, the President offers empty rhetoric and a distortion of his critics' position.

I am an engineer by education and training. Unlike politicians, engineers use logic and numbers to defend their positions. First, why is it that we cannot continue an energy policy that brought unparalleled prosperity to this nation and built the most powerful economy in the world? Second, if you can convince me with logic and numbers that we do have to change, what are the options and what is the cost? As addressed earlier, if one cannot express himself in numbers, he does not know what he is talking about. Since the President has no numbers and no facts to support his position, the following presentation of facts, numbers, and logic is provided to demonstrate the unsustainability of the arguments offered by the President and the supporters of alternative energy.

Fossil Fuels

Here is a simple question for the President and his supporters: What is wrong with fossil fuels, which have a multitude of industrial uses well beyond fueling vehicles? Fossil fuels are necessary to

---

[35] *From the President speech at Prince George's Community College Largo, Maryland on March 15, 2012*

make plastics, to fly planes, to propel construction equipment and turn generators to make electricity that keeps the lights on and your computer humming, and to support other vital aspects of the American economy. What is the most compelling argument for spending trillions of dollars to replace the sources of energy that have served us so well for the last hundred years? The President has two principal arguments: it is necessary to develop new sources of energy because the reserves of fossil fuels are diminishing, and global warming is reaching a disastrous level. Both arguments are demonstrably wrong.

Let's take the hypothetical diminishing supply first. It is worth pointing out that concerns about oil are not new. As early as 1885, various experts cautioned that oil would soon be depleted. The state geologist of Pennsylvania warned that "the amazing exhibition of oil was only a temporary and vanishing phenomenon—one which young men will live to see to its natural end." The experts were proven wrong back then, just as they were proven wrong in the 1970s and are being proven wrong today. This country and neighboring Canada are blessed with plentiful resources of oil, gas, and coal. Advances in the techniques of horizontal drilling and hydraulic fracturing, first applied to shale gas reserves, are now making it possible to develop U.S. oil in fields that previously were commercially unviable. Those fields could potentially make America energy independent.

Thanks to the new technology, the Bakken Formation in North Dakota could boost America's oil reserves tenfold, giving Western economies a trump card against OPEC's short-term squeeze on oil supply and making Iranian and Venezuelan threats of disrupting oil supplies futile. Texas, Louisiana, and the Gulf Coast, extending inland through west Texas, Oklahoma, and eastern Kansas, have important reserves, and there are also significant oil fields in Alaska along the central North Slope. Additionally, there is a super massive 200-billion-barrel oil reserve—almost equal to that of Saudi Arabia—sitting in Western Canada, ready for production and distribution to the marketplace from landlocked Alberta. Due to the new technologies and American entrepreneurship, in the last few years the United States has surpassed Russia as the largest gas producer in the world, and there is no reason the same cannot be accomplished with oil production.

As far as global warming is concerned, the previous chapter exposed the fraudulent nature of the theology. Still, fossil fuel is not a clean energy; it does pollute the environment. The real issue is whether it is practical, not to mention even possible, to replace fossil fuel for strictly environmental reasons, given the state of technology and the constantly growing demand. The answer is a resounding NO. What are commercially viable alternatives? The diagram below from the U.S. Energy Information Administration tells the story in numbers.

This diagram tells us that about 86 percent of our energy consumption (biomass included) is provided by fossil fuels. The major energy component of all fossil fuels is carbon. Therefore, one does not have to be a nuclear scientist or brain surgeon to conclude that our civilization is solidly carbon oriented, and unless we decide to return to caves, that picture cannot be altered significantly in the foreseeable future. Given the current energy demand to power this $17 trillion economy and constantly growing appetite for more energy, realistically speaking, there is no way the situation can change significantly over the next fifty years. Does that mean that we may eventually have to move from carbon to other types of energy? Most likely, yes. But when we do move, that change is not going to come from the government—just as fossil fuels were not invented by government. Therefore, ignorant environmental fanatics can write all the poems they want about global warming but they will not affect the prose of the fossil fuel reality, which is here to stay. All the drastic legislative measures to curb carbon production will not reduce the world's carbon use by any significant amount.

Can we at least reduce the fossil fuel component in our energy consumption? Let's examine the alternatives and try to find out what might and might not work, and let's do it using a logical, deductive approach.

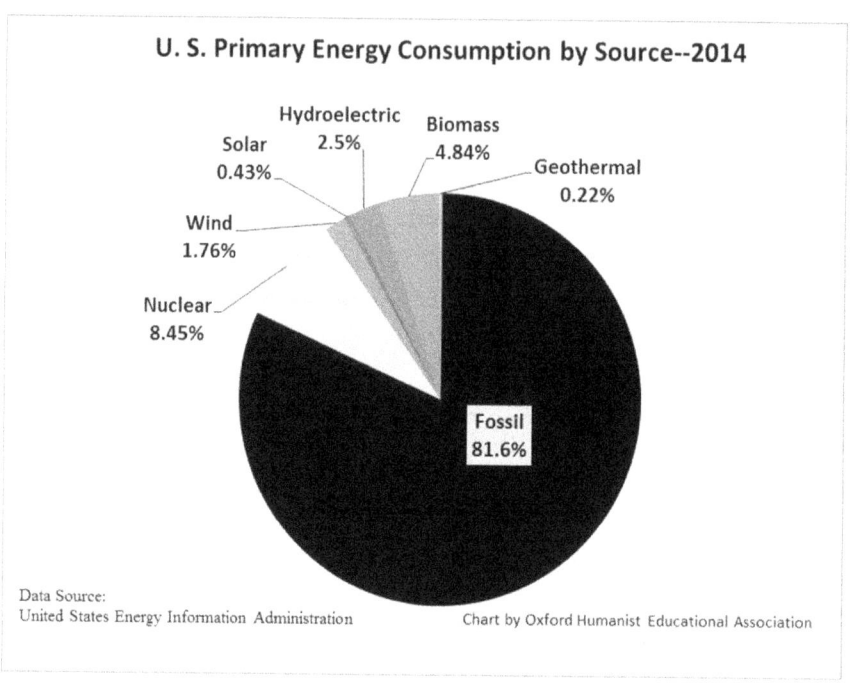

The U.S. Energy Information Administration diagram.

Hydropower

Hydropower is a very clean method of producing renewable energy, and Mother Nature does reasonably good job of supplying enough rain to run hydroelectric plants. The potential for building more hydroelectric plants in the United States, however, is basically exhausted. Hydropower plants need two components: a natural stream of water and a water reservoir. The reservoir is formed by a dam, and that requires a huge amount of land in order to hold a sufficient amount of water to equalize its use. Good examples are the Hoover Dam in Nevada and dams on the Columbia River in Washington State. However, there is a rare consensus between engineers and politicians that here, in the United States, we have already exhausted the land necessary for any more substantial plants or that would have to be flooded (and its residents relocated). Accordingly, the current level of hydropower use cannot be substantially increased.

Geothermal power

Geothermal power uses hot water and steam from the depths of the earth, where radioactive decay of various particles creates hot spots. Except for natural geysers of the sort we see in Yellowstone Park, in order to tap geothermal power we need to drill deep wells and pump hot streams to the surface. There, the steam and hot water run steam turbines to produce electric power. Despite the expense of drilling and cleaning underground water, and despite the high corrosiveness of those streams, it is still economically advantageous to use geothermal energy whenever it can be found at reasonable depths. The potential for geothermal installations is relatively small, however, and most of the streams are depleted over time. So, even if we double our current use of geothermal energy, it will remain a negligible part of our energy balance.

Solar Energy

Solar energy generated a lot of promise and solar plants are being built at an accelerating pace in Europe and the United States. Improving technologies have made solar production more economical than it was in the 1980s, when the first large-scale solar plant was built in the Mojave Desert in California. However, the fundamentals of solar energy production that limit its use have never changed: high costs, limited storage capability, low efficiency, and high maintenance.

The fundamental problem with solar energy is that it must have sunlight as a fuel. Even in the southern hemisphere, usable sunlight exists for no more than ten or eleven hours a day. Since we cannot store large amounts of electricity, solar plants are operable for only about half of each day. That said, they still could contribute to satisfying our daily peak usage that typically occurs around noon, especially in the summer when air conditioning use increases. Nevertheless, we cannot consider solar installations as a reliable power source, because they are subject to interruption of power production at any time. I personally observed the complete shutdown of solar production at the plant in the Mojave Desert when a small cloud drifted across the sun. Consequently, solar power requires standby capacity that can support the grid twenty-four hours a day. Utility companies do not advertise that fact, but when they contract to buy power from solar sources they quietly build in adequate fossil fuel backups capable of bolstering the solar-supported load.

The other inherent problem with solar power is its high maintenance requirement. All solar installations rely on a system of mirrors that concentrate the sunlight on a target that becomes heated and transfers that heat to a working fluid such as water. The mirrors have a tendency to get dirty, and the average solar plant has thousands of mirrors; the task of cleaning those mirrors takes time, reduces power production, and involves significant costs. Also, in the desert, where the most advantageous place to build is in the sand, frequent sandstorms can damage the mirrors to a degree that makes their effectiveness very low. Capital and maintenance costs would make construction of the solar plants prohibitive if not for the huge subsidies that states have legislated under pressure from environmentalists. I am not aware of a single solar plant that did not go bankrupt when the subsidies ended. Until we find a way to transmit sun energy wirelessly by a microwave link as cell phones do, the potential for solar energy remains limited.

Biomass

Biomass is a viable prospect. Biomass is the waste from agricultural products. It is burned in boilers, and the produced energy is converted into electric power. There are a number of biomass plants in this country. In the past, agricultural waste and even forest chips were burned in open fields, generating huge amounts of pollution. Burning waste in modern boilers, where pollution can be efficiently cleaned up, provides clear benefits to society. However, biomass is still a carbon-based fuel and produces CO_2 as all fossil fuels do. And it is highly unlikely that we will double agricultural production in the foreseeable future. Therefore, we should not expect the share of biomass in our energy balance to change.

Ethanol

Ethanol is an alcohol-based fuel made by fermenting and distilling starch crops, such as corn. Creating plant-based biofuels requires too much farmland to be practical or sustainable; the land would be better served growing food. Furthermore, producing ethanol and other biofuels takes more energy than the fuel can generate. Ethanol is too expensive to be used as a fuel, because according to the industry source, ethanol costs more than petroleum as a raw material. In any event, burning food for fuel has never been a good idea.

Wind Power

Wind energy's major drawback is the same as solar energy's: the lack of so-called dispatch-ability, the ability to generate such power at any time and in predictable and reliable quantities. Because wind power production varies due to the availability of wind, utilities cannot count on it as a reliable source of energy at this time. In addition, since we cannot store any significant amount of electric energy today (and probably won't be able to in the foreseeable future), wind power production, like solar power production, must have a backup, especially during peak hours. Consequently, when utilities buy wind power from suppliers, just as in the case of solar power, they must also provide a fossil-fuel backup, using fast-starting turbines burning (guess what?) natural gas.

There are some exotic technologies that wind power producers have been experimenting with, such as compressed air energy storage (CAES) plants alongside wind power facilities. The technology for CAES has existed since the early 1980s. The idea sounds simple: during the hours when the wind produces more energy than can be consumed, the excess of power is used to compress air and pump it to underground caverns such as salt domes and abandoned mines, which serve as energy storage. During peak hours, with increased demands for power, the air is released and heated using a small amount of natural gas. Heated air drives a turbine and produces electric power. This is an apotheosis of something that theoretically looks simple proving to be too complicated and impractical in a real-life environment.

Nuclear energy

Nuclear energy is among those energy sources producing very low levels of CO_2 emissions; in this respect it is closely comparable with renewables such as wind, solar, and hydro. The same people who advocate for a clean environment, however, aggressively oppose this reliable, cheap, and safe energy resource—safe because it enjoys an almost impeccable safety record. Nuclear reactors are routinely used for aircraft carriers and nuclear submarines that travel the world. Nuclear power is a major generator of electricity in Western Europe. It is responsible for manufacturing 78 percent of the electricity in France, 43 percent in Belgium, 36 percent in Spain, and so on. The opponents of nuclear power believe—and we say "believe" because the data tell us otherwise—that nuclear power poses a threat to people and the environment. They point to three nuclear accidents that have taken place over the last forty years: the Three Mile Island accident in 1979, which resulted in no damage or injuries; the self-inflicted Chernobyl disaster in 1986; and the Fukushima Daiichi disaster in 2011, which was exacerbated by improperly located and poorly designed reactors.

China has twenty-five nuclear power reactors under construction, with plans to build many more. Although nuclear power is proliferating and marching its way around the globe, local "true believers" of environmental policy will not be persuaded by the facts. Nuclear energy is truly an environmentally responsible source of energy, but environmentalists violently oppose it. Thus, nuclear power is out. Given the prose of reality, what is the President going to do? He will do what he does best: talk.

The reality is that fossil fuels, hydrocarbons, will maintain their economic and strategic significance way into the twenty-first century—the most significant being oil. Oil is the biggest business and the largest industry in the world in terms of assets, capital, and overall importance. With the exception of computers, the oil industry has been the source of the most important innovations in the areas of technology and manufacturing.

> *No other industry is big enough, sufficiently capitalized, and strong enough to address the economic and population growth of the twenty-first century.*

CHAPTER 9
The Politics of Immorality

You will never get rich counting other people's money.

The New World

Richard Nixon said, *"People have got to know whether or not their president is a crook."* Our country is undergoing a difficult period of economic and political uncertainty. Unfortunately, the "philosopher president" has neither the experience nor the inclination to lead a national debate about the future of this country.

> During his November 26, 2008 press conference Obama said, *"...understand where the vision for change comes from first and foremost. It comes from me. That's my job—is to provide a <u>vision in terms of where we are going</u> [emphasis added] and to make sure that my team is implementing it."*

Despite this impressive display of presidential ultra-ego, self-glorification, and epic oratory, eight years later, His Majesty does not dare to reveal his vision to the nation. His almost daily speeches are confined to populist slogans and vitriol of the alleged economic and social deficiencies. He purposely fails to articulate his intellectual tenets and philosophical doctrine. No specific meanings were ever given to CHANGE and FORWARD. But let's not quibble about words. The ambiguity of terms is used to conceal the agenda for the future. Anyone who does not see this has not grasped the full width of the ocean that separates secretive totalitarianism from a transparent democracy.

That explains why the President cannot detach himself from the world of George W. Bush; Obama constantly talks about overcoming the past, lauds his questionable accomplishments, never inspires confidence in the future, never talks about "a shining city upon a hill." Obama's pragmatism is understandable given that the future he envisions, in all essentials, is reminiscent of Greece and other Western European countries and even the Soviet Union, and runs contrary to American idealism and values. No wonder that when it comes to the economy, energy, immigration, the environment, foreign policy, or any other substantive issue, he lacks a coherent operational policy. Yet on each issue, Obama skillfully transforms liability into benefit. He offers ambiguous slogans and undefined objectives. This lack of direction leads to desperation, and desperation leads to continuation of national crises parlaying into acquisition of power, mimicking Lenin's path to usurpation. Demagogues and liars thrive in this type of environment.

Citing hypocrisy is just stating the obvious. We simply can't rely on anything Obama says, because he is doing most of the things of which he so vigorously disapproved in the past. He is constantly evolving falsehood into greater falsehood that is further begotten with even greater falsehood in order to conceal earlier falsehood. What has been historically regarded as an attribute of authoritarian regimes and African banana republics has become the normal process of governance. Perhaps future historians will have different explanations for the presidential disconnect between saying and doing, but as I see it through my red-colored communist glasses, it resembles communist practice at its worst. *"To rely upon conviction, devotion, and other excellent spiritual qualities; that is not to be taken seriously in politics,"* Lenin taught his apostles. This perspective elucidates why a key part of Obama's modus operandi is saying one thing and then doing the opposite.

President Obama would disagree with this characterization; predictably, he believes he has earned our trust. Speaking at a rally in Iowa during the last campaign, he said:

> *There is no more serious issue on a campaign than trust. Trust matters. And here's the thing: Iowa, you know me. You know that I say what I mean, and I mean what I say. There are some folks in this crowd that have probably been following me since I was running for the United States Senate. Like this guy right here, who I served with in the United States Senate, George Shatter. And you could take a videotape of things I said ten years ago, twelve years ago, and you could say, "Man, this is the same guy."*

The only truth in this speech is that he *is* the same guy—a guy who lacks devotion to the truth. There are numerous examples of the President's duplicity and dishonesty in this book; paraphrasing Mark Twain, "There are lies, big lies, and health care lies." Here are a few major promises about nationalized health care the President made and never intended to keep:

- The Affordable Care Act will cut the cost of health care. In reality, many Americans are seeing steep increases in the cost of their health care.
- Reduction of the deficit was a vital component of Obamacare. The president called the plan *"the single most important thing we could do in terms of reducing our deficit"* and he also promised that he "will not sign a health care reform plan that adds one dime to our deficits, either now or in the future." A sophist may ask, "Why would it add even a dime if it was designed to reduce the deficit???" Sure enough, the long-term federal deficit has increased by $6.2 trillion since the President made this promise, according to the Government Accountability Office, and likely will grow even higher.
- The president promised, "If you like your doctor, you will be able to keep your doctor. Period." The fact is that 83 percent of American physicians have considered leaving their practices because of President Obama's health care reform law, according to a survey released by the Doctor Patient Medical

Association. It seems we will have a difficult time finding *any* doctor, much less the one we prefer.
- "If you like your health care plan, you'll be able to keep it," the President promised. Yet we are getting daily reports of millions of people receiving cancellation notices from their insurers.
- Obamacare will create jobs. It will certainly create more government jobs, but as far as the economy is concerned, private enterprises are moving millions of full-time positions to part time in order to avoid additional costs associated with Obamacare.

And finally, the most outrageous lie was told to the American people in order to secure the necessary votes to pass the legislation. The issue was whether forcing people to obtain coverage would violate his campaign pledge against raising taxes on middle-class Americans. On September 20, 2009, in an interview with ABC's George Stephanopoulos, the President denied that the mandate to buy health insurance was a tax.

> *"For us to say that you have to take a responsibility to get insurance is absolutely not a tax increase,"* he said. When Stephanopoulos pressed further on whether the mandate was a tax, Obama said, *"I absolutely reject that notion."*

However, in a majestic sleight of hand, Obama's Justice Department absolutely *endorsed* that notion when it argued the constitutionality of this non-tax before the Supreme Court. U.S. attorneys shamelessly claimed that the penalty was in fact a tax and had prevailed on this argument. The Supreme Court agreed and ruled that the mandate is in fact a tax. The reason Obama so forcefully denied that the mandate was a tax was to give his fellow Democrats a "fig leaf," so they would not have to vote for a tax increase before the elections. The Democrats may learn eventually that this exposition of Marxist cleverness utterly undermined the legitimacy of the legislation. If those are examples of the President's definition of truthfulness, we can only imagine how he defines a falsehood.

Incomprehensibly, but factually, when our socialist president makes a promise we should expect exactly the opposite, to the point that if the President forecasts a sunny day we should expect rain. The Bolsheviks, who had a propensity for fancy names, called it "a monopoly on Revolutionary Truth."

In other words, the truth in the "decaying" capitalist world does not mean what it does in our bright socialist world. In practical terms, when Bolsheviks promised democracy, freedom, liberty, and inexorable "land to the peasants, bread to the hungry, peace to the people," those zealous Bolshevik slogans sounded great but the Russian people found soon enough that land to the peasants meant forced collectivization; bread to the hungry, man-made famine; and peace to the people, civil war. The question to ask yourself is, What do the Democrats actually mean when they speak of democracy, freedom, and liberty?

With this doublespeak in mind, if the President talks about reduction of the deficit, we should expect the deficit to rise.

If the President talks about reducing the size of the federal government, we should expect bigger government.

If the President talks about cooperation, we should expect more confrontation.

If the President talks about reducing the cost of health care, we should expect the cost to go up.

If the President talks about energy independence, we should expect moratoriums on drilling.

If the President talks about reducing taxes, we should expect taxes to go up.

If the President talks about banks lending more money, we should expect new rules that will tighten credit.

If the President promises transparency, we should expect cover-ups.

But if the President tells us that he wants to spread the wealth around, you'd better believe him!

These mass-produced lies oddly oppress our memories. It reminds me of a Russian anecdote of the Soviet era. A patient walks into a hospital to make a doctor's appointment. A receptionist asks him what type of doctor he needs to see.

"I need an eye-and-ear specialist," he says.

"Sorry," she says, "there is no such specialist." The patient insists.

"OK," she says, "let's assume we have one. What is your problem?"

The man replies, "I am suffering from complete disconnect between my vision and hearing. I hear our leaders saying one thing, but what my eyes see is totally different."

Jerry Kammer, a Pulitzer Prize–winning reporter, remarked with disappointment, "He promised to be a different kind of president." But of course he *is* a different kind of president. America is dancing to a new tune: unable to motivate the nation on the virtues of his ambiguous vision, Obama is using the powers of elocution to mobilize the constituency to accomplish his objectives through brute force, outmaneuvering critics in the process. A skillful demagogue, he mastered Marxist phraseology to energize his supporters and conceal his intentions. The President is not offering ideas; he is selling emotions and generating the emotional dynamic to advance his agenda. In this atmosphere, validity of arguments is irrelevant; therefore, the President may continue making passionate speeches from a copy of the election-year playbook, skillfully mixing emotions with ideology and telling people what needs to be done but not telling them how he plans to do it because he has no plans to do it.

However, if you, my reader, are willing to put on the Marxist red glasses you will see that despite the fact that Obama has refined his demagoguery into a high art reminiscent of Greek political oratory, the more he talks, the more he exposes his own "Poverty of Philosophy."

Thus, when business owners and CEOs complain that the Obama administration is the most anti-business administration in American history, they need to understand that this president's *"vision for change"* is not about business, it is about social justice; it is not about wealth creation, it is about wealth redistribution; it is not about law, it is about fairness; it is not about individualism, it is about collectivism; it is not about self-reliance, it is about dependence; and finally, whether they like it or not, it is not about capitalism, it is about socialism.

My point is that every time we get confused about what Obama is saying or doing, we should consult the works of Karl Marx or Vladimir Lenin; they will help to translate the President's ambivalence into clear and unambiguous terms. Based on the veracity of the forgoing evidence, any intelligent person who is even remotely familiar with the theories of Marx and Lenin would have unquestionably concluded that Obama's *"vision for change"* is actually Karl Marx's renewed version of the "Philosophy of Poverty."

It is impossible to underemphasize the centrality of Marxism-Leninism in Obama's policies, but I'm sure there are those who think I have not sufficiently substantiated my indictment and believe there's a more logical, calmer explanation. So, to anyone still having doubts and thinking that the author's assertions are far-fetched, I implore you to answer this critical question. Given the mountain of evidence that the President and Lenin share what Mr. Kloppenberg called a *"refreshing new way of thinking about the role of democracy,"* if Vladimir Lenin were elected president of the United States today, would President Lenin's *"vision in terms of where we are going"* be substantially different from President Obama's?

What Is "Social Justice," Anyway?

How to usher in a new harmonious era of global justice, fairness and equality? How to transform Obama's messianic hallucination into a majestic world in which the blind and the lame, the deaf and the dumb, the destitute and the sick are flocking for miraculous cures offered by the leader who is greater than God? How to introduce a new moral order that is dramatically opposite that of the Founders? Obama's novelty is to replace the Bolsheviks' "Land to the Peasants, Bread to the Hungry, Peace to the People" that reflected a substantively different historical era with the contemporary slogan "Viva Social Justice, Fairness, Economic Equality" that is just as euphoric and just as misleading as that of the Russian Bolsheviks.

We hear a lot about socialism and social justice from the Democrats and the press nowadays. What is "social justice"? The

International Labour Organization (ILO), an agency of the United Nations, defines social justice as a concept based on "human rights and equality and involves a greater degree of economic egalitarianism through progressive taxation, income redistribution, or even property redistribution." Furthermore, according to the ILO, "Redistribution of wealth is the transfer of income, wealth or property from some individuals to others by social mechanisms such as taxation, monetary policies, welfare or nationalization."

The similarities between the concept of social justice and socialism are readily apparent to anyone who is not hopelessly naïve: social justice is a code word for wealth redistribution and nothing less than socialism in disguise. It is worth pointing out that the ILO is an international body, and it is not talking about social justice in an individual country. It is talking about *world* social justice, the redistribution of wealth on a worldwide scale. It would not be difficult to figure out whose wealth the ILO is dreaming of redistributing. Whether you call it social justice or socialism, the fundamental goal is to build an egalitarian society. Whether it is done by the outright expropriation of property, the Bolsheviks' approach, or through taxation and regulation, the outcome is the same. The tactics and methods may vary, but the final objective is an "engineered" society. Said, Barack Obama,

> *Change will not come if we wait for some other person or some other time. We are the ones we have been waiting for. We are the change that we seek.*

Those words mimic the communist anthem, "The Internationale":

> *No one will grant us deliverance,*
> Not god, nor tsar, nor hero.
> We will win our liberation
> With our very own hands.

Supporters of social justice are trying to camouflage the issue, claiming that the moral justification for egalitarianism is deeply embedded in spiritual aspects of our lives and that ethics and social responsibility have a central place in Judaism and Christianity. It is worth pointing out that religion is separated from the state in this country. In this democratic society, the religious obligation to perform charity and philanthropic acts is not directed by the government. These acts of kindness are symbols of the individual goodness that is cherished in our society. The roots of this goodness have nothing to do with forcefully redistributing wealth or building egalitarian dreams.

Regardless of what these people call themselves—supporters of social justice, socialists, liberals, progressives, Marxists, or Bolsheviks—regardless of what lipstick they put on this pig, it is still a Marxist pig.

"You Didn't Build That"

When I heard the President say "You didn't build that", I thought his words must have been taken out of context. Only after I had read his statement myself—several times, in fact—did the significance of his comments become abundantly clear. It was in that unexpectedly lucid moment of sincerity from the President, who is otherwise a disciplined politician, that he provided profound insight into his real thinking. I am willing to bet that from now on he sticks to the teleprompter. His words are so revealing that I decided to quote the entire statement so I will not be accused of taking anything out of context. This is a case of the loyal student besting his teachers. Lenin and Trotsky would be proud of their pupil.

> *If you've been successful, you didn't get there on your own. You didn't get there on your own. I'm always struck by people who think, well, it must be because I was just so smart. There are a lot of smart people out there. It must be because I worked harder than everybody else. Let me tell you something—there are a whole bunch of hardworking people out there.*

If you were successful, somebody along the line gave you some help. There was a great teacher somewhere in your life. Somebody helped to create this unbelievable American system that we have that allowed you to thrive.

Somebody invested in roads and bridges. If you've got a business, you didn't build that. Somebody else made that happen. The Internet didn't get invented on its own. Government research created the Internet so that all the companies could make money off the Internet.

The point is, is that when we succeed, we succeed because of our individual initiative, but also because we do things together. There are some things, just like fighting fires, we don't do on our own. I mean, imagine if everybody had their own fire service. That would be a hard way to organize fighting fires.

So we say to ourselves, ever since the founding of this country, you know what, there are some things we do better together.

That's how we funded the GI Bill. That's how we created the middle class.

That's how we built the Golden Gate Bridge or the Hoover Dam. That's how we invented the Internet. That's how we sent a man to the moon.

We rise or fall together as one nation and as one people, and that's the reason I'm running for president—because I still believe in that idea. You're not on your own, we're in this together.

In this rare display of true candor, the President has accidentally unlocked a window into his soul and displayed his invincible prejudice against the individual business owner. What he is saying is "You did not build it alone, so you should not own it alone," or, more to the point, "We built it collectively, we own it collectively."

There are two types of society, based on very different premises. One society says, "You built your business, therefore you own your business"; and the other type of society says, "If you built your business, you built it because of our collective effort and therefore we all get to share the results of your success." One society says, "Wealth is a product of talent, perseverance, and hard work"; and the other type of society says, "You are poor not because you are an alcoholic or a drug addict, failed in school, or are just plain lazy; it is because you have been exploited. Therefore, all poor people shall unite and expropriate the expropriators."

One type epitomizes "can-do" individualism and is inspired by American idealism. The other type embodies the Marxist-Leninist philosophy of parasites, a philosophy all too familiar to former Soviet citizens: "If you made a scientific discovery, invented a new technology, or wrote a book—it is not your accomplishment. The government educated you, provided office space and laboratories. It does not belong to you, it belongs to society."

This psychological axiom of fairness has been a way of life for primitive tribal societies for thousands of years and was adopted by the Bolsheviks and now, as we have discovered, also by our president, who has primed it for this country. I was amused that the President purports to believe that if you succeed, it is only because you received help, and points out that "there are a whole bunch" of smart and hardworking people who did not succeed. If we drive the President's statement to its logical conclusion, we must conclude that if you are not successful, it is not your fault; you just did not get the help that successful people got. This perspective reveals a startling ideological reversal of the Democratic Party, as so eloquently expressed by a Democrat and great American, Daniel Patrick Moynihan:

The great corporations of this country were not founded by ordinary people. They were founded by people with extraordinary intelligence, ambition, and aggressiveness.

The President himself has had many great teachers in his life, no doubt; judging from his philosophy and actions, the two most gifted were Marx and Lenin. As stated earlier, the President believes the true origin of wealth is the exploitation of working people. In order to restore the equilibrium of fairness, the owners (the rich) have to transfer their unfair share of wealth back to society. The Russian Bolsheviks called it "expropriation of the expropriators."

The President is desperately trying to substantiate his argument for the fairness of wealth redistribution. But he is not doing a very good job. His statements are full of factual inaccuracies and insinuations. First, the implication that the government built capitalism is simply false. As was discussed at length in previous chapters, government had nothing to do with the Industrial Revolution, which precipitated the development of capitalism. America has become a great nation not because of some substantive government actions, but because of what individuals could accomplish for themselves and for the nation.

Or take this part of the President's statement: "Somebody invested in roads and bridges. If you've got a business, you didn't build that. Somebody else made that happen. The Internet didn't get invented on its own. Government research created the Internet so that all the companies could make money from the Internet." This is ridiculous, if not sardonic. The last time I checked the Constitution, it was "we the people" who established the government and enumerated its powers granted under the Constitution. Hence, the government is just a hired manager to perform certain "enumerated" functions. It is funded and supported by our tax dollars. "We the people" invested in the country's infrastructure. *We* made that happen. Government only administered the contracts—and did not even manage the projects. It was private enterprises that managed, engineered, supplied equipment and materials, and actually built the infrastructure, a monument to American ingenuity and the power of private enterprise. We all use the roads and bridges in America, and we all are still paying for them in the form of the gasoline tax and tolls. As for the government inventing the Internet, which is a distortion of the facts, and incidentally, Obama is not the first to claim this honor. Al Gore did it before, but that does not make the President's statement any less ridiculous. Indeed, government played an important role, as it has with the development of many other things that have revolutionized human life, but it is the individual who deserves the credit.

Here's another fallacious statement: "That's how we funded the GI Bill. That's how we created the middle class." Obama repeated this statement during an interview with Bill O'Reilly in February 2014 before the Super Bowl. Did the GI Bill create the American middle class? That implies there was no middle class in the United States prior to the mid-1950s. As was described in Chapter 7, the middle class in the United States emerged in the nineteenth century as a by-product of the evolution of capitalism, which lifted millions of people out of poverty. And, as emphasized earlier, not through government welfare, not by government handouts, nor the redistribution of somebody's wealth, but through the rise in productivity of capitalist enterprises and the hard work of millions of people engaged in trade, commerce, and other productive activities. The President does not care that he is at odds with the historical facts and it does not matter to him that the statements he makes are untrue! He knows that if he repeats them often enough, with the passion and vigor of Leon Trotsky, they will become as good as true. Hey, it worked for the Bolsheviks.

No civilization in history, be it the Romans, Greeks, Persians, or Soviets, has been able to provide the sort of upward mobility for every segment of society that the Western economic free-market model has done. The men who created the American system of government, in their wisdom, understood the undeniable truth that innovation and prosperity come from individuals, not from the government—not from the masses! Individualism is the essence of American idealism! However, our president continues to promote collectivism when he says, "I still believe in that idea. You're not on your own, we're in this together." It may be rhetorically accurate, but it factually is not true. Thanks to the President's policies, this country is almost equally divided between those who are pulling our economic wagon and those who are having a free ride on it. The fact that some people may be entitled to the free ride and some have earned it does not change the equation.

Today, collectivism exists in varying degrees around the world and is present in political movements like socialism, communism, and fascism. It is deeply embedded in the ancient roots and cultures of both Judaism and Islam. For the masses it creates an unfounded expectation to succeed collectively when they have failed individually. Inherently, collectivism trumps the individual's rights in favor of the interests of society, and shifts moral and social responsibilities from the individual to the state. The Soviet Union enacted a "liberal interpretation of law in favor of the State." In plain English, regardless of the individual's rights under the law, in the final analysis if there is a conflict of interest between individual rights and the interests of the state, the interests of the state trump individual rights.

Collectivism essentially replaces individual responsibility with collective responsibility and inevitably leads to coercion. It works both ways; nobody is personally responsible for anything, and we are collectively responsible for the fault of an individual. The Bolsheviks extended the concept of collectivism to new dimensions. Indeed, when Bolsheviks applied their responsibility doctrine, they applied it to distinct classes of society: proletarians and the bourgeoisie. The concept justified communist repression against various groups of people and against whole classes of the population. The propensity for collectivism can explain why our Liberal Bolshevik is dividing the country between the 1 percent and the 99 percent. He is trying to convince the nation that demonizing and suppressing 1 percent of the citizenry (just three million people) is no big deal and is fully justified, while doing so in favor of 99 percent of the people for the common good. To get the support of the 99 percent at the expense of the 1 percent is a canny political ploy. Thus, he hopes that the 99 percent of togetherness will resonate with the American people. It sounds great; no one wants to be alone. Obama is artfully playing on human insecurity, indulging people's hopes and fears.

Obama's Fairness Doctrine

In his 2012 State of the Union address the President laid out his version of America:

> *We can either settle for a country where a shrinking number of people do really well while a growing number of Americans barely get by. Or we can restore an economy where everyone gets a fair shot, everyone does their fair share, and everyone plays by the same rules.*

I must admit that those words rankle me, setting off an alarm bell in my Eastern European mind. Every time I hear the word "fairness" from a politician, I grab my wallet and get ready to move my assets overseas. Why? Because I am tired. I am tired of hearing that old socialist song about the inequities of capitalism. I am tired of listening to our president talking, in an intellectually arrogant manner, about fairness and everybody playing by the same, unspecified rules—as if we lived in a country with no laws! As if we have no Constitution or the Bill of Rights!! I am tired of hearing the Democrats demonizing people who pay their taxes lawfully and criticizing them for not paying enough. I am tired of politicians helping the middle class and saving Social Security. I am tired of promises made now to be fulfilled later. I am tired of mediocre lawyers and unemployable bachelors of art (government employees) insulting my intelligence. I am tired of hearing the same fairy tale for the last forty years; as a friend of mine is prone to exclaim, "I've had a bellyful of this baloney!!"

Once again, "If you can't express yourself in numbers, you don't know what you're talking about." It is no surprise that the President has failed thus far to define fairness in numbers. It cannot be defined; fairness is one of the most subjective philosophical notions. Fairness in politics has always been, and remains, pure demagoguery, a way to provide a moral justification for those of limited abilities to "demand" according to their unlimited needs. One cannot manufacture fairness; even God could not do it: he created an unfair world. Some people die young, children get cancer, some are born beautiful or rich, or both, and some neither. Fairness is neither a right nor a privilege nor something that can be legislated; it is a moral concept. A doctrine that purports to promote fairness is an excuse to override the rights of individuals and to override law. Any government interference that attempts to substitute a fairness doctrine for the rule of law will eventually lead to the destruction of society. The role of government is not to impose its interpretation of fairness; the role of the government is to enforce the law.

The President insists that for the sake of fairness the rich have to pay more, but he never tells us who they are, the rich. As a Marxist the President knows that class warfare—class struggle, Lenin called it—does work. The slogan brought into play by the French Revolution, "War to the palace, peace to the cottage," is alive and well today. The appeal of wealth redistribution has proved to be irresistible to the masses discontented by the inequities. It worked in France, it worked in Russia, it works in Venezuela, and it will work in the United States of America. The philosophy of envy and siphoning from the rich appeals to a large segment of the population that does not realize that the definition of "the rich" is a spiral of devolution that eventually will reach every business and every individual who works for a living.

I watched pollster Frank Luntz one day on FOX News. In a room full of people, he tried to quantify a fair tax rate for the rich. He started asking people, "What do you think is fair? Let's say I make ten million dollars. Would it be fair if I paid ninety percent?"

One lady said, "Of course. You can live pretty well on a million dollars."

Then he asked, "What is your household income?"

She said, "About three hundred thousand dollars."

I'm sure a person who makes $50,000 a year thinks $300,000 is a fortune and that she could probably live just fine on $90,000—so why not taxes her at 70 percent? The point is that someone making less is not the best authority on how wealthier people should spend their money, or be taxed. It is easy to be fair with other people's money. This woman obviously never had $10 million, so she treats it like a lottery ticket. But for the person who made that $10 million, the money represents sweat and sleepless nights and the torture of failure. It is an agony of responsibility for employees, their mortgages, private schools, and retirement. That money is used to replace outdated equipment and to weather downturns. But most importantly, *it is that person's money.*

After listening to Frank Luntz and doing some soul-searching, I have finally figured who "the rich" are: they are "everyone who lives better than me." Isn't that simple? I hope that eventually the President and Congress will agree with me.

The presidential rhetoric about fairness and calling for the rich to pay their "fair share" reminds me of a story about the Jewish gangster Misha Yaponchik who operated in the Russian city of Odessa in the early 1920s.

> Misha was an ordinary robber who invented racketeering in Odessa. Instead of robbing his victims, Misha decided to tax businesses. He did not offer protection; he just promised not to rob them in the middle of the night and not to use violence if payments were remitted to him in a timely manner. Misha kept half of the proceeds for himself and members of his gang; the other half he distributed among the poor in the form of food and other necessities. In this way Misha administered fairness by "asking" the rich to pay their "fair share." Misha Yaponchik was not a well-educated man; he was not familiar with the basics of "progressive" economics. It never occurred to him that by taking money from the rich and giving it to the poor he was stimulating the economy. The NKVD, the People's Commissariat of Internal Affairs (precursor of the KGB), did not share those economic theories either; they had Misha shot. If not for this unfortunate event, Misha Yaponchik today would qualify for a Nobel Prize in economics. Odessa's businessmen celebrated Misha's death prematurely. Shortly thereafter, the NKVD arrested the "exploiters of the working people," expropriated their "means of

production," and sent them to Siberian labor camps, where most of them perished. That was the Bolsheviks' idea of fairness. I wonder if the American socialists one day get to implement Obama's fairness doctrine of wealth redistribution, will they emulate Misha Yaponchik or the NKVD?

The President says that everyone should play by the same rules—a novel idea, coming from this government. So let us start close to home: if everyone should play by the same rules, then elected officials should start living by the same rules that apply to the rest of us. On what basis do congressional representatives receive a pension equal to 100 percent of their salaries after just one term in office while a military person retires after twenty years of risking his or her life with only 50 percent pay?

Or the so-called Affordable Care Act. Our elected representatives who voted for "affordable care" are beginning to realize that it is not as affordable as the President led us to believe it would be. So Congress has been giving an exemption for members of Congress and their staff, which preserves their very generous federal health insurance package that subsidizes approximately 75 percent of their premiums.

Or consider OSHA, the Occupational Safety and Health Administration, whose regulations do not apply to the government. And what about financial regulation? It is very telling that the Sarbanes-Oxley Act does not apply to Congress. The Act requires the chief executives of public companies to certify their financial reports; if they provide false or inaccurate information to the public, they could be fined up to $5 million and serve as many as twenty years in prison. Members of Congress (like all federal officials) are making up numbers as they go, passing laws based on false data, and misleading the public without any sanctions whatsoever.

Or perhaps the President in his "fairness" speech was talking about the bailout of General Motors? As a result of this so-called managed bankruptcy, the bondholders were shafted in favor of the United Auto Workers union, and the union pension fund received preferential treatment in violation of the bankruptcy law.

On a final note, how does affirmative action fit in, in an economy where everyone gets a fair shot and everyone plays by the same rules? Doesn't it represent reverse discrimination? What does it tell you about this country and our black president's vision? "Affirmative action means positive steps taken to increase the representation of women and minorities in areas of employment, education, and business from which they have been historically excluded."[36] Those steps involve preferential selection—selection on the basis of race, gender, or ethnicity. As a result, white applicants with good grades are not accepted in universities because universities receive bribes, in the form of federal and state benefits, for admitting minorities regardless of their grades. This is not so different from the way qualified Jewish students faced discrimination in the former Soviet Union.

Furthermore, affirmative action requires the government and large corporations to put aside a number of contracts for minority businesses. Here again, we see a pattern of awarding contracts to incompetent black and other minority contractors on a strictly racial basis. Why do I say incompetent? If they were competent, they would not need preferential treatment. The whole idea of preferential treatment is demeaning and should be insulting to blacks and other minorities. It sends a subliminal message that these people are inferior and need government assistance. It is morally wrong and it is wrong on substance. When was the last time Jewish people, who have been discriminated against for centuries, in this country as well as around the world, asked for preferential treatment? All they have ever demanded is equal opportunity to compete. Given an opportunity, they were confident that they could blow the competition out of the water. This confidence has helped the Jewish people survive under the most gruesome perils.

I remember my second day in the United States; we had a briefing at HIAS, a Jewish organization that helps immigrants to settle in the United States. "Perhaps you think there is no anti-Semitism in this country," we were told. "You are wrong. The beauty of this country is that you may be turned down for the job because you are

---

[36] *The Stanford Encyclopedia of Philosophy*

a Jew, but you can apply across the street and be accepted because you *are* a Jew." It was fair enough for us. We were seeking no privileges, no special status, no compensation for millennia of suffering; we were seeking equality of opportunity and we got it. Thousands of Jews who emigrated from the Soviet Union, most of whom did not even speak English, including the author, succeeded beyond anyone's dreams. If the President is sincere when he says he wants to have an "economy where everyone gets a fair shot," he should take advice from the chief justice of the United States, John Roberts, who said, *"The way to stop discrimination on the basis of race is to stop discriminating on the basis of race."*

The President's public speeches about fairness and the alleged deficiencies of the American capitalist system have never translated into sound economic policy. Even his most powerful arguments about fairness don't hold water. He says it is fair for the rich to pay more. Why is that fair? The rich did not get rich by paying less; they have always paid more. According to the IRS, the top 1 percent of the population contributes 37 percent of all taxes collected and the top 10 percent pays 50 percent of all taxes. At the same time, the lower 50 percent pays nothing. How is this fair? The bottom 50 percent enjoy the blessings of this country too.

As I said earlier, the President fanatically believes in his own righteousness and superior intellect. Perhaps we ordinary folks should entrust our lives to him so he can determine the rules and dole out our "fair share." Perhaps our president will become the "Father of All Nations," like Comrade Stalin, who called the Soviet people the screws of the state mechanism. And was Stalin ever right: we all turned in the same direction, we were inserted where our Father wanted to insert us, and we were removed when he decided it was convenient to remove us. And in the end, we were totally and completely screwed.

The American Constitution grants all citizens the same rights under the law. It prohibits discrimination based on race, gender, and religion. That is what gives all of us a fair shot at the American Dream, including our first black president. The American people don't need a "fairness doctrine" to grant what they already have. The country would be better served if the President committed himself to protecting the basic rights spelled out in the Bill of Rights and the Constitution instead of "fairly" violating the rights of some people in order to benefit others.

Inequality: Locomotive of Progress

> *Throughout the history of civilization people have been dreaming about a perfect world: full employment, fair distribution of wealth, full satisfaction of material and intellectual needs, and equality—only to discover, to their disappointment, that this utopian system does not exist on this side of the grave.*

Given President Obama's political persuasion, his obsession with inequality should surprise no one. In numerous speeches he has emphasized the alleged perils of inequality, including his 2012 State of the Union address, where he elevated the subject into *"the defining issue of our time."* Or, as he declared in December 2013, *"The combined trends of increased inequality and decreasing mobility pose a fundamental threat to the American dream."* He has never defined his own interpretation of equality or offered his own version of the American dream.

Since the President offers no specifics, let us look into the past and examine the historical precedents in order to gain some idea of what we may expect from economic equality and what the perils of egalitarianism are. Karl Marx, in his criticism of the Gotha Program in 1875, gave his vision of how "the co-operative commonwealth based upon common ownership of the means of production" would work. In this first phase (socialism), according to Marx, *the individual receives from society a voucher showing that he has done so-and-so much work.... On presentation of this voucher he withdraws from the communal storehouse of articles of consumption as much as this quantum of work is worth.*

What may come as a surprise to some Marxists is that this "advanced" society that Karl Marx primed for us existed 4,200 years before Marx's *Das Kapital* was published. The Akkadian king Sargon I (2335–2279 BC) founded an empire embracing Sumer, Babylonia, Elam, and Assyria, and established an economic system that Karl Marx imitated. Under King Sargon's rules, the products of labor were delivered to state depots and distributed to workers according to amount of work performed. Although this system did not prevent inequality, the mantra of equality lived on and as Marx himself pointed out in his writing, continued to have the same irreconcilable problems:

> *Thus if each individual were required to do an equal quantum of work, and all to receive an equal share from the social fund of articles of consumption, the man with dependents would be worse off than the single man, while the stronger and more clever individuals would be able to do the required amount of work with less effort than the weak.*

In the process of implementing the egalitarian dream in the Soviet Union, more problems came to light. How does society evaluate the labor of a general director and that of a janitor, as an example? While this issue might have been studied and debated by men of lesser initiative, it took Joseph Stalin's resourcefulness to solve this problem once and for all. He took all workers in a company regardless of status, from directors and janitors, and shipped them off to labor camps. In this way Stalin ensured full and complete equality…in slavery.

Primitive communism is another example of economic equality. Back then, before farming, people were forced to obtain food collectively. Under this arrangement there was no property, resulting in total economic equality—in poverty.

To sell the ideology, President Obama and his Democrat supporters insist they have no intention of creating an egalitarian society; they just want to reduce the gap between rich and poor. The elusive meaning of the term "reduce," however, leaves it open to endless interpretation, especially since they have failed to express their concept in numbers. Should the gap be a thousandfold, a hundredfold, tenfold—where does it stop? Furthermore, whether we shrink the gap a thousandfold or tenfold does not change the philosophical argument. The truth is that as long as there is a gap at all, the left will try to shrink it down to meet its ultimate objective, so unambiguously expressed in the communist slogan of the Soviet Union: "Economic Equality and Justice for All."

Economic equality and justice sound so appealing that the true believers do not even notice they are mutually exclusive because economic equality is in itself an intrinsically unjust concept. *The source of all wealth is the product of man's God-given ability to innovate.* This intellectual ability is a property of the individual and has not been given equally. God did not create a fair world. Or did He? If the world was full of people like Thomas Edison and Steve Jobs, we would have dirty toilets because nobody would clean them. Alternatively, we would have no toilets at all because there would be nobody to invent and build them. In His infinite wisdom God created a perfect world after all, indeed —"to each his own."

If society tries to "improve" God's world and equate the extraordinary contributions of great innovators such as Thomas Edison and Steve Jobs with those of millions of individuals not so gifted and talented, the enormous upward mobility of the last 200 years will immediately cease. As Aristotle observed 2400 years ago, *"The worst form of inequality is to make unequal things equal."* Freedom enables people to use their ingenuity to generate wealth, whereas coerced economic equality suppresses the very freedom required to innovate and begets poverty.

This is the reason the magical distribution formula did not work for the Bolsheviks and will not work for contemporary proponents of the egalitarian dream: liberals, social justice supporters, Social Democrats, and a few devoted communists, who refuse to accept the immutable fact that *freedom, inequality, hard work, and wealth are interdependent.* As stated earlier, capitalism, which embraces all these qualities, is the source of the greatest upward mobility in the history of mankind. Capitalism elevated the lumpen proletariat into a middle class, and in doing so, materialized the American Dream.

The President's policies, such as the Affordable Care Act, the Dodd-Frank Act, and new environmental regulations, are supposedly aimed at addressing the *"fundamental threat to the American dream."* But regardless of the positive spin Obama uses to promote these policies, they are not about freedom and creation of wealth; they are about suppression of freedom and redistribution of wealth.

In his quest for the egalitarian dream the President may choose to ignore the millennia of Aristotle's reality, but he cannot change it. *Inequality emanating from free enterprise is the ultimate expression of freedom and is the locomotive of progress.* It gives poor, rich, and everyone in between something to strive for.

This powerful locomotive has been pulling our economic wagon from the Industrial Revolution through modern-day free-market capitalism toward what Alexander Hamilton called "greater perfection and happiness than mankind has yet seen."

Paradoxically, the Founding Fathers and President Obama both aspired to equality. The Founding Fathers envisioned equality in liberty, while our president and the Democratic Party are driving the country into equality in poverty.

The Forgotten Seventeenth Amendment

> "The Constitution is not an instrument for the government to restrain the people, it is an instrument for the people to restrain the government—lest it come to dominate our lives and interests."—*Patrick Henry*

From time to time the world produces a demonic leader who challenges the legitimacy of established order with force or an impostor with seductive ideas. The Founders of the United States of America were painfully aware of human fallibility and, at the same time, refused to inhibit the individuals with radical views or hidden agendas from running for office within the legality of the democratic republic's framework. Hence, with their foresight they constructed the Constitution, NOT to prevent those individuals' rise to power, but rather to deter their destructive impulses via constitutional restraints, the two most important and interrelated of which were the principle of federalism and a doctrine of separation of powers that imposed a set of boundaries and restrictions on the activities of the federal government.

Federalism united divergent interests of different states around the common purpose and democratic ideals while offering self-government and preservation from interference of each other's affairs under the auspices of the limited federal government. Separation of powers was to ensure the longevity of the system and avoid usurpation of power. In order to preempt a potential threat, the authority of the federal government was split between three branches of equal weight.

Although not explicitly articulated by the Founders, the overriding impetus was to contain the Executive branch of government that, being in control of the armed forces and government bureaucracy, was the most prone to offer the principal challenge to other branches of government in attempt to alter the established pattern of constitutional authority. Those restraints were severely weakened following the ratification of the Seventeenth Amendment in 1913. And since then, every president has challenged, and for the most part succeeded, in expanding the boundaries, resulting in inexorable expansion of the federal government in size and influence.

Arrival of the socialist government has exposed the fatal flaw of the Seventeenth Amendment. Not bounded by constitutional constraints, devoid of morality, and unconcerned about the legitimacy of their actions, the Democrats rejected established concepts of balance of power between branches of government and proceeded with implementing "the right things," using surfeit of power rather than power of reason. Just like their Russian predecessors, guided by conviction that "power is always lawful, because power makes laws," the Liberal Bolsheviks are making a direct threat to the established law and order. The Democratic Party has now based its legitimacy on ideology—not effectiveness or virtues.

In this time of upheaval, it is critical that we revisit the provisions of the United States Constitution that laid the foundation for this great country. While there are many diverse opinions on this subject, the main reason for the mess this country has gotten itself into is that we have forgotten the principles upon which this country was built.

The U.S. Constitution emanated from the Great Compromise of 1787. It is worth being reminded of what was at stake and the essence of the compromise. At the time, the United States was a union of independent states that were trading some of their independence for common defense, collective security, and general welfare.

The real issue was the preservation of the states' sovereignty against a "tyranny of the majority." The Great Compromise provided that the people of each state would have one or more individual representatives in the House, with the number designated in proportion to the population of each state. In parallel, the Senate would represent the interests of each sovereign state, each state weighted equally with two representatives. The states joined the Union on the condition that their sovereignty would be protected. The House of Representatives was intended to be a "People's House," with representatives directly elected by the people in their respective districts. Senators were to be selected by state legislatures to represent the states and ensure their sovereignty.

The Seventeenth Amendment established the direct election of U.S. senators by popular vote. This effectively took power from the states, making a mockery of the original intent of the United States Constitution and de facto nullifying the Tenth Amendment, rendering it unenforceable. With the ratification of the Seventeenth Amendment the balance of power so carefully constructed by the Founders shifted irrevocably in favor of the federal government at the expense of the states' sovereignty. For the sake of beating a dead horse, the Senate was never intended to represent the interests of the people per se; it was intended to represent and zealously guard the interests of the states. In giving elective power to the states, the framers of the Constitution intended to protect the states' independence and constrain the role of the federal government, in accordance with the Tenth Amendment:

> *The powers not delegated to the United States by the Constitution, nor prohibited by it to the States, are reserved to the States respectively, or to the people.*

James Madison, the acknowledged father of the Constitution, explained in Federalist Paper No. 45:

> *The powers delegated by the proposed Constitution to the federal government are few and defined. Those which are to remain in the State governments are numerous and indefinite. The former will be exercised principally on external objects, as war, peace, negotiation, and foreign commerce.... The powers reserved to the several States will extend to all the objects which in the ordinary course of affairs, concern the lives and liberties, and properties of the people, and the internal order, improvement and prosperity of the State.*

Elected by the people, the senators de facto represented the electorate and no longer represented the interests of the states. Henceforth, the mechanism of deterrence against the mighty and powerful federal government was in practical terms abolished and subsequently the limitations on the role of government and restrictions on interference in state affairs were effectively removed.

With the removal of constitutional restraints, presidents could proceed with legislation and far-reaching regulations, in many instances harmful to the interests of the individual states, as long as they secured the support of both houses of Congress. Indeed, until lately, the presidents of both parties have, by and large, adhered to constitutional principles and recognized and respected the role of Congress in passing legislation, carefully balancing political activism with legitimacy.

A constitutional scholar, Barack Obama, imbued with the sense of a special and personal mission to fundamentally change and dismantle the established order and replace it with an ideologically inspired system, understood early on that there was practically no legal recourse for violating the Constitution and ignoring Congress. He condescendingly summarized his attitude thus: "I've got a pen and I've got a phone." Obama's pompous declaration was the fulfillment of the grim foreboding of the second president, John Adams: *"Our Constitution was made only for a moral and religious people. It is wholly inadequate to the government of any other."*

Having the federal bureaucracy, DOJ, courts, FBI, Internal Revenue Service, and the U.S. armed forces at his disposal, Obama can continue playing golf on Martha's Vineyard and do pretty much whatever he wants with impunity.

Ironically, elected for six-year terms, the senators are not bound to the interests of the people either. As the saga of health care legislation has demonstrated, the senators become committed to their respective parties' agendas and their own personal interests rather than the concerns and well-being of those who elected them. The Democratic senators never read the so-called Affordable Care Act before they voted for it, and for the years following their votes they knowingly or unknowingly perpetrated fraud on the American people.

Some may say that it is an exercise in futility to consider what could happen if... Nevertheless, if we didn't have the Seventeenth Amendment, the Senate would not be controlled by a political party and the states would have a say in any proposed legislation. The fighting about Obamacare, the skyrocketing deficit, generous welfare programs, the government-run education system, the departments of Energy and Agriculture, and a host of programs and executive orders, plus volumes of intrusive government regulations, would never have seen the light of day. Most importantly, with passage of the Seventeenth Amendment, the Senate lost not only its original intended purpose; it became redundant at best and an impediment at worst. Paraphrasing Churchill, "Never has so much been surrendered by so many to so few."

CHAPTER 10
The Politics of Delusion

"It is natural for man to indulge in the illusions of hope." —Patrick Henry

The Necessary War

Here I would like to invite our readers to move on to a different kind of misfortune that has befallen this country. While socialization, the new social order, represents an internal threat, Islam, which is in the process of constructing an intrinsically genocidal caliphate, poses both internal and external threats on the scale of Nazism and Imperial Japan in terms of potential mass death and destruction. Islam is conducting a war against the Western democracies with religious zeal and fanatical determination, using all resources available—from engaging in open warfare to spreading terrorism across the globe; from sponsoring radical ideology within Muslim communities to indoctrinating schoolchildren to hate Western values.

As Islam redraws the political map of the Middle East and terrorism gains in strength and audacity, the Democrats aren't just impervious to the immediate peril; they are trying to *"not allow a crisis to go to waste,"* taking advantage of the global chaos pushing the CHANGE.

Reprehensible as it might be, the spread of radical Islam, slow-motion wars in the Middle East and North Africa, and the subsequent upsurge of refugees serve the Democratic Party's political objectives. As identified in the preceding pages, the main political objective of the Democratic Party is the conversion of the American republic into a social democratic society. Backing up this ambitious goal requires perpetuation of Democratic Party rule. The Democratic scheme is to change the country's demographic with an emphasis on open borders and relaxation of the immigration laws, thus ensuring a continuous inflow of Latinos and Muslims to the U.S. The central premise of this policy is to entice the immigrants with welfare benefits, free health care, free education of children, and eventual citizenship in order to vote Democrat. Besides the Latin America the Middle East is the source of millions potential immigrants. Just since 9/11, the U.S. has accepted more than two million immigrants and refugees from Muslim nations. Therefore, any notion of closing the borders or restricting Muslims' flow into this country will be met with fierce opposition by the Democrats, who, in pursuit of electoral supremacy, refuse to recognize that immigration and terrorism are interrelated, and are perfectly willing to trade national security for votes.

As of this writing, the Democratic candidates for high office seeking strategic advantage are competing over who will be *more welcoming* to immigrants. It is becoming exceedingly obvious that despite dreadful consequences, the Democrats exhibit a greater hatred for capitalism than for Islamic terrorism, which makes them inherently incapable of safeguarding this country. The Democrats' policy of open borders or no borders is designed to open our country's gates to a tsunami of immigrants with morals and values diametrically opposed to those of Americans, promoting resentment instead of assimilation, polarization instead of unification, and ultimately making the United States of America not united, not states, and not even American. This is the vision of CHANGE that the Democratic Party and Islamists "Can Believe In."

But the Republicans are not far behind. As usual, totally oblivious to the political reality, they inadvertently offered support to the Democrats' plot and found themselves in cahoots with the advocates of Muslim immigration. In a bizarre interview with Sean Hannity on FOX News, House Speaker Paul Ryan declared that blocking Muslims from entering the country would not be "appropriate" and would be fundamentally un-American—proclaiming, "that's not who we are." Whether it was ideological exhortation or willful ignorance, the

Speaker has demonstrated an alarming aloofness of recent history. What we are is not defined by what we say, but what we do. By this definition, that is exactly *who we are*. In the next chapter I describe the saga of the European Jews who were denied entry into the United States and sent back to the Nazis' gas chambers. History is a cruel thing and in this instance it has repeated itself, "first as tragedy, second as farce." The only distinction between the two parties is that the Democrats are acting out of pragmatism without morality, while the Republicans are acting out of morality without pragmatism. But in the end, neither party's countenance is moral or pragmatic. The country is going through an interlude of disunity, challenged on all sides, driving disagreements to the edge of confrontation. Debilitated by Liberal Bolshevism politically, economically, and militarily, and lacking moral consensus, the United States is in no position to prosecute this war effectively.

World War III

The period of intermittent wars with terrorism began decades ago and went unrecognized, and in some instances was ignored or grossly understated, before it evolved into a global conflict. When Jeremiah Wright Jr., Obama's "spiritual mentor," proclaimed in a sermon that "America's chickens are coming home to roost," although it was a reprehensible statement, he may have had a point. Although within a different context, not as a result of alleged American misdeeds but rather as a consequence of American ignorance and complacency, the chickens are coming home to roost, and what a mess they are making. Pakistan, Afghanistan, Kurdistan, Egypt, Syria, Yemen, Iraq, Libya, Gaza—all engulfed in bloody battles accompanied by atrocities the world has not seen since World War II.

The degenerate Western democracies, having succumbed to inverted morality, neglected their security and permitted militant Islam to amass military capabilities, financial strength, and enormous human resources that it has converted into strategic gains well above and beyond what anybody could have imagined. The West erred in assessing that appeasement and pluralism are the answers to radical Islam and, as a result, opened the door to the invasion of

Western Europe. Just as it did centuries ago, Islam has launched itself across Europe, the Middle East, and North Africa in a relentless wave of religious acclamation and territorial conquest, fulfilling an inherent tenet of Islam that any land once ruled by Muslims remains Muslim land in perpetuity.

Via clever use of immigration and influx of refugees, entire areas of major European cities have been de facto annexed to the possession of Islam, and the sovereignty of the host states is no longer recognized in those sizable enclaves. The practical consequence has been that those areas of Europe have become the base of and fertile ground for Islamic radicalism. Like a cloud of locusts the Islamists are infesting continents, committing hijackings, kidnappings, murderers, and mass destructions in their fanatic determination to destroy Western civilization. As Islam has conquered more and more territories, subjugating whole countries in the Middle East and North Africa the war grew into a messy geopolitical conflict that involves the Middle East, Europe, Russia, and the USA, and threatens the established world balance of power.

In this insane war no demarcations between fighting factions can be established. Even those who find themselves on the same side of the war are pursuing mutually exclusive objectives. In Syria, besides the blood-soaked ISIS and the heart-eating Jaish al-Islam, there is a multiplicity of other Islamic factions arrayed against Assad's regime. The multiple shades of terror are fighting between themselves with constantly shifting patterns of alliances and swapping atrocities, but all are united in aspiration to flood the Earth with human blood. The so-called Western coalition, headed by the United States, is fighting ISIS and Assad while Assad is also fighting ISIS. The Americans and their partners, though bombing some terrorist groups, support others designated as moderate. Turkey, which is a member of NATO and part of the Western coalition, is facilitating the sale of illegal ISIS crude, assisting the terrorists with money laundering and supplying them with ammonium nitrate, a necessary ingredient for manufacturing explosives. Meanwhile, the Kurds, who have been fighting valiantly against ISIS and are supported by the U.S., are being bombed by the Turkish air force because they happen *also* to be an enemy of the Turkish government. In this war of all against all, only

Russia has articulated its position with clarity and consistency. Putin makes no bones about his strategic objective, which is to prevent the spread of Islam into Russia's controlled Muslim republics. He has pledged unwavering support for Assad, accused the United States and Turkey of arming the terrorists—whether deliberately or inadvertently makes no difference to him—and declared his policy, "Who is not with us is against us," which provides little comfort to all parties involved—with the exception of Assad, of course.

The administration, on the other hand, whether it is in Syria, Iraq or Afghanistan has been demonstrating its pitiful inability or unwillingness to identify the enemy. During an interview with *Newsweek* on December 19, 2011, Vice President Joe Biden told the magazine, "Look, the Taliban per se is not our enemy. That's critical." If the Taliban is not our enemy, who is? Why are our military men and women fighting and dying in Afghanistan? If we add to the equation Iraq, Libya, Pakistan, and Yemen, where various terrorist factions have established safe havens for their operations, it is easy to conclude that we are in a mess of biblical proportions.

Anatomy of the War

In this war America and the Western world are facing a type of peril they have never faced before. The West fails to recognize as immutable fact that radical Islam is not just a religion; it is also a political totalitarian movement, just like communism and fascism. The movement embraces a fanatical agenda that includes religious supremacy and a Marxist-type utopian/egalitarian standard of virtue. However, unlike communism and fascism, which were adopted by countries that could be defeated militarily, radical Islam is not a country, it is a mass movement sustained by an ideology embodied in unlimited human resources around the globe. Hence, diplomatic solutions cannot be found, nor is it possible to defeat in strictly military terms. The precariousness of this warfare is that the irrational zombies hate this world so much that they are perfectly willing to blow themselves up in order to meet seventy-two virgins (the latest irresistible offering) for killing infidels. This puts our conventional military forces at a serious disadvantage, having practically no defense against this kind of fanaticism. The Quran teaches its followers:

> *Strive hard against the unbelievers and the hypocrites and be unyielding to them; and their abode is hell, and evil is their destination.* Quran 9:73

or verse 9:29, which instills:

> *Fight those who believe not in Allah nor the Last Day, nor hold that forbidden which hath been forbidden by Allah and His Messenger, nor acknowledge the Religion of Truth, from among the People of the Book, until they pay the Jizyah with willing submission, and feel themselves subdued.*

If history is any guide, with the exception of the two preceding World Wars, religious wars have been the bloodiest in human history. This one, unfortunately, has the attributes of both types of war, and the contention that all wars eventually end may not be applicable this time. This one is dramatically different, exacerbated by the Islamic apocalyptic vision of the world and yearning for death, it may take generations, centuries, to end this war, especially given the high birth rate in the Muslim world. Since Sun Tzu wrote in his famous *The Art of War* two thousand years ago, "no country benefited from a prolonged war," *no country has benefited from a prolonged war*. At this juncture it is also impossible to predict how it may end. In previous world wars the winner out-produced the loser. During the Second World War Americans were losing, on average, six Sherman tanks for every German Tiger tank lost. But at the same time, American industry was manufacturing six Sherman tanks faster than Germans could produce one Tiger. Americans were producing more bombers than Germans were shooting down, and that was true for every other piece of military equipment. The United States, despite heavy losses at Pearl Harbor, not only replaced those losses in short order but also built a greater and more modern fleet than that of the Japanese. Imperial Japan and Nazi Germany were facing the unlimited industrial capabilities of the United States, further multiplied by the infinite human resources of the Soviet Union. There was not a chance that the Axis powers could possibly win the war; they were out-produced and out-manned. The longer the war went on, the weaker Germany and Japan became.

In this current world war, the past nostrum will not work. The strategic equation may not be in our favor, since the enemies' weapon of choice is a limitless supply of human bodies that they use with deadly efficiency. In this "arms" race, Islam will easily out-produce the civilized world, making our industrial and technological advantages inadequate. A new element of this war also challenges the conventional definition of victory. In conventional war the army loses if it does not win; in the war on terrorism, terrorism wins if it does not lose. And it does not lose, because it has nothing to lose; the purpose of terrorism is not to win but to terrorize, to break the will and paralyze the society into submission. It has worked through the centuries; it worked in Bolshevik Russia, Nazi Germany, Israel, and Belfast, just to name a few instances in which the country either completely surrendered or yielded to terror in one fashion or another.

Standing with Islam

As the battlefield spreads to the United States the Democrats are forced to reconcile multiculturalism with security concerns, especially in view of ferocious terrorist attacks in the U.S., Europe, and elsewhere; they appear disoriented and confused. Any suggestion there might be a connection between the terrorist attacks and Islam would destroy the politically correct narrative and provide fuel to the anti-immigration movement.

The willfully blinded Democrats, sticking to their open-door policy, espouse tolerance and amity and accuse opponents of xenophobia and racism. Living in a politically correct universe, they refuse to recognize the magnitude of this danger and are trying to reassure the nation that terrorism does not represent an "existential threat" to this country. The argument at this stage may sound theoretical, but the "existential threat" to American citizens is very practical indeed. The President and his party see appeasement as a panacea and insist that acts of terrorism are perpetrated by a few extremists and that organizations like ISIS and Al Qaeda are aberrations of Islam. Islam, they maintain, is a peaceful religion, and the majority of Muslims are law-abiding citizens—ignoring the fact that these peaceful citizens celebrated the 9/11 attacks, from the West Bank to Jakarta to Dearborn, Michigan, USA.

While waiting for the tolerant and peaceful Muslims to show up, we have been witnessing the almost daily ritual of tens of thousands of Muslims all over the world burning the American flag and chanting "Death to America." This manifestation of Islam's hatred toward Western civilization and particularly the United States is not a new phenomenon. Since 1776 and till the beginning of the nineteenth century, Islamic (Barbary) pirates targeted U.S. ships, capturing cargos and killing Americans or taking them hostage.

In May 1786, Thomas Jefferson, then the U.S. ambassador to France, and John Adams, then the U.S. ambassador to Britain, met in London with Sidi Haji Abdul Rahman Adja, the resident Tripolitan ambassador, to try to negotiate a peace treaty to protect the United States from the threat of Barbary piracy. These future U.S. presidents were making the point that America had done nothing to provoke any animosity from Muslims. To which Ambassador Adja answered them, as they reported to the Continental Congress, that the hostility "was founded on the Laws of their Prophet, as was written in their Quran, that all nations who should not have acknowledged Islam's authority were sinners, whom it was the right and duty of the faithful to plunder and enslave; and that every Muslim who was slain in this warfare was sure to go to paradise. He said, also, that the man who was the first to board a vessel had one slave over and above his share, and that when they sprang to the deck of an enemy's ship, every sailor held a dagger in each hand and a third in his mouth; which usually struck such terror into the foe that they cried out for quarter at once."[37]

The subsequent research into anti-U.S. Islamic terrorism conducted by John Quincy Adams, the sixth U.S. president (1825–29),

---

[37] *London, Victory in Tripoli, pp. 23–24*

confirmed that the core cause was Islam's endemic hostility toward the "infidel" as expressed in the Quran.

So, when Obama declared at Cairo University in June 2009, "Islam has always been part of America's story," he was correct. Indeed it has been and, unfortunately, still is.

Notwithstanding the historical facts and growing evidence to the contrary, the President is keeping with the ideological dogma, which is in line with the common theme of previous presidents' foreign policy doctrines, that terrorism is un-Islamic. As President Clinton expatiated during his address to the nation on August 20, 1998:

> *Islam [is] the faith of hundreds of millions of good, peace-loving people all around the world, including the United States. No religion condones the murder of innocent men, women, and children. But our actions were aimed at fanatics and killers who wrap murder in the cloak of righteousness; and in so doing, profane the great religion in whose name they claim to act.*

President Bush echoed Clinton in his speech to the Islamic Center of Washington, D.C., on September 17, 2001:

> *The face of terror is not the true faith of Islam. That's not what Islam is all about. Islam is peace. These terrorists don't represent peace. They represent evil and war. When we think of Islam we think of a faith that brings comfort to a billion people around the world. Billions of people find comfort and solace and peace. And that's made brothers and sisters out of every race—out of every race.*

But President Obama has outdone them all. He could qualify for the Nobel Prize for Duplicity in addition to his Nobel Peace Prize. In his near-pathological obsession in defense of Islam, which should come as no surprise given his upbringing, during a speech at Cairo University on June 4, 2009, Obama displayed a bizarre and illusory interpretation of facts and engaged in a deliberate distortion of history. Lecturing the crowd, the President of the United States of America stated that America and Islam

> *share common principles—principles of justice and progress; tolerance and the dignity of all human beings. ...Islam has demonstrated through words and deeds the possibilities of religious tolerance and racial equality. ...The U.S. and Islam share common goals of justice and tolerance and the dignity of all human beings.*

Are you kidding me? What are those common goals? Equality for women? Democracy? Freedom of speech? Freedom of religion? The right to bear arms? Perhaps tolerance for Judaism?

In his speech at Mumbai's St. Xavier's College on November 7, 2010, the President declared that

> *Islam is one of the world's great religions. More than a billion people practice Islam and an overwhelming majority views their obligations to a religion that reaffirms peace, fairness, and tolerance. I think all of us recognize that this great religion in the hands of a few extremists has been distorted by violence.*

These words were being said about a culture in which any member of a family can kill a woman suspected of having an affair. According to Sharia law, it is the duty of a brother to kill his sister if she "dishonors" the family. These words were being said about a culture that glorifies female mutilation—cutting off a little girl's clitoris with a dirty razor without anesthesia. These words were being said about a culture that hacks off the heads of "infidels" and relegates females to a status subordinate to farm animals. The President, who has been a strong defender of women's rights to have an abortion and free contraceptives, has never raised the issue of the horrifying treatment of women in the land of Islam. In his 2009 Cairo speech, Mr. Obama actually declared:

> *I consider it part of my responsibility as the President of the United States to fight against negative stereotypes of Islam wherever they appear.*

The examples cited above are not stereotypes, they are facts, they are Islam; and about these facts he is silent. Disregarding rational consistency, intellectual honesty, and adherence to historical facts by proclaiming that the United States of America and Islam "share common goals of justice and tolerance," the President exhibits signs of political intoxication, kissing Islamic tuchis. There is as much harmony between America and Islam as we had with Nazi Germany or Imperial Japan. Winston Churchill, the greatest statesman in history, who distinguished himself as a modern Nostradamus in his beautiful 1899 book, *The River of War: An Historical Account of the Reconquest of the Soudan*, offered his devastating indictment of Islam:

> *The fact that in Mohammedan law every woman must belong to some man as his absolute property—either as a child, a wife, or a concubine—must delay the final extinction of slavery until the faith of Islam has ceased to be a great power among men. Thousands become the brave and loyal soldiers of the faith: all know how to die but the influence of the religion paralyses the social development of those who follow it. No stronger retrograde force exists in the world. Far from being moribund, Mohammedanism is a militant and proselytizing faith. It has already spread throughout Central Africa, raising fearless warriors at every step; and were it not that Christianity is sheltered in the strong arms of science, the science against which it had vainly struggled, the civilization of modern Europe might fall, as fell the civilization of ancient Rome.*

Churchill's prophetic vision of 117 years ago is materializing before our eyes all over this world of fantasy, illusion, incomprehension, and denial. The proclamations of the President, who has tacitly given allegiance to Islam, should not deflect us from grasping the reality that the world is divided into two types of culture: one where violence is condemned and the other where violence is glorified, one which is built on the foundation of liberty and the pursuit of happiness and the other which worships destruction and death, one where success and respect are measured in capital and intellectual supremacy, and the other whose virtues are measured in power and violence.

The President and his leftist supporters maintain that all cultures are equal and as such are equally deserving of respect and celebration. That notion may sound noble, but in fact all cultures are *not* equal. This statement overlooks the fact that the cradle of freedom and democracy was the Western world, not the land of Islam. Western civilization governed by reason and guided by Judeo-Christian values, discovered science and technology and has subsequently produced a prosperous and relatively harmonious culture that the rest of the world envies and admires. Although the land of Islam is credited with the invention of time and the clock, the development of chemistry as a science, and the discovery of algebra (an Arabic word), in the last thousand years or so, governed by faith, it has contributed almost nothing to the advances of science and culture. Unable to progress with the rest of the world, Muslims wrap themselves in the seductive melodrama of eternal struggle, blowing themselves up, killing infidels and other Muslims under the banner of *Allahu Akbar* (God is Great), failing to realize that violence will not turn the clock which the Arabs invented back to their greatness.

I do not know whether our president deliberately ignores these important facts in an attempt to appease Islam or feels some inherent sympathy for Islam, or both. In his book *The Audacity of Hope* he wrote: "*I will stand with the Muslims should the political winds shift in an ugly direction.*" And so he does. One may think that our president took the oath of office to defend and protect Islam, not the United States of America.

Unlike in the areas of economic and political restructuring of the old USA, where the President is so faithfully following the teachings of his ideological precursors, in dealing with the issue of terrorism his policies are full of strategic blunders and the fertility of tactical inconsistencies. In Egypt he supported the Muslim Brotherhood, in Libya he supported groups associated with Al Qaeda, in Syria he supported the terrorists fighting Assad, and he wants to create a terrorist state on the West Bank and Gaza. For the illusion of democracy, the President is actively working to replace stable, autocratic, secular, and in many instances friendly-to-the-U.S. governments with unstable radical Islamist regimes whose stated objective is the destruction of American and Western values. In Egypt, President Obama continued efforts to reinstate the Muslim Brotherhood and president Mohamed Morsi even after Morsi was ousted. Why? As his argument goes, the Egyptians had an election and the Muslim Brotherhood was democratically elected; therefore, it is a legitimate government and we must support a democracy.

Paradoxically, this supposedly constitutional scholar is confusing elections with democracy. Elections are only an instrument of democracy, no more, no less. This instrument of democracy in many instances has malfunctioned and provided legitimacy to oppressive and totalitarian regimes. There are many examples where democratic elections failed to produce a democracy: Hamas in the West Bank, Salvador Allende in Chili, Hugo Chávez in Venezuela, and Adolf Hitler in Germany, to name just a few.

But the most repulsive examples of "standing with the Muslims" are the President's policies toward Israel and Iran. In a "bold gesture" for peace, this administration is lifting economic sanctions on Islamic Iran, which threatens Israel with nuclear annihilation, because Iran "promised" to postpone the development of nuclear weapons. At the same time, the administration was threatening to impose economic sanctions on and boycott the State of Israel because Israel is refusing to jeopardize its security and give up some territory in exchange for a piece of paper called a peace treaty with Palestinians, who are also committed to Israel's destruction.

To be fair, Obama is not the first president of the United States to actively support terrorists; it would seem that supporting terrorists has been a long-standing policy of the United States government and cuts across party lines.

The Politics of Delusion

President Jimmy Carter supported Ayatollah Khomeini and called him a "peaceful and holy man." In August 1982, Ronald Reagan sent Marines to Lebanon to save the Palestine Liberation Organization from complete annihilation when the Israelis cornered terrorists in Beirut. Just think about this utterly obscene picture: American Marines protecting PLO terrorists. America paid a heavy price for the involvement when 241 U.S. Marines died in a terrorist attack on their compound at Beirut International Airport in October 1983. And President Clinton turned down at least three offers by foreign governments to help seize Osama bin Laden.

Decades of frolicking with terrorists exact a heavy price. It is difficult to avoid the temptation, perhaps superfluous, to play the mental game of "if only." If only President Carter had not betrayed the Shah of Iran, contemporary Iran would not be run by ayatollahs. If only President Reagan had not sent the Marines to Lebanon, the Israelis would have eliminated the PLO once and for all and thousands of Israelis and 241 brave Marines would not have perished. If only President Clinton had killed Osama bin Laden, 9/11 might never have happened. If only America was more prudent, our leaders more determined. If only…our presidents and the American people had learned from history.

Obama's failure to call our conflict with Islam a war has resulted in widespread confusion. On the one hand, the President never misses a chance to release captured terrorists back into their environment, so they can continue killing. On the other hand, American drones are killing terrorists with deadly precision in Afghanistan, Yemen, and other parts of the world so efficiently that they cannot replace their commanders fast enough. At one point the administration decided to prosecute Al Qaeda leaders including Khalid Sheikh Mohammed as civilians in domestic U.S. courts even though there was a good chance that the terrorists would beat the rap on technicalities, just like Bill Ayers (a terrorist who is also Obama's friend), and walk free. Later, the President approved a raid in Pakistan to kill Osama bin Laden. It seems Obama is torn between his sympathies for Islam and the realities of war.

Once again, the President appears to be caught in conflicting currents. He insists that acts of terrorism are legal issues and must be dealt with by our legal system. Despite the fact that Obama refuses to call this conflict a war, he is sending drones abroad to kill people (even Americans) without due process. If this is indeed a war, no American civil or criminal law applies, and the President's actions are fully justified. However, if this is not a war, then how can the President execute people, including Americans, without due process? Although Obama does not call this conflict a war, he nonetheless personally chooses the drone "kill" targets, as revealed by the *New York Times*. Although deciding who lives and who dies may play well into the President's feeling of eminence, it is neither legal nor does it win wars.

Romance with Terrorism

Just as in domestic politics, the Democrats may choose to ignore reality, but they cannot alter it, nor can they avoid the consequences of ignoring it. The reality is that we are in a state of war: the Third World War. In order to win the war, we have to understand the enemy and its objectives. Napoleon once said, "If you do not understand your enemy, you have lost." His words should be taken as a warning, in effect, of worse to come. To say most Muslims are moderates and have nothing to do with the fanatical Islamic terrorists is like saying the Germans were a highly cultured, peaceful people and that the mass murder of Jews was perpetrated by National Socialist extremists.

There are many striking similarities between Nazi Germany and today's Muslim world, all of which this current administration and the left have chosen to ignore. The Nazis' doctrine called for supremacy of the Aryan race and extermination of the Jews. I am sure that the left (which has many Jewish supporters) would consider those policies "extreme." However, the left fails to recognize that, just like the Nazis' doctrine, the Quran segregates the human race into two groups: Muslims and infidels; and just like the Nazis' doctrine, the Quran calls for the killing of Jews. Just like Hitler's doctrine of the superior Aryan race, the Muslims' view of the world is that they alone possess absolute knowledge and the God-given supreme right over the infidels. Those who adhere to radical interpretation of Quran elevated the Quran's teaching into worldwide ideological and military conflict actively seeking to vanquish the blasphemies of the West and restore the glory of Islam over the world. As this concept of ideological pre-eminence is being projected into the United States and Europe, its integral component has been unnoticed or misjudged:

> *Radical Islam, through coercion and intimidation, united the Muslims of the world in its epic struggle to provide moral, financial, and logistical support to those who are on the front line of war with the infidels. That silent but effective network of support allows terrorists to avoid security forces, survive, plan, recruit new members, and provide training.*

The perilous truth is that there is a silent majority of Muslims that shares many of the same values of and evinces a favorable attitude toward radicalism. They are inseparable from the extremists.

The case of the Boston bombing is very telling. The two Muslim friends of the terrorists were not part of the conspiracy and did not know about the upcoming terrorist act, but when it happened they took it as a call of duty; they did not just fail to reveal the identities of the terrorists, they willingly and eagerly engaged in a cover-up. When Fatima Hadfi, the mother of terrorist of Bilal Hadfi, who blew himself up outside of the Stade de France in Paris, told a reporter that her son "was like everybody else," she inadvertently admitted the obvious: yes, he *was* like everybody else…in the Muslim community.

As we are ready to acknowledge that not all Muslims are terrorists, the Muslim community has to concede that all terrorists are Muslims and therefore the silent majority shares the moral responsibility for the terror attacks as long as it remains silent. The Romans' wisdom, *Qui tacet consentire vidétur*, "Silence is consent," is as relevant today as it was millennia ago.

Many Muslims who adhere to a peaceful and pluralistic interpretation of their faith insist that they had nothing to do with terrorism or mass murders perpetrated by Islamists in Syria, Iraq, and

---

[38] *Payment made annually under* Islamic *law on certain kinds of property and used for charitable and religious purposes, one of the Five Pillars of Islam.*

other places. The problem is they do not publicly condemn terror and continue to donate zakat[38] to the mosques, charities, and organizations that support those who "wage Jihad" and therefore quietly service radical Islam's geopolitical objectives. They, just like most Germans during the Nazi regime, pretend not to know. Despite the similarities between the Germans and Muslims, the pretense is fully apparent in the face of the twenty-first-century information reality that exposes a noteworthy difference. Unlike the Nazis, who went out of their way to hide the Holocaust, the modern savages are actually proud of genocide; they publicize and advertise atrocities as they record cutting off heads, burning people alive, and drowning infidels in cages on videos and on YouTube for the whole world to see. In the inherently violent Muslim world those videos are popular and inspirational, and widely used as a recruitment tool including in the United States and Muslim neighborhoods of Europe. Key word here is inspirational; these videos eloquently express the Islamic ideology and unveil the fundamental aspect of Islam's immoral enterprise.

I was in a hotel in Tripoli after the fall of Gadhafi, Arab TV showed gruesome images of beheadings. A few men were on their knees, blindfolded, with hands tied behind their backs. A young man took a butcher knife and started cutting the neck of the first victim. The executioner did not appear to know what to look for in order to cut through the spine quickly; it took him some time. It was horrific beyond belief! Finally, he found the spot, cut through, and severed the head. A huge crowd of bearded men and boys cheered loudly. That scene defined the contrast between Muslim extremists and moderate Muslims. The extremists carried out the execution, while the moderates cheered, recording the event on their iPhones and enjoying watching it on TV. We should not be apologetic for judging all Muslims by the behavior of most of them and we should not be confused by the Muslim silent majority regarding the true nature of Islam.

The left's position on the Muslim threat is inconsistent, immoral, and reprehensible. But that should not surprise us: the left did not consider Hitler extreme at the time, and supported the proposal to nominate him for the Nobel Peace Prize. The left has always had a natural attraction to totalitarian, bloody regimes. They admired Stalin, Mao, and in more recent times Castro, Che Guevara, and Hugo Chavez, and have consistently ignored the murderous nature of totalitarian regimes just as they currently ignore and deny Islamic terrorism.

Americans have been in denial about this threat since the early 1970s, when the Palestine Liberation Organization began committing terrorist acts against Israelis, but the world was silent because the victims were Jews and we are not Jews. Adding logs to that proverbial fire, the world endorsed and encouraged the terrorists by awarding the Nobel Peace Prize to PLO chief terrorist Yasser Arafat. Since then terrorists have taken to Europe, but we are not Europeans; and Asia, but we are not Asians. The evolving history of terrorism is captured well by what German Lutheran Pastor Martin Niemoller wrote about the Nazis:

> In Germany they first came for the communists
> and I didn't speak up because I wasn't a communist.
> They came for the Jews
> and I didn't speak up because I wasn't a Jew.
> Then they came for the trade Unionists
> and I didn't speak up because I wasn't a trade Unionist.
> Then they came for the Catholics
> and I didn't speak up because I was a Protestant.
> Then they came for me and by that time no one was left to speak up.

They Want to Die

Although it would require a fierce liberal skeptic to deny that terrorists are living among us, the Administration and the Democratic Party blame acts of terror on lack of gun control, not enough jobs, global warming, and individual pathologies—anything that would reframe the problem and shift the focus away from Islamic terrorism. The President telling the nation that "Americans refuse to be terrorized" is just another utterly pathetic attempt to spin inability to protect the country as an example of moral superiority. For those of us who do not travel in private jets or armored cars with security detachments, it is a challenge to not be afraid for our lives and the safety of our children when we read the latest news or sit next to a scarecrow in a black burqa on a plane. We are not cowards, but we are afraid.

The contenders for the White House from both parties continue projecting weakness and strategic incoherence. Gearing up for the presidential election, the prevailing strategy is to bomb ISIS, send American troops, create a new coalition with Arab countries, etc. The strategy is reminiscent of an anecdote about a drunken guy looking for something under a streetlight. Policemen approached the gentlemen and asked him what he was doing under the light. "I am looking for my watch," he replied. "Did you lose it here?" the policeman asked. "No, I lost it on the other side of the street," replied the man. "So, why you are looking for your watch here?" asked the policeman. "The other side is dark" was his response. As we stated, the terrorists are already here and if we think that if ISIS is defeated tomorrow, terrorism will magically cease and desist, we are hopelessly delusional.

The first order of making sense is to reject postmodern liberal thinking that Islam is peaceful and acknowledge that we are in the age-old struggle between freedom and tyranny. A key ingredient of this struggle is an understanding that the value of human life in the world of Islam is indescribably different from ours. Saddam Hussein said it best: "If you kill a man, you are a murderer; if you kill hundreds, you are a hero; but if you kill thousands, you are a conqueror." This is the mentality of the other society, where terrorism is an instrument of power and, paradoxically, if we are not prepared to kill thousands, we can be neither respected nor feared in the world of Islam. By contrast, the Liberal Bolshevik, by practicing the politics of appeasement, has a difficult time coming to terms with the teachings of the genuine Bolshevik and his ideological mentor, Vladimir Lenin. The father of modern terrorism, who was also on the receiving end of it, summarized his experience with Bolshevik brevity: *"Terror can be conquered only with greater terror."*

Whether this nation is prepared to conquer terrorists with greater terror is an open question. What is not in question is the imperative for survival of our civilization. This imperative shall be reconciled vis-à-vis Western thinking, which embraces the humanitarian principles that separate us from the barbarians, and the necessity of survival. Our contemporary American challenge is not the military aspect of killing a lot of people; it is the moral issue, regardless of reasoning and justification. Henry Kissinger addressed this dilemma when he wrote, *"While we should never give up our principles, we must also realize that we cannot maintain our principles unless we survive."*[39]

Whether we still possess the psychological stamina to do what needs to be done to *survive*, or we have watered down our genes and become impotent and ineffective, history will be the judge. But one thing is clear: we are doing neither the right things nor doing things right. In the past, civilized society had little hesitation to use all its might to protect and defend its ideals. Bombing Dresden in 1945 was, in contemporary terms, a clear act of terrorism aimed at German civilians in order to break the Germans' resolve. At the time Sir Arthur Travers Harris, Marshal of the Royal Air Force, speaking in reference to carpet bombing of German cities, summed up the dominant mood: "I do not personally regard the whole of the remaining cities of Germany as worth the bones of one British Grenadier." Dropping two nuclear bombs on Japan was hardly a humanitarian act either. However, whether it is a lack of historical perspective, or ignorance, or simply political insanity, or illusion, our folly is that we never learn from the lessons of history, including our own. Despite bitter experience, we ignore the positives and tend to repeat the wrongs.

The second order of making sense is to stop judging the whole world according to our own values. The West has consistently failed to balance its commitment for human dignity and distaste for repressive regimes with the realities of the Islamic world. Introduction of Wilsonian principles in the Arab world, calling for self-determination and democracy, without understanding the fundamentals of tribal societies, has proved disastrous for this country.

The idealistic goal of removing a tyrant and building democra-

---

[39] The American Encounter, p. 174.

tic nations in recent U.S. incursions in Iraq, Libya, and Afghanistan has proven insuperable in the face of an Islamic culture that violently rejects Western values. After millennia of bloody religious conflicts the imposition of democracy in this part of the world inevitably leads to sectarian violence. The competing parties see elections as a continuation of the struggle for domination by other means, paraphrasing Clausewitz, in which the loser would never accept the election results. Subsequently, we find ourselves in the middle of civil wars driven into protracted and costly military conflicts with no end in sight. As history has tragically recorded, by seeking democracy at the price of stability this country has been accomplishing neither. The mistakes of 1960s that led to overcoming difficulties of our own creation have been repeated with grave consequences.

> *Wilsonianism[40] of the early '60s had lured us into adventures beyond ourcapacities and deprived us of criteria to define essential elements of our national purpose.*

Thus wrote Henry Kissinger, the Goliath of American foreign policy, in his memoir, *Years of Renewal*. We should have learned from Kissinger that the most important task before our nation in this war on terrorism is to define our interests and shape our commitments—not to allow existing commitments to define our interests. Once we clearly define our interests and commitments, it will be time for Americans to find out, to paraphrase John F. Kennedy, whether we are free men standing up to our responsibilities and whether the United States has the will to face up to the enemy.

In order to face up to the enemy, we must recognize that the war on terror is not just a military confrontation, it is also an ideological and a political affair. First and foremost, this monster has to be defeated ideologically by superior principles advanced by Islam

---

[40] *Wilsonianism refers to the idealistic principles of conducting foreign policy by applying American democratic values, as set forth by Woodrow Wilson. It includes the notion of a new global order based on national self-determination and the proliferation of democracy.*

itself. Therefore, radical Islam can only be defeated by Islam. Indeed, across the Atlantic in Egypt, a new and different version of Islam is emerging. Egyptian president Abdel Fattah el-Sisi is assertively leading his country out of the Arab Spring. He has denounced Islamic terrorism and challenged religious clerics and scholars to "revolutionize the religion" and bring it in line with Western morality. The president of Egypt is a leader who exhibits moral clarity, courage, and charisma. With the enhanced stature of the restorer of stability, he is in a position to use his authority to isolate radicals ideologically and defeat them militarily. El-Sisi is the first and only Arab leader who has forcefully confronted terrorism by removing the "democratically" elected Muslim Brotherhood, supported by the United States and Europe, from power. Seizing power in a military coup and continuing to prosecute Islamic radicals made him anathema to those who, in their idealized version of the world, believe in reciprocity of appeasement.

The leaders of the Free World need to do much more than march in solidarity and make populist pronouncements. Having the overriding impetus of remaining free, they must recognize the fallibility of the democratic process and the imperative of eradicating radical Islam. The Free World should embrace el-Sisi and offer him moral support and unconditional financial and military assistance. Political posturing will not instill the fear of God in the Islamists, but el-Sisi, with Western help, will—if he lives long enough. Courageous leaders in this part of the world before him did not, so time is of the essence.

In the name of the missing Twin Towers and the thousands of victims of heinous terrorist attacks, in the name of the thousands of fallen men and women in the war on terror, in the name of the Israelis, who have suffered Islamic terrorism for decades, the United States must abandon denial, define the enemies, stop appeasement, face the threat, and acquire the will to use all means at its disposal to grant the ultimate wish to those who proclaim that they love death more than we love life.

CHAPTER 11

The Power of Demagoguery and Lies, or How the Democrats Win

"There are no morals in politics; there is only expedience." —V. I. Lenin

Two Monoliths and a Scam

The American electoral process consists of many facets and moving parts, but there are two voting monoliths and one election scheme the Democratic Party can always count on. Blacks and Jews are two segments of American society that, despite the Democratic Party's shameful record of racism and anti-Semitism, consistently vote Democrat regardless of issues, ideas, and political-social interests. Additionally, the voter scam helps the Democrats in heavily contested districts.

Devotion of Black Americans

Martin Luther King Jr., in his famous speech, envisioned: "I have a dream that one day on the red hills of Georgia, the sons of former slaves and the sons of former slave owners will be able to sit down together at the table of brotherhood." But the reality of the relationship between the sons of former slaves and the sons of former slave owners has been nothing short of a maelstrom of conflicting currents.

The authors of "all men are created equal" were slave owners governed by Plato's philosophy that it was right for the "better" to rule over the "inferior." Neither the Emancipation Proclamation nor defeat in a bloody Civil War that caused more American casualties than all other conflicts combined changed the moral convictions of slave owners. Although defeated militarily, they retained political power and used it to set the direction and tone of race relations for generations. The slave owners, the Democrats, never intended to let the slaves get too far from their plantations. They replaced emancipation with segregation that lasted for a hundred years, and most of them, like former Alabama governor George Corley Wallace Jr.—who infamously proclaimed, "Segregation now, segregation tomorrow, segregation forever" expected it to last forever.

But the leadership of the Democratic Party, faced with the Civil Rights movement of the 1960s, had no illusions that segregation would last. More importantly, they also realized that to be a slave one doesn't have to work on a plantation and have his existence dependent on a slave owner. Government entitlements would have the same effect of dependence on the sons of slaves as slave owners had on their fathers. At this point the Democrats made one of their most critical decisions, designed to ensure their electoral supremacy. If they had to let blacks into the voting booth, they needed to create a political process ensuring that blacks would vote Democrat.

In an act of political brilliance the Democrats abandoned segregation, stigmatized the sons of slaves as inferior, and portrayed them as victims of slavery who needed help and were entitled to redemption. They created government entitlement programs that provided assistance and offered privileges and protected class status to the sons of slaves, such as the landmark Civil Rights Act of 1964, which included the "affirmative action" provision that conveniently replaced civil obligations with rights and marked the start of a system of privileges. As LBJ put it, "I'll have these N—-ers voting Democrat for the next two hundred years."[41] With the proliferation of the culture of dependence, the Democrats have successfully

---

[41] The American Sentinel, September 1997, page 9. *Also:* You Don't say, by Fred Gielow, page 33.

replaced physical slavery with mental slavery. They corralled millions of black voters within the Democratic Party and continue to enact more government programs to ensure that the financial and emotional attachments of the sons of former slaves to the sons of former slave owners will never dissipate. This strategy has been proven effective over thousands of years, as the Greek historian Plutarch perceived: *"The real destroyer of the liberties of the people is he who spreads among them bounties, donations, and benefits."*

Two thousand years later, George Mason University professor Walter E. Williams validated Plutarch: *"The welfare state has done to black Americans what slavery couldn't do, what Jim Crow[42] couldn't do, what the harshest racism couldn't do. And that is to destroy the black family."* Hoover Institution Fellow Thomas Sowell concurs: *"The black family, which had survived centuries of slavery and discrimination, began rapidly disintegrating in the liberal welfare state that subsidized unwed pregnancy and changed welfare from an emergency rescue to a way of life."*

Moreover, the Democrats have effectively used the public education system to indoctrinate blacks in revisionist history. Subversion of the American education system is an ultimate crime because it is in fact subversion of the American mind. As a result, many black Americans don't know U.S. history. They believe that Abraham Lincoln was a Democrat and are surprised to learn that the Republican Party was formed for the purpose of abolishing slavery.

The Republican National Committee website states: "The Republican Party was born in the early 1850s by anti-slavery activists and individuals who believed that government should grant western lands to settlers free of charge." The Democratic Party, on the other hand, formed in 1792, identified itself as the "white man's party" while labeling the Republicans as the "party of the Negro." Black Americans would also be surprised to know that the first black U.S. congressmen were Republican. There was not a black Democrat in Congress until more than sixty years later. Those early black congressmen (during Reconstruction, after the Civil War)

---

[42] *The Jim Crow laws were racial segregation laws enacted between 1876 and 1965 in the United States at the state and local levels.*

were part of a Republican majority that passed comprehensive legislation outlawing any form of discrimination on the basis of race, color, religion, or gender a hundred years before the Civil Rights Act of 1964. They passed the Thirteenth Amendment, which abolished slavery, and the Fourteenth Amendment, which made freed slaves U.S. citizens, against unanimous Democrat resistance and a presidential veto.

To counter the Republican civil rights advances, the Democrats funded the Ku Klux Klan in 1866, which aimed at destroying the Republican Party infrastructure through terror and intimidation against Republican leaders and blacks. For those who consistently vote Democrat and want to learn the truth about camouflaged Democratic Party politics, I suggest *A Short History of Reconstruction* by Dr. Eric Foner.

So, when Vice President Joe Biden suggested that Republicans want to put black voters back in chains, he probably did not realize that he was talking about Democratic chains. What else? There were no others.

No wonder that every attempt of Republicans to break the chains of government dependence and liberate black Americans for the second time faces passionate hostility from the liberal media and has Democrats crying racism. Every time there is criticism of the system—such as that of Nevada rancher Cliven Bundy, who spoke from his heart in a straight, cowboy, no-nonsense way expressing his concern about the policies that encourage millions of people to rely on the government dole and do nothing while imported Mexicans "pick cotton"—the Democrats viciously attack such critics. They disparage their characters, question their motives, and demonize them, while intimidated Republicans and conservatives distance themselves from anti-socialists and run for the hills, offering no opposition to the Democrat offensive.

Community organizers and self-appointed leaders of the black community such as Jesse Jackson and Al Sharpton immediately get to work organizing rallies in support of the so-called victims of racism, making sure not that "all men are created equal" but that some are created more equal than others and are entitled to free stuff.

In the absence of a counterweight to this onslaught, Democrat policies are working as designed: black Americans have been supporting Democrats for the last fifty years, ensuring a continued culture of dependence, with disastrous results for both the black community and the nation.

A friend of mine, a black business owner, told me that his father insisted that he would always choose the Democrat, no matter what. "You do not have to bother yourself with the issues, just vote Democrat," his father told him. Roman Emperor Marcus Aurelius once famously said, "The opinion of ten thousand men is of no value if none of them know anything about the subject." Thus far, LBJ and the Democrats have proved the opposite. Black people have been voting Democrat for the last fifty years, discarding Marcus Aurelius' two-thousand-year-old wisdom for spurious advice from their fathers.

The Jewish Question

Winston Churchill called Jews "the most formidable and the most remarkable race which has ever appeared in the world." We are remarkable, all right. With superior intellectual prowess, a smart Jew predominates over the rest of the human race, but a dumb Jew is an insult to human intelligence. Here is my Jewish Question: Which of those remarkable Jewish-Americans voted for Obama in 2008?

As a Jew, I was perplexed: to me, it was completely obvious that the alternative choices for president in 2008 were clear and unambiguous. On the Republican side was a war hero, a strong supporter of Israel, an experienced politician with a strong track record and a commitment to public service. On the other side, for the Democrats, was a young man of Muslim background, an inexperienced politician with no track record of accomplishment whose personal files were mysteriously sealed. Moreover, this man had dubious connections with anti-Semites and America-haters. I was even more baffled in 2012. This time the Republican was a friend of Benjamin Netanyahu, a supporter of Israel, a man with impeccable business and civil service credentials. What could Obama do for Jews that Romney could not or would not do? What was it in the Democratic

Party platform that was so appealing to the Jews? Isn't something missing here?

After the shocking outcome of each election, I asked "Why?" many times, of many Jews.

The typical answer I received was "I did not (???) vote for him, but I am not going to vote for him this time." You ask a Jewish question, you get a Jewish answer. But they lied and did vote for him again in 2012. As prominent Zionist Max Nordau[43] once observed, "logic is a Greek art and Jews can't tolerate it. The Jew learns not by way of reason but from catastrophes. He won't buy an umbrella merely because he sees clouds in the sky. He waits until he is drenched and catches pneumonia." And, I should add, as he has already survived pneumonia, the umbrella can wait. The old saw, "There are two types of Jews—those who believe that Judaism is about social justice and those who know Hebrew," contains more than a kernel of truth. By and large, orthodox Jews voted for McCain in 2008 and for Romney in 2012.

Social justice, in terms of helping the sick and the poor, is deeply embedded in Judaism; for Jews it is a case of irrational obsession, and many of them believe that the only way to achieve a just society is through leftist policies. The problem is that their religion is not Judaism; it is almost every other possible ism, with the exception of conservatism and fascism—liberalism, socialism, feminism, environmentalism, and Marxism.

Speaking of which, the 1917 Bolshevik revolution in Russia that brought so much suffering to the people of Russia, including Jews, was in fact a Jewish revolution. Based upon socialist theories developed by a Jewish philosopher and economist, Karl Marx, the principal inspiration, organization, and driving power of the revolution came from Jewish leaders. Most of them changed their Jewish names to Russian ones to conceal their Jewishness, such as Trotsky (Bronstein), Zinoviev (Apelbaum), Kamenev (Rosenfeldt), Sverdlov (Rubenstine), Larine, Uritsky, Steclov (Nakhamkes), all of whom later assumed major positions in Lenin's government. In effect, Jews

---

[43] *Zionist leader, physician, author, and social critic (1849–1923). He co-founded the World Zionist Organization with Theodor Herzl.*

founded and shaped the Soviet state. Yet these same Jewish Bolsheviks quickly became the first victims of the Soviet state. Over the next twenty years, by 1937, practically all of them had become targets of Stalin's repressions and were executed or murdered abroad, like Leon Trotsky. Still, they would not abandon their devotion to socialism.

In the late 1920s, German Jews voted for Hitler's National Socialist Party, only to become victims of the Holocaust a decade later. They chose to ignore Hitler's anti-Semitic rhetoric, believing that it was merely for domestic consumption. They doubted that Hitler could be bad, much less evil. After all, he was a socialist!

Jews passionately supported and continue to admire FDR, who denied entry for Jews seeking asylum from Nazi extermination just before World War II. The most telling is the tragedy of the German ocean liner MS *St. Louis*, whose captain, Gustav Schroder, tried to save 937 German Jewish refugees after they were denied entry to Cuba, by bringing his ship to Miami only to learn that the U.S. refused his Jewish passengers a safe harbor. Finally the Jews were accepted by various European countries and eventually ended up in Auschwitz and Sóbibor. By refusing to allow Jews to enter the United States, Roosevelt offered Hitler a propaganda coup: justification of the persecution of Jews. The Nazis could say that they were not alone in their hatred of Jews; the rest of the world, and especially the United States, did not want them either. Nevertheless, Jews voted for FDR and still love him—after all, the New Deal was a giant step toward socialism.

It does not get any better nowadays. In their almost religious devotion to the Democratic Party, American Jews support the Democrats welcoming thousands of illegal children from Latin America into the USA with open arms and loving hearts. As Barack Obama asserted, *"These children are America's hope for the future"* and I am afraid he may be right.

The Power of Demagoguery and Lies, or How the Democrats Win

SS St. Louis: The ship of Jewish refugees nobody wanted.

In an act of colossal memory loss, American Jews choose to forget the tragic destiny of millions of Jewish children whom the Democrats deprived of the chance to be part of the American future. As a matter of fact they were deprived of any future, ending up in Nazi gas chambers because the Democrats refused them asylum in the United States. This is a frightening reflection of Jewish unwavering intellectual and spiritual commitment to socialist causes prevalent even among Holocaust survivors.

The Jewish love affair with socialism that began in Russia continued in Germany and endures in today's America. An examination of the current socialist Obama administration reveals a similar Jewish pattern. Living in ghettos for two millennia, the Jewish people have been struggling to reconcile their tragic history with the logic of contemporary reality. They have a difficult time coming to terms with the freedom and equal opportunities that America offers. They continue to fight for social justice, refusing to recognize that, as far as Jews are concerned, what they have accomplished goes well beyond their

Liberal Bolshevism

Jewish children not wanted in America

wildest expectations. Sons and daughters of the first immigrants, who dug trenches and washed dishes in New York, became doctors, lawyers, senators, bankers, industrialists, and influential politicians.

Unfortunately, the descendants of the first immigrants inherited the genetic memories of their ghetto ancestors. They appear to have nurtured and maintained a sense of guilt, even more so in the face of their success; they feel guilty for achieving a standard of living as good as or better than any other ethnic group in this country. They are constantly seeking forgiveness for their survival. They are prisoners of insecurity. The guilt associated with their success has led them to take on, and support, the cause of every underdog and liberal movement in sight, no matter how undeserving, no matter how irrational or against their own interests or even survival. As Jewish sociologist Milton Himmelfarb observed, *"Jews earn like Episcopalians and vote like Puerto Ricans."* Over the last century, no social macrocosm in America has more consistently voted against their self-interests.

> *Socialism, which began with the fanaticism of the grandparents, has been transformed into fear in the parents and subsequently into habits in the children and grandchildren; it is embedded deeply in the Jewish DNA.*

The unequivocal Jewish commitment to the Democratic Party makes them irrelevant during the elections. Republicans do not care about Jewish interests because Jews do not vote for them regardless of whether or not Republicans address their concerns. Democrats take the Jewish vote for granted and essentially do not care about Jewish votes because the Jews will vote for them regardless of their position on Jewish issues. Even among the Jews who emigrated from the Soviet Union there are many supporters of Obama and his socialist policies. That confirms the Russian saying *"You can take a Jew out of socialism but you cannot take socialism out of a Jew."*

Despite the obvious, Jews continue to neglect the teachings of Karl Marx, their fellow member of the tribe, that socialism is about redistribution of wealth. Redistribution means taking from one group of citizens and giving it to others. Bolsheviks took from the bourgeoisie; Nazis took from the Jews. The contemporary Liberal Bolsheviks' aim is to take from the rich, even though there are many Jews among them. Immediately before the 2012 election, I was in a Las Vegas restaurant with some of my Jewish friends, talking politics over dinner. At an adjacent table was another Jewish gathering. One of them turned around and asked one of my friends if he really was going to vote for Romney. My friend replied that he would vote for a cockroach if it ran against Obama. I thought that perhaps this expression, which I personally enjoyed, reflected a glimmer of hope that the Jews might emerge from their intellectual ghetto and commence a wave of voting based on logic, not habit. In the end, however, habit proved to be stronger than logic and, once again, emotional attachments trumped Jewish interests. In retrospect, I was picking up the dinner tab, which may have tilted the table in my philosophical direction.

"It Is Not Important Who Votes…"

I thought Nancy Pelosi's statement that food stamps and unemployment insurance are the best economic stimulus—as she put it, "the biggest bang for the buck"—was the pinnacle of absurdity. But when I heard President Barack Obama attacking laws requiring voters to show some form of identification at the polls I had to change my mind. Here are a few recent presidential quotes that outline the President's position, or lack of it, on the subject and reveal the depth of demagoguery and lies the opponents of IDs are prepared to employ to deny the obvious and defend the indefensible. Obama, speaking to his supporters, raised the alarm. "The stark, *simple truth*, is this: The right to vote is threatened today in a way that it has not been since the Voting Rights Act became law nearly five decades ago" and "Across the country, Republicans have led efforts to pass laws making it harder, not easier, for people to vote" and "I want to be clear: I am not against reasonable attempts to secure the ballot. We understand that. There has [*sic*] to be rules in place. But I am against requiring an ID that millions of Americans don't have."

What is really astounding is not that the President's position is supported by his Party, no surprise, but that it is not regarded with anything but ridicule by anyone of average intelligence. He is not offering anything except brilliant verbal facility while saying nothing of substance. Obama tells us what he is against, but never what he is for. Because the President is not there to solve problems or offer solutions; he is there to misrepresent issues and demonize those who disagree with him. This is the guy who gave us "If you like the health care plan you have, you can keep it," promised to cut the deficit in half, and perpetrated at least two dozen more documented lies, now telling us the *simple truth*. And what is the President's *simple truth*? "The right to vote is threatened," the President says, "because the Republicans are making it harder to vote." Characteristically, the President is having a problem with the truth, even the "*simple truth.*" He can shout and clamor about the right to vote being threatened, but the truth is that elections are not threatened by an ID requirement; they are threatened every time an illegal vote nullifies a legitimate vote by an American citizen. Republicans are not making it harder to vote, they are making it harder to steal the vote.

Then the President says that he wants to be clear he is "not against reasonable attempts to secure the ballot…but I am against requiring an ID." Is he for indelible ink? If anything is clear, it is that his statement is an oxymoron. How can such an attempt possibly be reasonable without IDs? Aren't IDs are the most reasonable and widely accepted way of identifying a person?

The president also says, "There has [sic] to be rules in place." Yes, indeed! There *are* rules in place, but our president is obviously not aware of or does not want to know that

- Only American citizens are allowed to vote
- A person has to be 18 years of age and meet residency requirements of the state in order to vote
- The person has to be alive

The *simple truth* is that the supporters of IDs simply seek to safeguard the voting process by enforcing the rules. Perhaps the President doesn't, but the rest of us have to use photo IDs constantly in everyday life. No matter how absurd, no matter how ridiculous, no matter how preposterous it all is, the most puzzling aspect is how in the face of common sense and overriding reality the Democrats could possible get away with this nonsense. What are the arguments of the Democratic Party in defense of the indefensible? What are the Democrats' arguments for NOT having a photo ID requirement? Let's take them one at a time.

Argument #1. *The American people* [citizens] *have the constitutional right to vote, and no impediment to exercise that right shall be tolerated.*

Well put, but there are three problems with this argument.

First, as stated above, there are rules in place that must be complied with.

Second, the American people have the constitutional right to bear arms. Shall we eliminate the ID requirement for the purchasing of firearms on the basis that it may be an impediment to exercising that right? Sorry, my fellow Democrats, I do not hear you.

Third, in April 2008 the Supreme Court, in a 6–3 ruling, upheld Indiana's state law requiring voters to produce photo identification. The Court specifically ruled that the voter ID law does not violate voters' constitutional rights.

Argument #2. *Approximately 23 million citizens of voting age lack proper photo ID and, as a result, could be turned away from the polls on Election Day.*

Those without photo ID, the Democrats claim, are disproportionately low income, disabled, and young. It is a bogus number to begin with; there is no reliable statistic to confirm the number of citizens without photo IDs. Be that as it may, one might wonder what is so distinct about low-income people that prevents them from having IDs? Because it is a citizen's right to vote, it is also a citizen's responsibility to obtain proper documentation in accordance with the law. Furthermore, citizens' civic responsibilities do not end at a lower income bracket.

And how it is possible to function in this country without an ID? If a person is gainfully employed, he has an ID regardless of income. He would not be able to get a job without ID or deposit a check in a bank. If a person does not work, he or she gets some form of government assistance such as welfare, unemployment, food stamps, that the Democrats love so much, all of which require ID. Elderly and disabled citizens get SSI, Social Security checks, welfare, disability, etc., all of which require ID. Students get IDs as well. By the way, students and elderly get discounts in movie theaters and restaurants, which low-income people would especially appreciate but would not get without IDs.

But this last one is the trademark of Democrats' mental and moral cretinism: the Democrats propose IDs for illegal aliens so they can prove that they are illegal. On a serious note, the Democrats have failed thus far to produce a single U.S. citizen who does not possess an ID. Just to be clear, as the President says, the Democrats are not against IDs in principle; they are against them as a tool for safeguarding elections.

Argument #3. *Some would not have the time to get an ID.*

Besides the fact that those who do not have time to get an ID likely would not have time to vote anyway, this one could be the most bizarre and ludicrous argument of all, demonstrating the extent of the absurdity to which the Democrats are prepared to go in order to defend their silly position. The Associated Press reported that the Justice Department called a witness in the Texas Voter ID trial in Washington, D.C., to testify. The eighteen-year-old witness complained that she couldn't find the time to get her parents to drive her to get the free photo ID. Astonishingly, the Democrats did not note the obvious absurdity that she found the time to get her parents to drive her to the airport and fly with her to Washington, spend a day in Washington, and fly back home. Since she was a Justice Department witness, taxpayers picked up the bill. One more thing: she needed an ID to get on a plane.

Argument #4. *There is no evidence of voter fraud; therefore, there is no need to secure elections with IDs.*

The *simple truth* is that a whole range of voter fraud cases has been documented in the well-researched book *Who's Counting?* by conservative journalist John Fund and former Bush Justice Department official Hans von Spakovsky. The authors disclosed a huge docket of electoral and voter fraud cases, many of which have been successfully prosecuted.

One case stands out as a poster child of the Democrat manipulation of election results. In the 2008 Minnesota Senate race, Republican Senator Norm Coleman was running for reelection against Democrat Al Franken. It was impossibly close; on the morning after the election, after 2.9 million people had voted, Coleman led Franken by 725 votes. Franken and his Democrat allies dispatched an army of lawyers to challenge the results. After the first recount, Coleman's lead was down to 206 votes. That was followed by months of wrangling and litigation. During the controversy a conservative group called Minnesota Majority began to look into claims of voter fraud. Comparing criminal records with voting rolls, the group identified 1,099 felons—all ineligible to vote—who had voted in the Franken-Coleman race. The state Democratic judiciary exhibited little interest in investigating potential voter fraud. After a number of recounts, Franken was declared the winner by 312 votes. He was sworn into office in July 2009, eight months after the election, and placed a decisive vote for Obamacare. As "the great democrat" Joseph Stalin used to say, "It's not important who votes; what's important is who counts the votes." The U.S. Supreme Court seemed to agree with "the great democrat" in its 2008 ruling upholding the voter ID law; it stated that *"flagrant examples of [voter] fraud...have been documented throughout this nation's history."*

Argument #5. *At a time when states are experiencing huge budget shortfalls, it would be an enormous waste to spend hundreds of millions of taxpayer dollars to disenfranchise voters.*

That one is laughable. This is the administration that wasted $862 billion on stimulus and billions more on Obamacare and alternatives energies; the administration that takes hundreds of millions or perhaps billions of dollars in bags to the governments of Afghanistan and Ukraine. It seems as if the administration has the money for all kinds of wasteful spending, but there is no money to ensure the integrity of the election process.

Given the ferocity of the Democrats' activism in defense of the indefensible, the false logic, and the enormous political capital and millions of dollars invested in this utterly made-up issue, one may be curious as to what is behind this no-ID nonsense.

The ancient Romans called it *cui prodest?* "Who stands to gain?" When it is not immediately apparent which political or social groups, forces, or alignments advocate certain proposals, measures, etc., one should always ask: "Who stands to gain?" I have a fact and I can offer a hint: *President Obama didn't win a single state in 2012 that required a photo ID to vote.* Could it be just a coincidence? Could it be that there are some other reasons for this phenomenon? Or perhaps the Supreme Court issued us a warning in 2008 that we choose to ignore.

They Are Ignorant. But They Vote.

The Americans who are still in a state of shock and disbelief over the election of Barack Hussein Obama would like to know the answer to this question: How did a man with no substantive experience at anything, and with no record of proven accomplishments in any field of endeavor, propel himself in so short a time into the position of president of the United States?

Obama sprang into prominence at the right time in history. American voters were well prepared for a socialist candidate and he skillfully exploited a favorable alignment of circumstances; lack of education and historical perspective, together with a proliferation of political illiteracy against the background of the impending economic crisis, created fertile ground for a talented demagogue to seduce the nation. "Ignorance is power" has replaced "Knowledge is power."

The 2008 elections were not just Barack Obama's personal achievement but also a historic victory for the progressive movement in this country. For the past fifty years, the progressives have been waging an all-out war against American institutions such as education, religion, and family values. Early on, they realized that there is no better way to subvert America than to have a degraded and broadly inferior education system. Unable to persuade contemporaries to accept their fanciful ideas, they conspired to steal new generations from their parents via education and indoctrination.

During 1930s, when communist influence in the United States was at its zenith, the whole generation of Americans called "Red Diaper" babies was brainwashed by Soviet propaganda and their cultivated offspring became contemporary adherents of socialism. Communists and former terrorists of the sixties who dreamed of overthrowing capitalism through violent revolution with old age became teachers and university professors making American schools, after the breakup of the Soviet Union, the largest concentration of Marxists in the world. Without even noticing it, we have submitted our youth to Marxist tutors, who distort U.S. history and shape young minds toward glory of socialism and animosity toward this country.

Their tireless efforts have paid off and are reflected in the dramatic transformation of American values during this period. They succeeded in centralizing and subsequently socializing American education. Not too many people realize that centralization and government control over the education system was originally the Bolsheviks' concept. The Russian Bolsheviks understood the importance of education and indoctrination on future generations. *"Give me four years to teach the children,"* Lenin said, *"and the seed I have sown will never be uprooted."*

In 1983, the Reagan administration published a report titled "A Nation at Risk: The Imperative of Education Reform." The report warned that the decay of American schools was becoming a threat to the very survival of the country. But the powerful amalgamation of teachers unions, state bureaucracies, and the Democrat establishment defeated the initiative.

Committed to preserving the status quo, this special interest group became the guardian of American education, maintaining complete control of the education curriculum and using its position to subvert innovation in education. No surprise, this group enjoys the systematic support of the Obama administration. Recently, the U.S. Justice Department sued the state of Louisiana to block a very successful school voucher program for students in public schools, an action effectively defending the substandard public school education system and pouring cold water on the efforts of other states, such as Indiana, New Hampshire, and Texas, to implement education reform.

The government's action should come as no surprise. For generations, the federal government has denied parents the option of choosing a school for their children. The following numbers tell us about the deplorable state of American education. Just over 100 years ago, in 1913, 2 out of every 10 adults, 20 percent, couldn't read or write and only 6 percent had graduated from high school. Today the average graduation rate is 75 percent, but 14 percent of adults can't read, according to the U.S. Department of Education. I think you get the picture.

Ironically, it was the Civil Rights movement of the 1960s that subverted the education system by offering equal opportunities in education and employment. As usual, the left confused equality of opportunity with equality of results. Integrated schools were supposed to provide quality education for all children regardless of color. In reality, there were large gaps between the education, behavior, and performance of white and black children. Instead of recognizing these differences, enforcing discipline, and providing black children with additional help and assistance, the schools geared their curricula and educational standards to the lowest common denominator. In doing so, they indeed did produce an equality of results: equality in illiteracy.

In stark contrast with the rest of the world, these newly integrated schools became factories of illiteracy, producing inferior students year after year. The rest of the world, particularly the Soviet Union and China, realized the supreme importance of education in modern economies, which were becoming more and more complex and knowledge intensive. The rise of China and the decline of the United States can be traced directly to the quality of education in each country.

Thinking about the significance of education, I recall my first day of school in the Soviet Union. The principle made it clear, in words no child would ever forget, the educational values she expected of seven-year-olds. *"Children,"* she said, *"No one will get out of here illiterate; those who want to learn, we will teach you; those who don't, we will force you."*

I still feel a chill down my spine every time I think of those words. This is not the place to make specific suggestions for improving the American education system or to suggest that we emulate the Soviet system, but you get the point. As concerned Americans we must recognize and understand that the system has been in decline for many years, producing a poorly educated electorate that gravely endangers our democracy. In order to become a U.S. citizen, a foreigner must demonstrate a basic level of civic knowledge. But if you are a U.S.-born citizen you need not be troubled with knowledge of your country's history, the Constitution, or even geography. According to a recently released Gallup-Harris poll, a full 37 percent of American citizens are incapable of identifying their home state on a map of the United States. And 22 percent think it is "a place to definitely explore when I finally get my passport." Some are proud that "America defeated Hitler during the Vietnam War in Iraq." They are so ignorant, it is frightening. But they vote.

As Americans in the midst of this "fait accompli," we can appreciate the Founding Fathers' apprehension about the American public, as expressed in statements from the Constitutional Convention of 1787. Here is one expressed by delegate Elbridge Gerry: "The people are uninformed, and would be misled by a few designing men." And another, by delegate George Mason: "The extent of the country renders it impossible that the people can have the requisite capacity to judge of the respective pretensions of the candidates." The apprehension of the delegates at the Constitutional Convention came to fruition and by 2008 the American electorate was well prepared for CHANGE.

The statistics produced by both the U.S. Department of Education and the United Nations demonstrate the deplorable state of American education. However this may be, the numbers themselves do not tell the full story. I have had firsthand experience with the American education system since the mid-1970s, when emigrants from the Soviet Union began sending their children to public schools. Children who were in the sixth and seventh grades in the USSR were tested and accepted, despite poor English, into the eighth and ninth grades, respectively. By the 1990s the situation was getting progressively worse. The story of one exchange student from Kazakhstan reveals the depth of the problem in very personal terms. The following is a true story.

The Power of Demagoguery and Lies, or How the Democrats Win

In 1995, I was working for an international engineering and construction company in Houston. We did a lot of work in Kazakhstan, one of the former Soviet republics. In the course of my work, I established a very good relationship with the Deputy Minister of Energy. His daughter, Irina, was a straight "A" student in Almaty, at the time the capital of Kazakhstan. She won the privilege of becoming an exchange student and was invited to spend a year in an American school. This was considered quite an honor. The girl had just finished ninth grade and was accepted to the tenth grade for the following school year.

She arrived in Wichita, Kansas, where she was met by an American family. She stayed in their home and was well taken care of. A few weeks later, her father called me, sounding desperate. "Alex," he said, "Irina was assigned to a class for mentally retarded kids. Please help me transfer her to a regular class. Please explain to them that she is a bright girl, she just has a poor command of English." It just happened that I was having lunch in my office. I lost glasses, a sandwich stuck in my throat, and spilled coffee made a small lake on my desk. I was ready to laugh and cry at the same time. I understood immediately what was going on. I should have warned the man about American schools, but he was so proud of his daughter being awarded a spot in the exchange program that I just couldn't bring myself to do it. "Boris," I said, "Irina is not in a class for mentally retarded students. That's just what a typical American class is like." He was shocked. "Alex," he pleaded, "You have to help me. She's a tenth-grader. What they are teaching her she learned in the sixth grade. When she comes back home she will never be able to graduate, not to mention be accepted in the university." Fortunately, my employer was originally headquartered in Kansas, and many executives had friends and relatives in Wichita. One of the company's executives knew a dean at Wichita University and asked him to intervene. After an interview, the girl was allowed to take courses at the university. The story has a happy ending. This young lady graduated with honors, got married, and today lives happily somewhere the United States.

However, there is no happy ending for the millions of American kids whose advances in education are measured by the tests supplied by the Department of Education. If anyone thinks that the situation has improved after the government has poured billions of dollars into public education since 1995, think again. This is another true story, from 2014. The following is an instruction given by a teacher to students at one of the finest private schools in Texas.

> *People, as you already know, you will have to take the SAT test. I know, I know, you think you've worked hard and you're ready for it. Wrong. In order to do well on the SAT, you have to dumb down; everything I've taught you does not apply. It is a test designed for morons. We do not teach you in this school to be idiots; therefore, you are woefully unprepared.*
> *Your smart analytical thinking skills DO NOT WORK!!! They will only confuse you. Remember, this test is not based on real-life logic, so don't think! The most obvious answer is the right one. For example, if a question says "What can you infer from the line "The teacher walked into class with her hair wet?" you may think, "Well, the answer is she just took a shower or the answer is she got caught in the rain," both of which are answer choices. You will be wrong. The answer is "Her hair is not dry." No, really. This is your answer. So for this test, forget those lovely analytical skills I've taught you! Forget those useful inference skills your elementary school teachers drilled into your heads! Basically, go for the most thoughtless, shallow, obvious answer and you will be fine.*

The question is whether we, as a nation, will be fine. If we are raising one of the dumbest electorates in the world today, how can we expect to make intelligent decisions about tomorrow?

Representation without Taxation

The slogan of the Boston Tea Party, the original Tea Party, was "No taxation without representation." At the time, Americans objected to being taxed and not having a say in their governance. Today we face a different and more subtle problem: "representation without taxation." Currently, about 50 percent of Americans do not pay income tax. It's been said that Americans are voting with their wallets, but the truth is that too many Americans are voting with other people's wallets. The Democratic Party has successfully corralled these voters with promises of a better life, free health care for all, better job benefits for workers, stronger unions, and a government passing the laws to pay for all of this out of the Treasury. In this case the representative democracy is making the government responsive to the will of an irresponsible majority. If those who fought with George Washington had known that they were fighting for this eventually ludicrous republic, I wonder if they would have supported the Continental Army against the British Crown.

Thomas Jefferson said, *"A democracy is nothing more than mob rule, where fifty-one percent of the people may take away the rights of the other forty-nine."* Jefferson's trepidation was shared by the other Founding Fathers, who rejected the concept of democracy and voted for a republic. Jefferson pointed out the problem facing modern America: we have more people voting for a living than we have people working for a living.

Within this context, a new era of the Republic is beginning to take shape. This era, reminiscent of the end of the Roman Empire, was the subject of a prophetic warning by Ben Franklin when he said, *"When the people find they can vote themselves money, that will herald the end of the republic."* Around the second and third century CE Roman citizens, who used to be proud warriors and independent producers, discovered democracy. Instead of capturing slaves and acquiring wealth through conquest and manufacturing goods, they endeavored political process and began to vote benefits to themselves. The politicians took full advantage of this trend and start buying elections, offering more and more benefits to the masses to the point that free food was handed out daily. The high point came in the year AD 274, when Emperor Aurelian declared that the right to government assistance was hereditary. The Roman Empire had become an ultimate welfare state that could not sustain itself and eventually and inevitably collapsed.

CHAPTER 12
"Forward" with Socialism

"[T]he worst advertisement for Socialism is its adherents." —George Orwell

The Second Coming of Barack Obama

In the words of Nikolai Bukharin, *"We asked for freedom of the press, thought, and civil liberties in the past because we were in the opposition and needed these liberties to conquer. Now that we have conquered, there is no longer any need for such civil liberties."*

The Second Coming of Barack Obama, or frightening narration of *Apprehension* [44] has been characterized by arrogant indifference for the rule of law and a massive assault on democratic institutions and individual liberties. The intellectual concept of truth has been challenged. Falsehood confronts reason, and intimidation replaces consensus. The aftermath of Obama's "refreshing new way of thinking about the role of democracy" is an immense transfer of power away from the democratically elected representatives of Congress to the executive branch, thereby increasing its power above and beyond constitutional limits and producing an extraordinary imbalance between power and legitimacy. The application of power based on dubious legitimacy is threatening the coherence of our society and signifies the "point of departure" from the democratic principles that made the United States a pinnacle of liberty. Power founded on

---

[44] *The three phases of socialism cited in Chapter 2: Euphoria, Apprehension, and Despair.*

principles is being replaced by principles founded on power. The series of recent scandals validates this notion as the administration is suppressing freedom, persecuting political opponents, spying on the American people, disrespecting the Constitution, and militantly disregarding the Congress, all combined within an authoritarian polity.

The abuse of power is so blatant that it feels as if we have gotten to the point reminiscent of an Orwellian future, with "a boot stamping on a human face—forever." The government does anything it pleases: it ignores congressional inquiries and suppresses dissent by the brute force of its agencies, including the power of the Justice Department to bring frivolous lawsuits and bankrupt its victims. A red blanket of tyranny is covering America. The people and businesses are beginning to fear the all-powerful government that is perfectly willing to deploy a full arsenal of state weaponry, such as FBI, IRS, EPA, DOJ (Department of Justice), DOE (Department of Energy) and its powerful FERC (Federal Energy Regulatory Commission), DHS (Department of Homeland Security), DOL (Department of Labor), and other assets we may or may not know about. However, Obama is not satisfied with the changes he brought to Washington. In a *60 Minutes* interview aired September 2012 he admitted, "*And, you know, if you ask me what's my biggest disappointment, [it] is that we haven't changed the tone in Washington as much as I would have liked.*" Since that interview he has made more changes to Washington, and for someone who came from a communist country, it feels as if I never left.

Speaking in July 2014 in Los Angeles, Obama, referring to American corporations using legal procedures to avoid excessive U.S. taxation through overseas mergers and acquisitions, passionately reaffirmed the Bolshevik's attitude on how he intended to "faithfully execute the law" when he declared, "I don't care if it's legal—it is wrong." Soviet leader Nikita Khrushchev used to say, "There are two opinions; one is mine and the other is wrong."

As this socialist government becomes more autocratic with time, we should expect abuse of power and lawlessness to become even more pronounced, further exacerbating the conflict between government bureaucracy and democracy. We can envision what will happen then by what is happening now. The following, is a small part of an unending list of government abuses that exemplifies and brings into focus Obama's *"vision in terms of where we are going."* This matter-of-fact illustration dramatizes the administration's cynicism as well as the paucity of wisdom of the American electorate.

- **Targeting of political opponents.** The administration used the IRS, FBI, OSHA, and other agencies of the government to target political opponents prior to the 2012 election. Questions are being raised why this occurred, who ordered it, whether there was any White House involvement.
- **Benghazi.** This is actually three scandals in one: the failure of the administration to protect the Benghazi mission; the changes made to the talking points in order to suggest that the attack was motivated by an anti-Muslim video; and the refusal of the White House to say what President Obama did to protect the consulate and his people during the attack.
- **Intimidation of the press.** The Justice Department performed a massive gathering of Associated Press reporters' phone records as part of a leaked investigation. Who can say now that the government doesn't listen to the people?
- **Rosengate.** The Justice Department lied to a federal judge, claiming that FOX News reporter James Rosen was a criminal, in order to get a warrant to monitor his phones and emails.
- **Potential Holder perjury I.** Attorney General Eric Holder told Congress he had never been associated with the "potential prosecution" of a journalist, when in fact he signed the affidavit that termed Rosen a potential criminal.
- **Potential Holder perjury II.** Holder told Congress in May 2011 that he had just recently heard about the Fast and Furious gun-walking scheme, when there is evidence he may have known about it much earlier.
- **The ATF "Fast and Furious" scheme.** Federal agencies allowed weapons from U.S. gun dealers to "walk" across the border into the hands of Mexican drug dealers. The ATF

summarily lost track of scores of those weapons, many of which were used in crimes, including the December 2010 killing of Border Patrol Agent Brian Terry.

Each of the above issues has national significance, and based on information available at this time, Obamacare and the Benghazi disaster are the most telling demonstrations of government abuse of power. They expose the depth of duplicity and the extent of falsehood and deception perpetrated by the administration.

Many of the hazards of Obamacare have been exposed in previous chapters; nevertheless, it is worthwhile to set forth its ideological character as a poster child for the perils of socialism. The enacted reforms clearly undermine the economic and political stability of our country. The administration, guided by ideology and rotten with incompetence and corruption, has produced economic and political turmoil, arguably on the scale of the Cultural Revolution in China or Khrushchev's Virgin Land Program in the Soviet Union. The first destroyed China's economy and the second deprived the USSR of grain. Just like the other socialist calamities, the Affordable Care Act will leave deep scars on the American economy and our way of life for years to come.

And, just like any other socialist creation, Obamacare is based on tyranny: the government used coercion to force the consumer to either do what government has defined as "the right thing" or face the consequences of state enforcement power. Obama's justification for enforcement is that "the right thing" serves the common good and, therefore, the consumer's freedom of choice and the grievances of the minority can be ignored. It is a familiar Marxist tune about sacrificing liberty for the common good that the President has been singing since his inauguration. The philosophy of doing "the right thing" at the expense of individual rights is not new; as stated earlier, it has been tried innumerable times, always with disastrous consequences.

To be sure, this time is no different. The product was well sold. The President wrapped his stinking merchandise up in an overabundance of promises so the public would not detect the socialist smell inside. It passed the Congress and was validated by the Supreme

Court, to become the Law of the Land. When it was unwrapped, Americans, who expected the scent of "a new car" and instead smelled the decaying odor of socialism, understood that it was "the Lie of the Land." Although humiliating to have fallen for it, this gigantic ruse was actually very instructive because of its homely boldness and primitiveness.

Has the President lied? Yes, he has. As delineated in previous chapters, there were lies, all lies, nothing but lies. The masses chose to believe the President's socialist nonsense. The voting herd of Democrats blindly followed the President the way ducklings follow a mother, the liberal media were elated about socialized health care, unions supported the legislation because they thought it would not affect them, insurance companies had been promised an additional 30 million policyholders and subsequent windfalls. It would be a mistake, however, to blame it on the "stupidity of American voters" devoured by the "intellectual preeminence" of Obama and his gofers, as the lead engineer of Obamacare, MIT Professor Jonathan Gruber and members of the liberal academia believe. The truth is that Obamacare is nothing short of the American version of the Bolsheviks' "land to peasants." The only difference is that unsophisticated Russian peasants called it a lie, while American supporters of Liberal Bolshevism elegantly called it "lack of transparency." In both instances it offered culprits "a huge political advantage"[45] and confirms what my father referred to as the enormous power of demagoguery and lies.

After three years and a billion dollars spent on developing the website, the program was not ready for prime time and its launch was a public relations disaster. The ultimate embarrassment was that the President had been consumed with depriving "we the people" of our voluntary decision to procure the product that meets our individual needs, instead forcing us to buy what we do not need. After an extraordinary disruption to the economy and people's lives, and after millions of people who lost their health insurance finally discovered that now they have no choice and they do need it, the system would not work anyway. As usual, for a while Obama denied his

---

[45] *Jonathan Gruber, "Lack of transparency is a huge political advantage."*

prior knowledge of the problems associated with the website. He insisted that nobody had told him about it. Finally, during a press conference, under relentless pressure from reporters, Obama claimed that nobody had told him about it "directly." Directly or indirectly informed, the President directly admitted that he did know about the problems with the website. Getting the truth from the President is like pulling teeth from an elephant.

The mystifying question is, if Obama knew that the introduction of the program was doomed to fail, then why did he fight the Republican proposal to delay it for a year? Why did he turn down the helping hand and let the country suffer the government shutdown and Republican filibuster when he was offered an easy and legal way out of his predicament? A month later it took a revolt from his fellow Democrats, terrified of voter backlash in 2014, to force him to delay some of the facets of the program that he had fought so hard not to delay.

As a Marxist-Leninist, Obama is driven by a rationale that is diametrically opposed to the Western mentality. Unlike Western thinking that endorses conflict avoidance through consensus and compromise, Obama, as stated earlier, believes that change is a product of conflict. Consequently, if there is no conflict, there is no victory—no real change. The ideology constantly drives him away from compromise to supremacy via grand pronouncements and confrontation. Most importantly, whether the website works or not doesn't fundamentally change the outcome of the assault on the American health care industry. The industry as we know it will cease to exist and eventually will be replaced with the socialist version, whether the site works or not. Given the "historical inevitability," Obama was committed to go FORWARD regardless of risks and sacrifices.

The Benghazi affair is the apogee of cynicism and total disregard for the truth. President Obama, former Secretary of State Hillary Clinton, and other top administration officials willfully and deliberately perpetrated a false story to the American public. The Benghazi cover-up was motivated by the looming election, but it has the feel of the Watergate cover-up, with Iran-Contra undertones. There are troubling similarities between the Iran-Contra affair, which took place during the Reagan administration, and the Benghazi disaster, which happened on Obama's watch.

For those of you too young to remember, the Iran-Contra scandal in the Reagan administration involved selling weapons to Iran in exchange for Iranian assistance in releasing the American hostages taken by Hezbollah in Lebanon. The proceeds from the sale were used to provide arms to the Nicaraguan Contras (rebel groups fighting the Sandinista communist government in Nicaragua). The Democrats accused the President of paying ransom to kidnappers in violation of the U.S. policy of not negotiating with terrorists and of the Boland Amendment, which forbade the U.S. government to provide military assistance to the Contras. The Democrats were having a field day trying to impeach the President for seeking release of the Americans and assisting the anti-communist movement in Nicaragua. After multiple congressional inquiries and seven years of investigation by a special prosecutor, Judge Lawrence Walsh, no evidence was presented that would implicate President Reagan in diverting funds, ordering the cover operations, or even having knowledge of any of it. Though it was understood in the White House that the President was taking the release of the hostages very personally. During a December 7, 1985 meeting in the Oval Office, Reagan expressed this sentiment: "The American people will never forgive me if I fail to get these hostages out over this legal question." Reagan, in his determination or even obsession in pursuing that objective, may have inadvertently violated certain laws and statutes, but his purpose was noble.

In sharp contrast, one president was prepared to risk jail or impeachment in order to save American hostages, the other did not lift a finger to save Americans who were courageously defending the Benghazi compound against overwhelming terrorist forces. Obama went to bed that night in Las Vegas, where he had attended a campaign fund-raiser, knowing full well the compound was under assault and that Americans were dying.

One president went to extraordinary lengths to save the lives and secure the freedom of two Americans, the other Commander in Chief and his Secretary of State both grossly neglected their fiduciary duties, which resulted in four Americans dead and a number of others wounded.

At this juncture, the press and Congress could have stepped forward and demanded truth and accountability. The facts of these cases should have been laid out on front pages all over the country, but instead the mainstream media, with the notable exception of FOX News, chose to genuflect to the notion that this president who is "sort of God" could do pretty much whatever he wanted, with an arrogant sense of impunity. In this new moral order, as Bukharin said, *"there is no longer any need for such civil liberties."*

Bob Woodward, in the Introduction to his book *Shadow*, wrote of the impact of the Nixon presidency on the future of our democracy. "Congress…was determined to play a more prominent inquisitorial role. The media was going to dig deep and incessantly because much was hidden before. And quite naturally prosecutors and ethics investigators were more and more determined. The habit of deception and hedging practiced by presidents would no longer be acceptable." Yes, most of us at the time wanted to believe President Ford, that "our long national nightmare" was over, but it was only the beginning. Watergate looks like child's play in comparison to any one of the above scandals.

In a brazen display of the coalescence of tyranny and lawfulness, Congress, controlled by the President's party, became an accessory to the presidential misconduct and blocked investigations into alleged financial, ethical, and criminal violations by the President and members of his administration. The ideologically driven prosecutors would not bring criminal charges for the most evident and outrageous violations of the law. The press suppressed institutional memory and voluntarily abrogated its First Amendment responsibility. A sense of impunity has been acquired by the Democrats in the House and Senate and in the executive branch. The exultant desperadoes are acting like a cartel rather than a political party, consistently supporting the President's actions and non-actions and ferociously defending the cover-ups.

The President responds in a manner of reciprocal obligation. Every time a new allegation of government wrongdoing comes to light, the President confines himself to partisan political speeches and expressing verbal indignation, but taking no action against the alleged perpetrators.

At the same time, Obama himself maintains implausible deniability; he was not aware of impending problems because nobody reported to him about the abuses and criminal misconduct in his government. We have been witnessing the familiar pattern: "The President is frustrated and nobody wants to get to the bottom of this [whatever it is] more than the President," but the President cannot be responsible for something he did not know about. In criminal law it is called "willful blindness," a term used to define the acts of a person who intentionally fails to be informed about matters that would make the person criminally liable. Over and over again, Obama is the man who "was not there."

> *Yesterday upon the stair*
> *I met a man who wasn't there.*
> *He wasn't there again today;*
> *Oh, how I wish he'd go away!*
> —Hughes Mearns

In May 1987, Laurence Tribe, a liberal Harvard law professor and expert on constitutional law, published an article in the *New York Times* providing the legal basis for the Democrats to prosecute President Reagan. He said that in the Iran-Contra affair the President had failed in his constitutional duty to "take care that the laws are faithfully executed." Tribe wrote,

> *In other words, if the puppets are subject to the law and violated it, the puppet master cannot escape accountability.*

Better words could not be spoken about President Barack Hussein Obama.

Irreconcilable Ideological Demarcation

The years of the Obama administration were like living on a volcano. The country went from one crisis to another. The skyrocketing deficit, health care reform, immigration policy, Social Security, and environmental regulations were just a few of the issues on which the Democrats and Republicans were far apart. Americans have been suffering a catastrophic loss of trust in their government, democratic institutions, and the President. In September 2011, Obama said he hoped

> *in the midst of a crisis like this that we could pull America together to move forcefully on behalf of the American Dream and on behalf of all those who aspire for something better for their kids. And what has been clear over the last two and a half years is that we have not had a willing partner.*

Apparently, more than half of the country does not share the President's peculiar vision of the American Dream.

After experiencing years of infighting, not the least of which were the government shutdowns over the debt limit and Obamacare, Americans might be likely to name dysfunctional government as the most important problem facing this country. Yet Americans don't seem to be able to identify the major cause of this dysfunction. Some think it is the Tea Party, some blame Republicans in general or Democrats or both, some blame the President. Americans continue to emphasize the obvious over the important. The obvious is the inability of Republicans, Democrats, and the President to come together and solve the nation's problems. The important, once again overlooked, is that the current brinkmanship is another chapter in the epic struggle between socialism and freedom.

President Thomas Jefferson declared in his inaugural address that *"we are all Republicans, we are all Federalists."* Many years later another president reconfirmed the sentiment. In his State of the Union address in January 1989, President Reagan said, *"Yes, we will have our differences. But let us always remember: what unites us far outweighs whatever divides us."*

The point both presidents were making was that we are all Americans and we all share the same ideals and aspirations: self-reliance, belief in a free-market economy, and commitment to the democratic process. Nixon summarized it best in reference to John F. Kennedy, "We agreed on our goals but we disagreed on the means." It was the key reason that previous administrations, Democrat and Republican alike, despite ideological differences over a wide spectrum of issues, including the role of government and a variety of social concerns, could work out their disagreements and get important legislation passed.

The current political environment, however, is fundamentally different. The rise of left radicalism that culminated with the election of a Marxist socialist government, which is taking control over the economy, proliferating the welfare state, and fostering replacement of self-reliance with dependence, led to the emergence of the Right radicalism that is committed to the preservation of the Constitution and the capitalist free-market economy. The radicalism on both sides became too intense, and as a result the ideological Great Divide became impossible to bridge. "The bonds of affection" Abraham Lincoln talked about in his inaugural address were broken. Any attempt to negotiate a settlement between Democrats and Republicans is doomed from the start because they are pursuing diametrically opposed visions of America. Republicans and Democrats are not just disagreeing on the means; they are disagreeing on the goals.

This is a struggle directed from two bitterly opposed and ideologically hostile, irreconcilable camps. Both sides are consumed by excess expectation. The administration's excess expectation runs on the conviction that the new order can be imposed without general consensus, through a combination of brute force and ideological assault. The Republican opposition's excess expectation assumes that standing on ideological principles may stop an avalanche of carefully mascaraed populist legislations. One side is frantically trying to preserve the old political reality and the other is aggressively fighting to replace it with a new order.

The government is not dysfunctional; the separation of powers embodied in the Constitution ensures permanent conflict as a guarantee of freedom. Therefore, it functions as should be expected in these desperate hours of a highly polarized environment.

Impending Catastrophe and How to Avoid It

Abraham Lincoln cautioned that *"America will never be destroyed from the outside. If we falter and lose freedoms, it will be because we destroyed ourselves."* The lessons of the 2012 presidential election must have left their imprint on the strategic thinking of the leaders of the Republican Party. The Obama victory could not be explained by conventional thinking. How was it possible that despite a dismal economy, high unemployment, soaring gas prices, staggering debt, millions on food stamps, unpopular health care legislation, and a host of international debacles, the President was reelected? Furthermore, Republicans, for the second election in a row, fell short in their efforts to win control of the Senate, a goal that seemed within reach. Republican strategic analysis thus far has been limited to a flood of excuses and finger-pointing, such as the following:

"Democrats cheated!"
"Obama spent millions on vicious attack ads!"
"It was Romney's '47 percent' remark!"
"Conservative 'purists' stayed home!"
"It is all the fault of social conservatives!"
"It is all demographic!"
"Obama lied!"
"It was the liberal press!"
"Hurricane Sandy upset the campaign's momentum!"

I am not going to list the whole gamut of excuses. Even a list three times as long would not explain such a devastating defeat. Traditionally, given the state of the economy and the country, a solid candidate like Romney should have been at least ten points ahead, but according to public opinion polls he was behind during the entire election cycle, with the exception of one brief period when he was slightly ahead. Hence, his loss should not be surprising at all.

Republicans made two strategic errors during the last election. First, where the Republicans and supporters of capitalism were wrong during the last century was in thinking that most people like to work. Conventional wisdom was that in order to be reelected, the

President needed to get the economy going and reduce unemployment, but his anti-capitalist agenda was in conflict with the laws of economics. Obama's unrestrained spending, high taxation, and government regulation of industry and financial services effectively impeded any significant expansion of the economy. Therefore, emphasis on the economy looked like a safe bet.

Second, the Republicans made a fundamental error of judgment; they used common sense. As discussed earlier, the President is not governed by conventional wisdom. To understand him, one has to get into the mind of a Marxist. On the surface, the President was facing the awkward task of reconciling the irreconcilable, but the political gurus underestimated the Liberal Bolshevik's sinister nature. Although the economy was not in any danger of improving, the President did not need a good economy to get reelected; all he needed were good economic numbers. Since his administration was producing the numbers, and oftentimes the numbers were adjusted in subsequent reports, this political high-wire act was not a "mission impossible." As a matter of record, in my book *Anatomy of a Bolshevik*, published before the 2012 election, I predicted that the unemployment numbers would be falsified before the election. Since Romney based his entire election strategy on the unemployment rate, he effectively set himself up for defeat. The cornerstone of Obama's reelection strategy was not an improved economy but increased dependence. A bad economy justifies the expansion of entitlements and the proliferation of dependence.

The President's strategy was to get reelected, not in spite of the bad economy, but because of it.

The President skillfully used the ongoing economic crisis to shore up his base. The Republicans' folly in not recognizing Obama's reelection strategy can hardly be overstated. Obama was taking a page from FDR's playbook and Lenin's teachings. FDR successfully exploited economic difficulties to appoint himself president for life. His formula of tax, spend (buy votes), and get elected proved to be unbeatable. Democrats controlled the House for sixty years, and there is a good chance that if they regain control of the

House, they will keep it for another seventy (the life span of socialism). There is one not-so-subtle difference, however: FDR's America was a country of predominantly self-sufficient individuals who were not accustomed to, and did not live off of, government handouts. Hence, at the end of FDR's tenure, America was ready and willing to go back to free markets and could easily have abandoned the idea of "regulated" capitalism that FDR introduced.

As discussed earlier, about 50 percent of Americans today don't pay any income tax, and millions receive welfare checks, food stamps, and other forms of government assistance. Obama needs to increase this number by only a few percentage points to put this country in an irreversible decline. Expanding government programs such as welfare, food stamps, free health care, and student loan forgiveness do just that. Obama's task is quite easier than FDR's. Exploiting the economic crisis served the President's reelection strategy and will serve the Democrats in the future.

Over the years the Democrats have built an army of supporters and a diversified arsenal of election weaponry. The millions of Americans who depend on the government one way or another are Obama's army. Candidly, in this zero-sum game, the Republicans appear to have been asleep at the wheel!

Government employees are one of the many divisions of Obama's army. Obama greatly expanded this part of his army in the years prior to the 2012 election and increased their pay scale. Nearly 3 million Americans, roughly 2 percent of the U.S. labor force, are employed in more than 800 occupations for more than 100 federal government agencies! An additional 5 million Americans work for state governments, and 14 million are employed by local governments. That's a total of 22 million Americans—14 percent of the labor force—employed by governments at the local, state, and federal levels. Let's not forget the elderly. As many as 61 million Americans collect Social Security and Supplementary Security Income (SSI) payments. Most of these people don't care about Social Security going broke; it has been going broke for decades. They just want to get their checks and feel comfortable that there will be enough Social Security for their lifetimes. Any talk about prospective changes, modifications, or improvements raises their anxiety. No surprise that most of them voted for the status quo.

These strategic advantages for the Democrats were augmented by the most destructive weapons in Obama's arsenal—demagoguery and lies. In this context I would like to offer this clipped-tail history lesson.

The leader of the Bolshevik opposition, distinguished admiral Alexander Kolchak[46], was defeated on the battlefield, betrayed by the Allies and captured by the Bolsheviks. During interrogation, the Bolsheviks were trying to understand how they could defeat the well-supplied regular army, led by experienced military commanders. They asked him, "Admiral, why didn't you promise land to peasants? You could have won this war." (Russia was an agrarian country and the ownership of land was one of the most compelling issues of the revolution.) "I would not promise what I could not deliver" was the admiral's response. The interrogators smiled. Lenin, who characterized the civil war as "We have only one controversial issue—land: who buries whom," did promise "land to the peasants" and buried the opposition, literally.

Obama's campaign was about burying the opposition. Whereas Obama was working hard offering people a dole, Governor Romney found himself in Admiral Kolchak's predicament—he was threatening them with jobs. While Obama and the Democrats created the environment where having employment was not a prerequisite for making a living, Romney was talking about the high rate of unemployment. But who cared? Many Americans, just like the citizens of Rome, were happy to substitute guaranteed "bread and circuses" for gainful employment. I am not sure about circuses—perhaps political—but bread and freebies were certainly plentiful. As my late father said, demagoguery and lies "move nations," and this nation most certainly was no exception.

---

[46] *Alexander Vasilyevich Kolchak (November 4, 1874–February 7, 1920) was a polar explorer, admiral, and commander of the Imperial Russian Navy. He established the anti-Bolshevik Provisional All-Russian Government in Siberia and was recognized as the "Supreme Ruler and Commander-in-Chief of All Russian Land and Sea Forces" by the other leaders of the White movement (1918–1920). He was executed by firing squad on February 7, 1920 in Irkutsk, Siberia.*

More to the point, the President offered a very powerful contemptuous anti-capitalist message to the country: while millions of people suffered, the millionaires and billionaires were enjoying lower tax rates, pocketing "money they do not need." Since Obama had already decided for them what they needed, as the rationale went, we should invest more money in entitlements and solar energy.

Moreover, while advancing FORWARD, Democrats argued that high unemployment was George Bush's fault, not Obama's. And the Republicans wanted to cut the duration of unemployment benefits and make millions of Americans suffer. And the Republicans would reform entitlements and deprive grandma of Medicare and poor children of food stamps. And finally, the Republicans would make everybody pay some income tax (raise taxes) while preserving low taxes for the rich.

These were some of the reasons compelling those who enjoyed "representation without taxation" to reelect Comrade Obama. This segment of the population was happy to have Obama make those of us "who are unequally rich equally poor," as FOX News political analyst Brit Hume put it. The political landscape was definitely shifting in favor of socialism.

Anyone who hoped that CNN would be "keeping them honest" was greatly disappointed. The mainstream media, whose opposition to the Republicans is a permanent part of the current political landscape, took pride in unmercifully attacking a honorable man who genuinely dissented from the President's views and policies.

What was disturbingly appalling was that Mitt Romney was not attacked for his shortcomings or vices; he was venomously attacked for his virtues and his success. The success was portrayed as immoral and the virtues as dishonorable. The liberal press adeptly moved the political discourse from debating policies to recycling the smears, demagoguery, and distortions brought on by the Democrats, with no sense of proportion, just as Lenin taught:

> *The press should be not only a collective propagandist and a collective agitator, but also a collective organizer of the masses.*

And the American press during the last election season was well prepared to carry out Lenin's directive. No lie was too big to tell, no promise too outrageous to promote. The press did not find it distasteful to replace the ancient Roman tenet *"Asserted without proof shall be denied without proof"* with Lenin's rule, *"A lie told often enough becomes the truth."*

The election of Barack Obama in 2008 manifested the arrival of a new world, economically and politically. The reelection of the President in 2012 confirmed that the threat of socialism has become a dark reality in the United States of America. The Republican Party and the public at large, suffering from lack of knowledge and the intellectual weaponry to confront socialism, appear to be in denial about the social and political tsunami that is already beginning to engulf them.

Strategy for 2016

The Republicans must be mindful that Bolsheviks do not relinquish power voluntarily, as Lenin proclaimed after the victory of the October Revolution: *"We are taking power, and we are taking it for a long time."* Although Lenin did not say "forever," it still took the collapse of socialism in the Soviet Union to force the Bolsheviks out of power. In recognition of this historical premise and the "copycat" approach employed thus far, we should not expect Obama to leave the presidency quietly. *If in 2008 Obama sought power to make "fundamental change," in 2016 he will seek "fundamental change" to keep the power.* The President will make a determined effort to come up with an arrangement that will ensure his access to power and policy making after the 2016 election, should the Democrats win. As the Democrats are gearing up for the 2016 elections, most political pundits aver it a forgone conclusion that Hillary Clinton, with the support of Barack Obama, has effectively secured her nomination.

As with many instances in the political process, however, what is perceived as obvious and assured at the time only exposes the limitations of human foresight. There is no evidence that Obama ever considered Hillary to be his successor. If that were the case, he would have asked her to be his running mate in 2008 or 2012. The vice presidency offers a high-visibility, low-risk reward, and the vice president is seen as a natural successor to the sitting president and can count on the support of his own party. Instead, Hillary received the high-risk position of secretary of state, a post that can be easily undermined by the President and, for a person inexperienced in foreign affairs, such as Hillary, carries a host of potential liabilities. Being assigned to a position of responsibility and authority above the level of her competence, she became an actor in a play written by Barack Obama. Effectively programmed to fail, she did not disappoint her master.

Although during her tenure she schlepped almost the entire world, visiting 112 countries and running up a million frequent-flyer miles, she has nothing to show for it. The infamous, childish "reset button" with the Russians, which Russian Foreign Minister Sergey Lavrov most likely dumped in the first trash can he came to; the series of political calamities in the Middle East culminating in the all but complete collapse of the U.S. international position: hardly a track record to be proud of. Being an unaccomplished secretary of state makes her extremely vulnerable to challenges within her own party, not to mention those from Republican opponents.

The Clintons obviously are not aware of the Bolsheviks' motto: "A forgiven enemy never becomes your friend." Obama's feeling toward Bill Clinton is a combination of awe and envy. Awe because of what Bill Clinton is and envy because of everything Barack Obama is not. As the most respected Democrat, one who enjoys popularity even outside the Democrat universe, Bill Clinton challenges Barack Obama's dominance. As stated earlier, Marxists are monopolists of power and there is no room for two Führers in the Marxist Brotherhood. The White House has compiled a sizeable file of incriminating information on Hillary—the private server, the Clinton Foundation, and the most troublesome, the Benghazi tragedy—as they have been coming to light, like drops of water on a stone, slowly eroding her standing with the electorate and projecting the sense of imminent rendezvous with disaster.

Benghazi is Hillary's Chappaquiddick. Just like Senator Edward Kennedy, who cowardly fled the scene of an accident he caused and failed to organize a rescue that might have saved Mary Jo Kopechne's life, which in consequence cost him the White House, Hillary left the Benghazi consulate unprotected and cowardly failed to provide rescue during the attack that cost four American lives, also ruining her chances for the presidency. As Chappaquiddick was for Kennedy, Benghazi is a gruesome testament of another liberal Democrat's lack of character, integrity, competence, and leadership.

So, if not Hillary, then who? I do not know who, but I venture to offer a conjecture.

There is no one else in the Democrat universe that has Barack Obama's stature and theoretical acumen to lead the country through the transition to the socialist paradise Therefore, power of reasoning and political logic indicate that the easiest and most reliable approach is for Michelle Obama to run. The self-assured, energetic, articulate, and unmistakably ambitious first lady would be a formidable opponent to any Republican nominee. Her qualifications are just as "solid" as Hillary's when she ran in 2008. Both women are lawyers and the wives of former (or to-be-former) presidents. The Democrats will be ecstatic about Michelle, who will not only ensure the transition to socialism, she will also be the first woman president—and she is black. But above all, she is an Obama!!! Who could be a better candidate for the Democratic Party? Why would the Democrats buy a generic when they can have the brand? Michelle will enjoy the support of Obama's army of Democrats, augmented by the even greater number of those who enjoy representation without taxation, plus more women and feminists. Michelle's frequent denials about a potential presidential run shall not be taken too seriously because she is not the one making this decision.

The changing 2014 post-election political landscape represents interesting political dynamics for the President and his party. The ideological bond, the blind devotion to a leader, the superhero, a person of unlimited ability, strength, and charisma, who is according to Evan Thomas a "sort of God," contains the seeds of its own destruction. As I pointed out earlier, Obama's strategy is based on permanent confrontation, which in the long run inevitably reveals its fatal flaw—unsustainability. In a free, democratic society that cherishes pluralism and tolerance, confrontation cannot be sustained indefinitely.

The 2014 midterm congressional election is a case in point. As the electorate becomes tired of partisan speeches and political cleverness that proved ineffective at forging positive transformations of the society, the God loses his charm, and his confrontational attitude becomes too precarious for the public at large. While Obama is losing touch with the emerging legislatorial reality and grows more and more isolated, the voting herd is losing its shepherd and, with him, it is losing internal cohesion, forcing each sheep to fight for its own political survival. At this stage the herd is the most vulnerable and for the sake of self-preservation may be willing to temporarily support Republican initiatives as a tactical necessity and as long as they do not challenge established socialist programs.

Although the political landscape seems to be shifting away from socialization and support for social engineering is dwindling, none of it, including the recent shellacking, seems to have diminished the President's determination or shaken his convictions. Even in the instant of his greatest weakness, Obama remains defiant. He knows that he is right; he knows that his seductive ideas are popular with the two-thirds of people who did not vote. (In Russia in 1917 only 10 percent of the population supported the Bolsheviks.) He knows that despite maneuvering for a tactical advantage he and his democratic socialists are engaged in a common enterprise and share a mutual antagonism of capitalism. He knows that the elections have in no way changed his Party's social democrat vision for America. And finally, Obama knows, and his minions know, that even without congressional support the President still enjoys the elements of power that he can use to advance his policies FORWARD.

Having been unable to complete his fundamental transformation by subterfuge, however, the President is desperately running out of time. At this juncture Obama is being forced to recognize that imperatives of egalitarianism and impetus to translate socialist achievements into permanent components of American life must override any pretense of legitimacy. Consequently, he decided to enforce the CHANGE by a series of executive orders exacerbating the already growing conflict between power and legitimacy. From now on there is no room for ambivalence—socialism has to be enforced and nothing should prevent Obama from the fulfillment of his messianic vision.

At this writing, the 2016 presidential election campaign is in process and the brinkmanship presents the Democrats with a radical reinvention of American values and democratic traditions. It also makes them vulnerable to an ideological challenge during the election cycle that they are hardly prepared to accept: if the Democrats do not condemn the illegal usurpation of power that belongs to Congress, they become de facto co-conspirators in subverting constitutional principles of separation of power. On the other hand, after the years of consistently supporting the President's policies, the Democratic Party cannot challenge the President unless it first reexamines its internal doctrine and redefines itself from Obama's "what your country can do for you" back to JFK's "what you can do for your country." How the Party synthesizes this intractable dilemma between political necessities and possibilities will be driven in large part by the presidential elections. Thus far it does not look as if the Democrats are going to abandon socialism. The Democratic candidates firmly adopted a socialist platform and are competing by mowing further and further to the left—until there will be no more left to the left.

The Republicans' Road to Calvary

The Republicans have a daunting challenge of their own. They must offer programs protecting individual liberty while preserving the social and economic advancements. They have to expose the Democrats' objectives and offer superior rationality. And Republicans have to understand this fact of historical record: socialism cannot be defeated; it self-destructs. Therefore, only socialism can defeat socialism—if the Republicans just let it happen. But until recently the Republicans, intoxicated by their 2010 and 2014 midterm election victories, have been drifting down a path of miscalculations and political failures. As a consequence they have too often found themselves in a position called Zugzwang in chess. This is a situation in which a player has to make a move, but any possible move will worsen his position. And when the House Republicans have moved, too often they have chosen the Alamo-like strategy of standing on principle and being destroyed when they would have been better suited, given the political landscape, to choose the ancient Greek strategy of "live to fight another day."

Right and wrong in politics cannot be judged in abstraction apart from the underlying circumstances. Those who are prone by temperament and character to stand up on high principles and be ready to accept inevitable destruction are not always right, and those who seek patiently and faithfully the amicable resolution of a conflict at the cost of some principles are not always wrong. The winds of politics are changing unpredictably and those who could wait, in many instances over time, have been proven right.

While waiting for the winds to change, the Republican Party needs to engage in ideological soul-searching. Conservatism, the prevailing ideology of the Republican Party, began losing ground with the introduction of "compassionate conservatism," which surreptitiously assimilated the tenets of liberalism.

In case some are confused about the collocation of conservatism and compassion, George W. Bush in his preface to the book by "the godfather of compassionate conservatism," Marvin Olasky, *Compassionate Conservatism: What it is, What it does, and How it Can Transform America*," defined Olasky's ideological discovery as "*Conservatism must be a creed of hope,*" where <u>government</u> [emphasis mine] "*acts as a clearinghouse and catalyst for the natural compassion that is a hallmark of the American people...the creed that promotes social progress through individual change.*"

This subtle attempt of balancing elements of social liberalism with conservatism achieved neither ideological legitimacy nor moral supremacy. Failing to produce a record of sustainable accomplishments, conservatism suffered a series of devastating electoral defeats in 2008 and 2012, when the traditional conservative principles and values of limited government, self-reliance, and individual liberty were rejected. Oddly enough, they were rejected first and foremost by the Republican Party, which got lost in conflicting temptations and nominated a de facto Democrat in 2008 and a pseudo conservative–moderate Republican in 2012. During the 2012 campaign Republicans viciously attacked capitalism by calling

Mitt Romney a "vulture" capitalist, corroborating Obama's socialist arguments against capitalism. Moreover, in the course of the 2012 campaign the gold standard of ideological purity, *The National Review*, denounced Newt Gingrich, an effective candidate with a flawless conservative record and impressive accomplishments, as too radical and threw its considerable weight behind Mitt Romney. But the lesson of ideological inconsistency was not learned. During the current election cycle *The National Review* savagely attacked Donald Trump for not being "truly conservative." Go figure.

The 2016 elections offer Republicans an opportunity to avoid prior mistakes and develop a new operating strategy. This new strategy must derive from the recognition that almost half of the country is addicted to socialist programs; thus conservative orthodoxy would hardly be an effective vehicle to economic and fiscal sanity. In this ideologically polarized environment the Republicans must ask, Is there a necessary correlation between ideology and the strategy toward which it is directed? Or, better yet, to rephrase Henry Kissinger's famous maxim: *"While the conservatives should never give up their principles, they must also realize that they cannot implement their principles unless they win."*

Only time can tell whether a nascent ideological evolution emanating from the election campaign is sufficient to bridge the current sociopolitical divide.

In regard to the Democratic Party, as the midterm elections demonstrated, the Republicans do not have to wait too long. Obama and his party are not in a strong position. After years of Keynesian economics the economy is struggling, and good economic numbers produced by the Administration are no substitute for a good economy. There is no light at the end of this tunnel; the deficit is going into the stratosphere, and "affordable" health care is having a rendezvous with disaster. The country is deeply divided over race, income, and most domestic issues: religious freedom, the Second Amendment, domestic terrorism, emigration, and abortion. While the American house has been divided, our alliances have weakened, our friends have become ambivalent, our enemies emboldened.

If in the field of domestic policy Obama had a script to follow, there is no guidance in Marxism-Leninism for managing foreign policy. Since foreign affairs became more prevalent in his second term, the perception of a weak presidency by our adversaries led to further challenges. The inexperienced president with a limited outlook on the world scene and his amateur State Department bureaucracy, unable to distinguish between the desirable and the achievable, let alone decide what is desirable, caused the total collapse of America's position and prestige in the world.

The dominant political fact is that in this competition of ideas for the future of America, the Democrats have nothing to offer but unemployment, food stamps, Obama phones, alleged racism, and more welfare. They have no new ideas, and no record of accomplishments. Obama's vision for the future is "equality in poverty." The President exhibits authoritarianism, and his administration is soaked in corruption and serious scandals that threaten the nucleus of our republic.

After years of relentless lying to the American people in order to conceal the administration's offenses and misconduct, the truth finally caught up with Barack Obama. By consistently and profoundly violating the trust of the American people in deceiving them about the benefits of Obamacare, the President exposed himself and effectively destroyed his party's credibility. Obamacare was "the straw that broke the camel's back." In addition, revelation of the series of scandals and subsequent cover-ups placed Obama in the humiliating position of being forced to shield criminal activities, putting the Democratic Party on the defensive.

Obama's credibility shattered, he is no longer innocent until proven guilty; he is now guilty until proven innocent. *The truth in politics is not what can be proven, it's what cannot be avoided.* Hence, there is no need to spend energy and resources in searching for evidence of wrongdoing by the President and his administration; the cover-ups and inadequate responses to congressional inquiries are the evidence. Republicans just have to make sure, during the 2016 elections, that the American people do not forget about Obamacare, Benghazi, "Fast and Furious," numerous perjuries by government officials, and other offenses. The President is weak and the Republicans just have to let this drama play itself out, adopting Napoleon's credo, *"Never interfere with an enemy while he's in the process of destroying himself."*

Ultimately, the administration and the Democratic Congress provide Republicans with ample opportunities for the upcoming presidential elections if the Republicans choose to fight on philosophical grounds. In this unfolding American drama, however, Republicans, blindfolded by implacable hostility toward Obama's agenda, have failed to comprehend his ambitions, objectives, and methods of operation. Reluctant participants in the perpetual contest of wills, they are preoccupied with tactics, trying to capitalize on individual issues and spending all of their energy and political capital attacking Obamacare, global warming, the bad economy, etc., and have failed thus far to make intellectual adjustments to stop America's descent into socialism. As Lord Salisbury stated, *"The commonest error in politics is sticking to the carcass of dead policies."*

CHAPTER 13

¡No Pasaran!

"A democracy is always temporary in nature; it simply cannot exist as a permanent form of government. A democracy will continue to exist up until the time that voters discover that they can vote themselves generous gifts from the public treasury. From that moment on, the majority always votes for the candidates who promise the most benefits from the public treasury, with the result that every democracy will finally collapse due to loose fiscal policy, which is always followed by a dictatorship"
—Alexander Tyler[47]

Bolsheviks Are at the Gates

While walking among some Greek and Roman ruins with my daughter, I experienced a mixture of melancholy and deep anxiety. Melancholy because we, all of us—the entire human race—should be grateful to the Greeks and Romans for their contributions to our culture, language, science, and philosophy, which became the basis of our civilization. Anxiety because of the inescapable parallels between those ancient democracies, which created and nurtured their own demise, and our contemporary American society. The downfall of the Greek and Roman civilizations was caused by their

---

[47] *Scottish history professor Alexander Tyler wrote these words in 1787, around the time our country was founded.*

leaders' greed and the voting citizens' lack of responsibility. The old adage that "those who do not learn from history are bound to repeat it" applies to our country in spades.

Contrary to universal acumen, the presidency of the United States was not the final destination of Obama's political journey; it was a ticket to his final destination—the egalitarian dream. America has tasted only half a bottle of the envenomed drink called "Ism"; it has not felt the full lash of Marxism, but it has been given a foretaste of what is yet to come.

Alarmingly, Barack Obama is coming within measurable distance of accomplishing the centerpiece of his presidency. The aspirations of the Bolshevik Revolution are being reincarnated in Vermont and exported to New York and California, as the country has become inured to the world of radicalism. The most obvious sign is the rise of the socialist movement, especially among young people, within the Democratic Party, which opened a door to populist demands that no future administration will be able to sustain. The seeds of Marxism have successfully sprouted.

Obama has every reason to be triumphant. He sees himself as a political genius whose talent far exceeds that of his ideological forefathers, Lenin, Stalin, and Mao, who saw the horizon of communism and murdered tens of millions on their way to the egalitarian paradise only to discover that it was indeed a horizon—an imaginary line that gets further as one gets closer, and therefore beyond their reach. Obama is getting there without firing a single shot, making these men historical pygmies. He dreams of his name written in the history books and, unlike his infamous predecessors, it will not be written in blood. He will be remembered and admired for a thousand generations, like Jesus Christ, Julius Caesar, Alexander the Great, and Napoleon Bonaparte. In the country's history, there will always be Before Obama and After Obama. This is the lasting legacy Barack Hussein Obama hopes to leave behind.

But not everything is going as planned; Obama's reach exceeded his grasp—he and his democratic socialists had grossly underestimated the U.S. economic vitality. The U.S. economy, although struggling, can endure even a $20 trillion deficit for a while; the massive money printing has not produced hyperinflation yet, and the dollar is somehow still relatively strong. The energy industry, with the discovery of new domestic oil reserves and deployment of innovative technologies, is thriving despite draconian environmental regulations; the financial sector has proved to be more resilient than expected; the implementation of the Affordable Health Care Act is facing serious hurdles and will take longer to implement than anticipated; not all of Mexico, Central, and South America crossed our open borders into Texas, Arizona, and California, and unlike some European cities, Chicago, Detroit, and New York are not yet annexed to the possession of Islam and our schools are not teaching children the direction of Mecca. Unlike the bust of Churchill, the Stature of Liberty has not been sent back to France. Even more importantly, despite a huge strive, socialism has not yet attained political meaning and the concept of equality still has little reverence in American society.

In order to ensure their legacy, Obama and his minions need more time; they need more than two terms to complete the "fundamental change." Therefore, the upcoming elections are not really about Democrats or Republicans. They are not about universal health care, the national debt, the price of gasoline, or the rate of unemployment. Those are the consequences of the progressive's socialist policies that, despite the doomsday scenarios of this writing, could be temporary and overcome with the passage of time—provided that Americans stop taking their liberty for granted. Obama's reign is a divine omen of what has become the fatal dilemma for the American people: What kind of country are we going to be: "One nation under God, indivisible, with liberty and justice for all" or "One nation under debt, with equality in poverty for all"? "The land of the free" or "The land of the voting herd"?

Fifty-two years ago, in 1964, Ronald Reagan gave a speech on behalf of presidential candidate Barry Goldwater that would become known as "A Time for Choosing." His words resonate even more today:

> *You and I have a rendezvous with destiny. We will preserve for our children this, the last best hope of man on earth, or we will sentence them to take the*

first step into a thousand years of darkness. If we fail, at least let our children and our children's children say of us we justified our brief moment here. We did all that could be done.

The enemies are at the gates, the fifth column is already inside ready to open them to welcome in the Marxist socialist future. The challenge of our time is to acquire adequate knowledge and to comprehend the social democratic agenda and its consequences for the future of this country, for our children and grandchildren. It is imperative for our survival and the preservation of American idealism. A prominent Russian journalist, Stanislav Mishin, gloomily wrote after the 2008 election,

The proud American will descend into slavery without a fight, beating his chest and proclaiming to the world how free he really is.

Mishin could still be proved wrong; the socialist's overreach could turn out to be a political wake-up call for this nation, like Pearl Harbor or 9/11. Although the specter of communism is haunting America, it does not have to take root here; the fall of the American empire is not inevitable and the third phase of socialism — *DESPAIR*—may still not materialize.

It was another Russian, immigrant and novelist-philosopher Ayn Rand, who in 1946 wrote a novel, *Anthem,* which has acute relevance today:

The greatest guilt today is that of people who accept collectivism by moral default; the people who seek protection from the necessity of taking a stand, by refusing to admit to themselves the nature of that which they are accepting; the people who support plans specifically designed to achieve serfdom, but hide behind the empty assertion that they are lovers of freedom, with no concrete meaning attached to the word; the people who believe that the content of ideas need not be examined, that principles need not be defined, and that facts can be eliminated by keeping one's eyes shut. They expect, when they find themselves in a world of bloody ruins and concentration camps, to escape moral responsibility by wailing: "But I didn't mean this!"

I trust there will be a time After Obama when communist "CHANGE" and "FORWARD" will be replaced with a new era of "RECONSTRUCTION"— the revival of economic prosperity and the rebirth of almost forgotten constitutional principles.

You may say I'm a dreamer, but I'm not the only one.[48]

---

[48] *From the song "Imagine," by John Lennon, an English musician.*

Acknowledgments

Setting the stage for the idea and ultimate creation of this book was a wonderful blog I participated in for several years; it was started by my friend and gifted engineer Edvig Gershengoren, who is, unfortunately, no longer with us. The blog debated politics from all points of view, from the furthest left to the hardest right—and had a great time stretching those boundaries and occasionally reaching agreement on certain points. Many of the ideas in this book were first tested or developed there, and much of my inspiration for this work has come from the blog.

Many thanks to my fellow bloggers, especially Rich Batey, Elliott Lyon, Al Kasper, Jennifer Keller, Irine Dean, and Amin Shakill, for the ideas that emanated from the heated discussions and for deepening my understanding of the issues.

Special thanks to Ted Belman, an Israeli journalist and the editor of Israpundit, for his invaluable advice and support. Ted reviewed the early version of the manuscript and made substantive improvements. Without Ted's input this book would not be the same. I am also appreciative of Cliff Kincade, president of American's Survival, for offering his platform for early book promotion.

I want to thank the following friends and business associates who read parts of the manuscript and offered useful comments: Simon J. Wachsberg, George W. Arzymanow, Joel Goldberg, Richard A. Olliver, Victor Nevik, and Peter Maffitt.

I would like to acknowledge a group of people who one way or another contributed to this book, among them award-winning writer Joan Swirsky, who introduced me to the world of book publishing.

Special thanks to Dog Ear Publishing for getting the book published in record time.

For this book and a host of articles I have published over the last few years, I owe particular gratitude to my editor in chief, Rita Samols, who possesses great editing skills perfectly suited to my unconventional writing. She went over the manuscript tirelessly several times and is responsible for many improvements.

I also must thank my lovely wife, Elena, for her support and inspiration. Finally, I have to thank my teenage daughter, Rebecca, my first and best editor, and the person for whom I wrote this book in the hope that America, in which she will raise her children, will be as joyful and rewarding for her as it has been to Elena and me. I can still hear her cry in exasperation, "Daddy, who writes like this?!"

Bibliography

Books

Bukharin, Nicolai. *Economics of the Transition Period.* 1920

Bulgakov, Mikhail. *The Master and Margarita,* 1967.

Churchill, Winston. *The Gathering Storm. Volume I of The Second World War,* 1948, p. 403.

———. *The River War: An Historical Account of the Reconquest of the Soudan,* 1899.

Colmes, Alan. *Thank the Liberals for Saving America,* 2012.

Cooper, Luke and Simon Hardy. *Beyond Capitalism? The Future of Radical Politics,* 2013.

Engels, Friedrich. *Socialism: Utopian and Scientific,* 1880.

Fund, John, and Hans von Spakovsky. *Who's Counting? How Fraudsters and Bureaucrats Put Your Vote at Risk,* Encounter Books, 2012.

Foner, Dr. Eric. *A Short History of Reconstruction, 1863–1877.* New York: Harper & Row, 1990.

Gielow, Fred. *You Don't Say.* Freedom Books, 1999, p. 33.

Gingrich, Newt. *To Renew America,* Harper Collins, 1995, p. 29.

Goldstein, Fred. *Capitalism at a Dead End: Job Destruction, Overproduction and Crisis in the*

High-Tech Era. World View Forum, 2012.

Hayden, David. *Muhammad and the Birth of Islamic Supremacism: The War with the Jews 622-628 A.D.* Bird Brain Productions, 2012.

Hayek, F. A. *The Road to Serfdom*. Chicago: University of Chicago Press, 1944, p. 24.

Horvat, Branko. *The Political Economy of Socialism*, 1983. Chapter 1: "Capitalism, The General Pattern of Capitalist Development," pp. 15–20.

Kengor, Paul. *The Communist: Frank Marshall Davis: The Untold Story of Barack Obama's Mentor*. Mercury Radio Arts Publishing, 2012.

———. *All The Dupes Fit To Print: Journalists Who Have Served as Tools of Communist Propaganda*. CreateSpace Independent Publishing Platform, 2013.

Keynes, John Maynard. *The Economic Consequences of the Peace*, 1919, pp. 235, 236.

Keynes, John Maynard. *The End of Laissez-Faire*, 1926.

Kissinger, Henry. Essay in Hoge, James F., and Fareed Zakaria. *The American Encounter: The United States and the Making of the Modern World*, 1998, p. 174.

———. *World Order*, 2014.

———. *Years of Renewal*, 1999, pp. 108, 791, 802, 803, 807.

Kloppenberg, James T. *Reading Obama: Dreams, Hope, and the American Political Tradition*, 2012.

Krugman, Paul, and Robin Wells. *Economics*, 2005.

Lenin, Vladimir. *Lenin's Selected Works*. Moscow: Progress Publishers, 1963. Volume 1, pp. 667–766.

———. *The Three Sources and Three Component Parts of Marxism*, 1913.

———. *To the Rural Poor*, 1903. (Pamphlet)

———. *What Is to Be Done?* 1901.

London, Joshua. *Victory in Tripoli: How America's War with the Barbary Pirates Established the U.S. Navy and Shaped a Nation*. Wiley, 2005.

Loudon, Trevor. *Barack Obama and the Enemies Within*, 2008.

Martin, Rose. *Fabian Freeway: High Road to Socialism in the U.S.A.*, 1968.

Marx, Karl. *Critique of the Gotha Program*, 1875.

———. *Das Kapital [Capital]*, 1867. Volume 1, Chapter 1: "The Commodity."

———. Preface to *A Contribution to the Critique of Political Economy*, 1859.

———. *Value, Price, and Profit*, 1865.

———. *Wage Labour, and Capital*, 1847.

———. *The Poverty of Philosophy*, 1847.

Marx, Karl, and Friedrich Engels. The Communist Manifesto, 1848.

———. *Selected Works*, 1973. Volume 2.

Obama, Barack. *The Audacity of Hope: Thoughts on Reclaiming the American Dream*, 2007, p. 261.

———. *Dreams from My Father: A Story of Race and Inheritance*, 2004.

Pozner, Vladimir. *Parting with Illusions*, 1990, pp. 160, 346.

Proudhon, Pierre-Joseph. What Is Property? An Inquiry into the Principle of Right and Government, 1840.

Proudhon, Pierre-Joseph. *System of Economical Contradictions: or, The Philosophy of Poverty*, 1847.

Raico, Ralph. *Great Wars and Great Leaders: A Libertarian Rebuttal*, 2010.

Rand, Ayn. *Anthem*, 1946.

———. *Capitalism: The Unknown Ideal*, 1966.

———. *For the New Intellectual*, 1961.

Ricardo, David. *On the Principles of Political Economy and Taxation, 1817*. Chapter 1: "On Value."

Schlesinger, Arthur M. Jr. *The Imperial Presidency*, 1973.

Smith, Adam. *The Wealth of Nations*, 1776.

Sun Tzu. *The Art of War.*

Trotsky, Leon. *On Democratic Centralism and the Regime*, 1937. (Letter to the Editor of *Socialist Appeal*)

———. *The Revolution Betrayed: What Is the Soviet Union and Where Is It Going?* 1937, p. 283.

Wells, H. G. *Russia in the Shadows*, 1921, p. 157.

Wood, Gordon. *The American Revolution: A History*, 2003.

Woodward, Bob. Introduction to *Shadow: Five Presidents and the Legacy of Watergate*, 1999.

Peer-reviewed Papers

Michaels, Patrick J., and Paul C. Knappenberger. "Scientific Shortcomings in the EPA's Endangerment Finding from Greenhouse Gases." *The Cato Journal* 29, no. 3 (2009): 497–521.

Soon, Willie H., Sallie L. Baliunas, Arthur B. Robinson, and Zachary W. Robinson. "Environmental Effects of Increased Atmospheric Carbon Dioxide." *Climate Research* 13, no. 2 (October 1999): 149–64.

Magazine Articles

"American capitalism gone with a whimper." *Pravda*, April 2009.

American Sentinel. September 1997, page 9.

"Another Ice Age." *Time* magazine, June 24, 1974.

Chernus, Ira. "Eisenhower's Ideology in World War II." *Armed Forces & Society* 23, no. 4 (June 1997): 595–613.

Obama, Barak Sr. "Problems Facing our Socialism." *East Africa Journal*, July 1965.

Roosevelt, Franklin D. "Appendix A: Message from the President of the United States Transmitting Recommendations Relative to the Strengthening and Enforcement of Anti-trust Laws." *The American Economic Review* 32, no. 2, Part 2, June 1942.

Roubini, Nouriel. "Karl Marx was right." *The Wall Street Journal*, August 19, 2011.

"Talk with Bolshevist Head." *New York Times*, April 23, 1919.

"The Coming Ice Age." *Newsweek*, April 28, 1975.

Speeches and Presidential Addresses

Churchill, Sir Winston. Speech at Hansard, November 11, 1947.

———. Speech at Kinnaird Hall, Dundee, May 4, 1908.

Eisenhower, Dwight D. Farewell Address to the Nation, 1961.

Obama, Barack. Presidential Inaugural Addresses, 2009, 2010, 2011.

Roosevelt, Franklin D. Address to Congress, April 29, 1938.

Government Reports

Moynihan, Daniel Patrick. *The Negro Family: The Case for National Action*, 1965.

Reagan, Ronald. "A Nation at Risk: The Imperative of Education Reform," 1983.

Roosevelt, Franklin D. "Recommendations to the Congress to Curb Monopolies and the Concentration of Economic Power," April 29, 1938.

U.S. Department of Education, National Institute of Literacy, April 28, 2013.

U.S. Energy Information Administration Annual Energy Review, 2009, 2010.

Television News Reports and Programs

Evan Thomas interview, MSNBC, June 9, 2009.

President Obama interview with Steve Kroft on 60 Minutes, December 11, 2011

"U.S. Bridges, Roads Being Built by Chinese Firms." ABC News, September 23, 2011.

Press Releases

Morris, Michael G. (American Electric Power's Chairman and CEO) June 9, 2011.

Other Miscellaneous Reports

International Labour Organization (ILO), "Declaration on Social Justice for a Fair Globalization," 2008.

Social Labour Party, "The Socialist Programme."

Government Acts and Laws

American Clean Energy and Security Act

The American Recovery and Reinvestment Act of 2009

Cap & Trade Bill

Dodd-Frank Wall Street Reform and Consumer Protection Act

APPENDIX I

"Talk with Bolshevist Head"

"Aim of Every Party Must Be to Convince the Majority That It Is Right."

A HINT ON HOW TO CONVINCE

"When a Revolution is Most in Danger Dictatorship Must Be Most Pitiless."

HIRES HIGHLY PAID EXPERTS

Admits It's Almost Backsliding—Prints Money to Make It Useless—Reads Confucius
Copyright 1919 by The New York Times Company
Special Cable to *The New York Times*
GENEVA, April 22, Dispatch to *The London Daily Chronicle*. I am able to send authentic notes of an interview with Vladimir Ulyanoff Lenin, high priest of Bolshevism, which were communicated to me by a recent visitor to Moscow.

Lenin has aged since his advent to power. There are gray threads in his short black beard and his naturally high forehead is made to appear still higher through increasing baldness. He speaks with calm, dictatorial deliberation, using only the simplest phrases. His voice and manner are authoritative. He sweeps aside all arguments and objections, inexorably pursuing the thought in his mind. There is a gleam of hard, fanatical intelligence in his eyes.

According to minute notes made by my informant, Lenin explained the policy in the following terms:

"The first aim of every political party must be to convince the majority of people that its program is right. This task, although far from being absolutely achieved, is now in a great measure solved, for the majority of the Russian workmen and peasants today consciously adhere to the principles of Bolshevism.

"The second problem is the conquest of political power and the suppression of resistance on the part of the capitalist classes. This problem could only be solved by means of a dictatorship of the proletariat, which consists, so to say, in a permanent state of war against the bourgeoisie. The people who protest against acts of terrorism committed by the Communists entirely forget what the term dictatorship means. Revolution is in itself an act of terrorism. The word dictatorship in all languages means simply the rule of terror. It is likewise evident that when the revolution is most in danger the dictatorship must be most pitiless.

"At first the danger was very great in Russia and the dictatorship proportionately severe. Today it is considerably less and we can almost dispense with terrorism. We have committed many errors in the past, but our disappointment and difficulties were inevitable, for it was impossible to foresee how the social philosophy of Marx, which had never been put into practice before, would work out in actual government."

Paper Money to Destroy Money's Value

Lenin is obsessed at present by a plan for the annihilation of the power of money in the world. He outlined his ideas on this subject thus:

"Hundreds of thousands of ruble notes are being issued daily by our Treasury. This is done not in order to fill the coffers of the State with practically worthless paper, but with the deliberate intention of destroying the value of money as a means of payment. There is no justification for the existence of money in a Bolshevist state, where the necessities of life shall be paid for by work alone.

"Experience has taught us it is Impossible to root out the evils of capitalism merely by confiscation and expropriation, for however ruthlessly such measures may be applied, astute speculators and obstinate survivors of the capitalist classes will always manage to evade them and continue to corrupt the life of the community. The simplest way to exterminate the very spirit of capitalism is, therefore, to flood the country with notes of high face value without financial guarantees of any sort.

"Already even the hundred-ruble note is almost valueless in Russia. Soon even the simplest peasant will realize that it is only a scrap of paper not worth more than the rags from which it is manufactured. Men will cease to covet and hoard it so soon as they discover it will not buy anything, and the great illusion of the value and power of money on which the capitalist state is based will have been definitely destroyed.

"This is the real reason why our presses are printing ruble bills day and night without rest. But this simple process must, like all measures of Bolshevism, be applied all over the world in order to render it effective. Fortunately the frantic financial debauch in which all the Governments have indulged during the war has paved the way everywhere for its application."

Questioned concerning the plans of world conquest entertained by the Bolsheviks, Lenin replied:

"A communist state cannot exist in a world of capitalist states. This is politically and economically impossible. The communist state must either convert the capitalist state to communism or succumb itself to capitalism. An apparent compromise between the two is conceivable for a short time, but it can never be real and lasting. They exclude each other mutually, but it is with ideas, not with armies we shall conquer the world."

Sees Capitalism Destroying Itself

"Capitalism carries on a more effective propaganda for us among the masses than we ourselves could even hope to achieve by our own efforts. The international profiteer is our best propagandist. It is true we owe much to war, but I do not fear peace, for the incurable avidity and corruption of the capitalist classes will survive it and paralyze its healing effects. The cost of living, instead of diminishing, is still increasing steadily in most countries. The lust of gain of international exploiters, bourgeois financiers, manufacturers, and tradesmen is still unslaked, and they are conspiring to prevent return of normal conditions, totally unconscious of the fact that they are preparing their own destruction."

To his visitor's observation that the Bolsheviks are nevertheless now inviting the bourgeois classes in Russia to participate in the administration of the Soviet Republic Lenin replied:

"The transformation of the capitalist state into the communist state is impossible without the assistance of scientific and technical experts. Inevitably these experts are today bourgeois. We have, therefore, been forced to adopt bourgeois methods and to secure the services of the most competent bourgeois specialists by paying them high salaries; it is evident that this measure represents a departure from the principles proclaimed by the Paris Commune, which established that all salaries without exception shall be reduced to the level of an ordinary workman's wage. To a certain extent the employment of bourgeois specialists may even be said to signify a truce in the midst of our offensive against capitalism and a retrograde movement on the part of our Socialist Soviet Republic, which from the first had promised and has already carried out a leveling of high salaries in accordance with the principles of the Paris Commune. However, it is but the truce inevitable in a period of transition."

Lenin entertains vast and partly mystical agricultural plans in the conception of which he has been influenced by Confucius, whose works are at present his favorite study:

"Russia's economic part in the future life of Communist Europe," he declares, "must be based on the development of agriculture. Enormous wealth which can largely contribute to the prosperity of mankind lies hidden in Russian soil. In other countries the development of industries will supply the needs of the International Soviet community, but Russia will produce the workers' daily bread.

"In order to intensify agricultural production in Russia it is necessary to employ scientific methods on a vast scale. Special attention is being given at present to the manufacture of agricultural machinery. Numerous new plants have recently been constructed and are running satisfactorily, some of them under direction of foreign specialists. It is a fact that several foreign firms which had established branches In Russia before the revolution are at present overwhelmed with orders for agricultural machines and implements by the Soviet rulers."

Bolshevist mentality is characterized by an extraordinary mixture of Utopianism and Machiavellianism. The following reminiscence, narrated by Lenin in a most matter-of-fact way, illustrates what the Bolshevik has in his mind when he condescends to cooperate with the bourgeois.

"When the German imperialists hurled their armies in February 1918 against defenseless demobilized Russia, who had placed her trust in the solidarity of the international proletariat before the international revolution had ripened completely, I did not hesitate a moment to conclude a sort of agreement with the French monarchists. A Frenchman, Captain Sadoul, who sympathized with the Bolsheviki in words but in reality served French Imperialism faithfully, brought a French officer named de Lubersac to see me.

"'I am a monarchist, my sole aim is the defeat of Germany,' announced de Lubersac at once. That goes without saying,' I answered.

"His declaration did not hinder me in the least from concluding an agreement with him concerning the services which French military engineers could render us by destroying railroads and blowing up bridges to retard the German advance. This is a perfect example of compromise which every sensible workman must sanction, a compromise in the interests of socialism and of French monarchists, and we shook hands, although we knew each of us would have liked to have the other banged. But our interests for the time-being were coincident, to ward off the menace of German imperialism. We did not scruple to use equally imperialistic French officers as our instruments in order to safeguard the threatened interests of the Russian and of the international Socialist revolution.

"Thus we furthered the interests of the working classes of Russia and of all other countries; thus we strengthened the proletariat and weakened the bourgeoisie all over the world. We merely adopted a perfectly legal and approved method of maneuvering, resting and biding our time until the rapidly ripening proletarian revolution should break out in all countries."

Such are Lenin's opinions, conscientiously recorded. It is evident that in expressing them he was fully aware that he is himself his most effective propagandist. Nevertheless some of his remarks are sufficiently frank and illustrative of the sinister form of moral insanity which distinguishes the Bolshevist mind to be a terrible warning to Western Europe.

APPENDIX II
Sampling of Reports from the 1970s Warning of Global Cooling

National Academy of Sciences issued report warning of coming ice age in 1975.

Excerpt: "A major climatic change would force economic and social adjustments on a worldwide scale," warns a recent report by the National Academy of Sciences, "because the global patterns of food production and population that have evolved are implicitly dependent on the climate of the present century." Peter Gwynne, "The Cooling World," *Newsweek*, April 28, 1975

NASA warned of a coming human-caused ice age in 1971.

Excerpt: The world "could be as little as 50 or 60 years away from a disastrous new ice age, a leading atmospheric scientist predicts," read a July 9, 1971 *Washington Post* article. NASA scientist S. I. Rasool, a colleague of James Hansen, made the predictions. The 1971 article continues: "In the next 50 years"—by 2021—fossil-fuel dust injected by man into the atmosphere "could screen out so much sunlight that the average temperature could drop by six degrees," resulting in a buildup of "new glaciers that could eventually cover huge areas." If sustained over "several years, five to 10" or so, Mr. Rasool estimated, "such a temperature decrease could be sufficient to trigger an ice age." *Washington Times*, September 19, 2007

New York Times: Obama's global warming–promoting science czar Holdren "warned of a coming ice age" in 1971.

Excerpt: In the 1971 essay "Overpopulation and the Potential for Ecocide," Dr. Holdren and his co-author, the ecologist Paul Ehrlich, warned of a coming ice age. They certainly weren't the only scientists in the 1970s to warn of a coming ice age, but I can't think of any others who were so creative in their catastrophizing. Although they noted that the greenhouse effect from rising emissions of carbon dioxide could cause future warming of the planet, they concluded from the mid-century cooling trend that the consequences of human activities (such as industrial soot, dust from farms, jet exhaust, urbanization, and deforestation) were more likely to first cause an ice age. Article by John Tierney, *New York Times*, September 29, 2009 (See also: "Obama Science 'Czar' John Holdren's 1971 warning: A 'New Ice Age' likely," **New York Times**, September 23, 2009.)

1977 book **The Weather Conspiracy: The Coming of the New Ice Age** *says CIA feared global cooling.* Excerpt: In the early 1970s, top CIA thinkers concluded that changing weather was "perhaps the greatest single challenge that America will face in coming years." As a result they ordered several studies of the world's climate, the likely changes to come, and their probable effect on America and the rest of the world. The studies concluded that the world is entering a difficult period during which major climate change (further cooling) is likely to occur. That is the consensus of the Central intelligence Agency, which highlights the fact that we are overdue for a new ice age. Many climatologists believe that since the 1960s, the world has been slipping towards a new ice age. ...the evidence suggests that change will be a return to a climate that was dominant from the seventeenth century to about 1850. Soviet weatherman Mikhail Budyko believes that a drop of 2.8 degrees Fahrenheit in the average global temperature would start glaciers on the march. If the temperature should fall by another 0.7F, it could usher in a 90,000-year tyranny of ice and snow.

Sampling of Reports from the 1970s Warning of Global Cooling

"*The Cooling World*," Newsweek, *April 28, 1975, by Peter Gwynne.*
Excerpt: "The evidence in support of these predictions has now begun to accumulate so massively that meteorologists are hard-pressed to keep up with it. In England, farmers have seen their growing season decline by about two weeks since 1950, with a resultant overall loss in grain production estimated at up to 100,000 tons annually.... The central fact is that after three quarters of a century of extraordinarily mild conditions, the earth's climate seems to be cooling down. Meteorologists disagree about the cause and extent of the cooling trend, as well as over its specific impact on local weather conditions. But they are almost unanimous in the view that the trend will reduce agricultural productivity for the rest of the century. If the climatic change is as profound as some of the pessimists fear, the resulting famines could be catastrophic. 'A major climatic change would force economic and social adjustments on a worldwide scale,' warns a recent report by the National Academy of Sciences, 'because the global patterns of food production and population that have evolved are implicitly dependent on the climate of the present century.'... Climatologists are pessimistic that political leaders will take any positive action to compensate for the climatic change, or even to allay its effects. They concede that some of the more spectacular solutions proposed, such as melting the Arctic ice cap by covering it with black soot or diverting arctic rivers, might create problems far greater than those they solve."

Professor Stephen Schneider converted from warning of a coming ice age in the 1970s to promoting man-made global warming fears today.
In the 1970s Professor Stephen Schneider was one of the leading voices warning that the Earth was going to experience a catastrophic man-made ice age. He is now, however, a member of the UN IPCC and a leading advocate warning that the Earth is facing catastrophic global warming. In 1971, Schneider co-authored a paper warning of a man-made "ice age." (See: Rasool, S. & Schneider, S. "Atmospheric Carbon Dioxide and Aerosols—Effects of Large Increases on Global Climate," *Science* 173 (9 July 1971): 138–141.) Excerpt: "The rate of temperature decrease is augmented

with increasing aerosol content. An increase by only a factor of 4 in global aerosol background concentration may be sufficient to reduce the surface temperature by as much as 3.5 deg. K. If sustained over a period of several years, such a temperature decrease over the whole globe is believed to be sufficient to trigger an ice age." Schneider was still promoting the coming "ice age" in 1978. (See: Unearthed 1970s video: Global warming activist Stephen Schneider caught on 1978 TV show 'In Search of…the Coming Ice Age,' September 20, 2009.) By the 1980s, Schneider reversed himself and began touting man-made global warming. "The rate of [global warming] change is so fast that I don't hesitate to call it potentially catastrophic for ecosystems," Schneider said on UK TV in 1990.

1975 **New York Times***: "Climate Changes Called Ominous," by Harold M. Schmeck, June 19, 1975, p. 31.*

Excerpt: "The most drastic potential change considered in the new report is an abrupt end to the present interglacial period of relative warmth that governed the planet's climate for the past 10,000 years…. The report also noted that periods of benign climate comparable to the present are unusual and have existed for about 8 percent of the last 700,000 years."

1974 **New York Times***: "Climate Changes Endanger World's Food Output," by Harold M. Schmeck, August 8, 1974, p. 35.*

Excerpt: "A recent meeting of climate experts in Bonn, West Germany, produced the unanimous conclusion that the change in global weather patterns poses a severe threat to agriculture that could lead to major crop failures and mass starvation…. The drop [in global temperatures] since the 1940s has only been half a degree, but some scientists believe this is enough to trigger changes that could have important effects on the world's weather and agriculture."

Sampling of Reports from the 1970s Warning of Global Cooling

1975 **New York Times***: "Scientists Ask Why World Climate Is Changing, Major Cooling May Be Ahead," by Walter Sullivan, May 21, 1975.*

Excerpt: "Sooner or later a major cooling of the climate is widely considered inevitable. Hints that it may already have began are evident. The drop in mean temperatures since 1950 in the Northern Hemisphere has been sufficient, for example, to shorten Britain's growing season for crops by two weeks."

1974 **Time** *magazine: "Another Ice Age," June 24, 1974.*

Excerpt: "However widely the weather varies from place to place and time to time, when meteorologists take an average of temperatures around the globe they find that the atmosphere has been growing gradually cooler for the past three decades. The trend shows no indication of reversing. Climatological Cassandras are becoming increasingly apprehensive, for the weather aberrations they are studying may be the harbinger of another ice age.... Man, too, may be somewhat responsible for the cooling trend. The University of Wisconsin's Reid A. Bryson and other climatologists suggest that dust and other particles released into the atmosphere as a result of farming and fuel burning may be blocking more and more sunlight from reaching and heating the surface of the earth.... Whatever the cause of the cooling trend, its effects could be extremely serious, if not catastrophic. Scientists figure that only a 1% decrease in the amount of sunlight hitting the earth's surface could tip the climatic balance, and cool the planet enough to send it sliding down the road to another ice age within only a few hundred years."

On October 24, 2006, **Newsweek** *admitted it erred in reporting on predictions of a coming ice age in the 1970s.*

Excerpt: It took 31 years, but *Newsweek* magazine admitted it was incorrect about climate change. In a nearly 1,000-word correction, Senior Editor Jerry Adler finally agreed that a 1975 piece on global cooling "was so spectacularly wrong about the near-term future." Even then, Adler wasn't quite willing to blame *Newsweek* for the incredible failure. "In fact, the story wasn't 'wrong' in the journalistic sense of 'inaccurate,'" he claimed. "Some scientists indeed thought the Earth might be cooling in the 1970s, and some laymen—even one as sophisticated and well-educated as Isaac Asimov—saw potentially dire implications for climate and food production," Adler added. However, the story admitted that both *Time* magazine and *Newsweek* were wrong on the subject—*Newsweek* as recently as 1992.

Climatologist Dr. Patrick Michaels, a prominent critic of the man-made global warming fears today, recalls how pervasive the coming ice age scare was when he was in graduate school. "When I was going to graduate school, it was gospel that the Ice Age was about to start. I had trouble warming up to that one too. This (greenhouse) is not the first climate apocalypse, but it's certainly the loudest," Michaels said.

1970: First Earth Day promoted ice age fears.

Excerpt: At the first Earth Day celebration, in 1970, environmentalist Nigel Calder warned, "The threat of a new ice age must now stand alongside nuclear war as a likely source of wholesale death and misery for mankind." C. C. Wallen of the World Meteorological Organization said, "The cooling since 1940 has been large enough and consistent enough that it will not soon be reversed."

1976 book **The Cooling: Has the Next Ice Age Already Begun?** *by Lowell Ponte.*

Excerpt: "This cooling has already killed hundreds of thousands of people. If it continues and no strong action is taken, it will cause world famine, world chaos and world war, and this could all come about before the year 2000."

Earth Day 1970: Kenneth E. F. Watt on air pollution and global cooling: "If present trends continue, the world will be about four degrees colder for the global mean temperature in 1990, but eleven degrees colder by the year 2000.... This is about twice what it would take to put us in an ice age."

Atmospheric Scientist Dr. Reid Bryson, the founding chairman of the Department of Meteorology at the University of Wisconsin (now the Department of Oceanic and Atmospheric Sciences), who was pivotal in promoting the coming ice age scare of the 1970s (See

Time magazine's 1974 article "Another Ice Age" citing Bryson and *Newsweek*'s 1975 article "The Cooling World" citing Bryson) converted into a leading global warming skeptic before his death in 2008. On February 8, 2007, Bryson dismissed what he termed "sky is falling" man-made global warming fears. Bryson was on the United Nations Global 500 Roll of Honor and was identified by the British Institute of Geographers as the most frequently cited climatologist in the world. "Before there were enough people to make any difference at all, two million years ago, nobody was changing the climate, yet the climate was changing, okay?" Bryson told the May 2007 issue of *Energy Cooperative News*. "All this argument is the temperature going up or not, it's absurd. Of course it's going up. It has gone up since the early 1800s, before the Industrial Revolution, because we're coming out of the Little Ice Age, not because we're putting more carbon dioxide into the air," Bryson said. "You can go outside and spit and have the same effect as doubling carbon dioxide," he added.

Fire and Ice: Journalists have warned of climate change for 100 years, but can't decide whether we face an ice age or warming," by R. Warren Anderson and Dan Gainor **Business and Media Institute,** *2006.*

Excerpt: The media have warned about impending climate doom four different times in the last 100 years. Only they can't decide if mankind will die from warming or cooling.

1978: Harley, W. S. "Trends and Variations of Mean Temperature in the Lower Troposphere." *AMS Monthly Weather Review* 106, no. 3 (March): 413–416.

1971: Mitchell, J. Murray Jr. "The Effect of Atmospheric Aerosols on Climate with Special Reference to Temperature near the Earth's Surface." *J. Applied Meteorology* 10: 703–14.

1975: Mitchell, J. Murray Jr. "A Reassessment of Atmospheric Pollution as a Cause of Long-term Changes of Global Temperature." In *Global Effects of Environmental Pollution*, edited by S. Fred Singer.

CPSIA information can be obtained
at www.ICGtesting.com
Printed in the USA
BVHW060137090319
542136BV00001B/48/P